THE BLEAN

The Woodlands
of a Cathedral City

THE BLEAN

The Woodlands of a Cathedral City

SAWD BOOKS

DEDICATION

To: William (Bill) Holmes

The rights of the Canterbury Woods Research Group to be identified as the authors of this work has been asserted by them in accordance with the Copyright Designs and Patent Act 1998. All rights reserved. No part of this publication may be reproduced, stored in a retrieval system, or transmitted in any form or by any means, electronic, mechanical, photocopying, recording or otherwise, without prior permission of the copyright owner, application for which should be addressed to the publisher.

British Library Cataloguing-in-Publication Data.
A catalogue record for this book is available from the British Library

SAWD BOOKS is an imprint of SAWD Publications

Plackett's Hole, Bicknor,
Sittingbourne Kent ME9 8BA

Copyright 2008

ISBN: 978-1-872489-01-8

Contents

Acknowledgements

List of Illustrations and Colour Plates

Foreword - Oliver Rackham, OBE

        INTRODUCTION 1

Chapter I - THE BLEAN 3

Chapter II - WOODLANDS MYTH AND REALITY 10

Chapter III - GEOLOGY AND SOILS 23

Chapter IV - ARCHAEOLOGY AND HISTORY 31

Chapter V - TREES AND WOODLAND PRODUCTS 51

Chapter VI - BLEAN TIMBER FRAMED BUILDINGS 64

Chapter VII - FLORA AND FAUNA 72

Chapter VIII - THE WOODS FROM EAST TO WEST 134

Chapter IX - THE FRENCH CONNECTION 173

Chapter X - THE BATTLE OF BOSSENDON WOOD 180

Chapter XI - A SUSTAINABLE FUTURE 191

        GLOSSARY 195

ACKNOWLEDGEMENTS

The Blean Group extends its grateful thanks to Dr Alexander Wheaten who, during the period of research, led and inspired their endeavours.

The Group would also like to thank the following who have freely given of their expertise to complete this study in local natural history: Fred Booth, Ian Clark, Ian Garraway, Dr Oliver Rackham OBE, Geoffrey Roberts, Russell Smith, Michael Walter and Malcolm Watling.

The original members of The Blean Research Group were: Dr Alexander Wheaten, (leader), Elizabeth Birmingham, Christopher Cherry, Gerry Flack, Robert Foster, Mary Fox, William Holmes, Irene Marchant, Margaret Matherne, David Maylam and Heather Nightingale OBE.

Sadly Geoffrey Roberts and Bill Holmes have both died since the first edition. They are sorely missed by the group.

Back Cover photograph: Canterbury Cathedral from the University Woodland - Elizabeth Birmingham

List of Illustrations & Colour Plates

Illustrations

Chapter I
An example of a medieval document
Recording Assessments in Botanical Surveys
Summaries of Representative Botanical Surveys

Chapter III
Geological Time Scale
Section through the Weald
Geological Section through the Blean
Ecocene Deposits
Soil Particle analysis from the Blean
Sites of Soil Analysis

Chapter IV
Scrapes and Flints found in the Blean
Manors with Woodland in the Blean

Chapter V
Carpinus betulus - Hornbeam
Sorbus torminalis - Wild Service Tree
David Maylam's survey of Earthworks

Chapter VI
Estimated sizes of trees in the Faversham Barns

Chapter VII
Tilia cordata - Small-leaved lime
Trees found in the Blean
Ancient Woodland Indicator species
Luzula pilosa - Hairy Woodrush
Species recorded in the Blean
Mnium hornum
Hypnum jutlandium
Fungal species in the Blean
Species List for Blean Butterflies
Wood Ant areas
Ant Nests number changes
Ant Nests volumes
Spiders from the Blean
Bird Habitats in the Blean
List of Breeding Birds
Mammals of the Blean

Chapter VIII
Ellenden Wood
Mincing Wood

Chapter IX
French Translations

Chapter X   *The village of Dunkirk and Bossendon Wood*
The Battle of Bossendon Wood

Plates
I	*A mediaeval map of Church Wood*
II	*Stone age artefacts found in the Blean*
III	*15th Century Roof Timbers*
IV	*A rare spider*
V	*Heath fritillary*
VI	*Pyramidial Orchid*
VII	*Yellow Archangel*
VIII	*Primroses*
IX	*Common Spotted Orchid*
X	*Fly agaric*
XI	*Stinkhorn*
XII	*Great Spotted Woodpecker*
XIII	*Female Whitethroat*
XIV	*Bluebells*
XV	*Coppice Stools*
XVI	*Old Marker Tree*
XVIII	*Eroded Way*
XIX	*Woodland Boundary*
XX	*Part of Old Beech Hedge*
XXI	*Beech Pollard*
XXII	*Woodbank*
XXIII	*Woodbank and Ditch*
XXIV	*19th Century Road*
XXV	*Former Disused Road*

Foreword

Wite ye nat wher rther stant a litel toun
Which that y-clepped is Bob-up-and-doun
Under the Blee, in Canterbury weye?
  Chaucer - *The Manciples Prologue (referring to Harbledown)*

The Blean is the name given to the north-western half of the great ring of woods that surrounds Canterbury. Nobody knows what it means. For a thousand years Blean has been the second biggest concentration of woodland in Kent after the Weald: ten miles of near continuous hornbeam, chestnut, oak and beech, trees horizontal, trees vertical, great coppice stools, muddy and mysterious between great banks and little boggy streams.

Blean in some ways echoes other big concentrations of medieval woodland. It is not on land that is good for growing trees, but on land that is bad for anything else; a ridge of sterile gravel and acid clays, soggy in winter and draughty in summer. But it was not just prehistoric wildwood: like other big wooded areas it has ample evidence of prehistoric and Roman settlement and field systems. Farming has retreated and the woods were once less extensive than they are now. Woodland, however, brought its own values and practices, which to some extent still continue. Scores if not hundreds of times the trees have been cut down and have grown again from their permanent bases.

I once described Hatfield Forest, Essex as a microcosm of English history.[1] Maybe the Blean is too but in a different way. Like Hatfield it has a prehistoric dimension going back to the Mesolithic. But it was never a Royal Forest nor associated with deer-parks: the cult of the deer as status symbol, which had far reaching effects on the English landscape, passed Blean by. (It is still one of the few wooded areas of England not to have deer). Hatfield, like other big wooded areas, had a large component of wood-pasture, cattle and sheep grazed not in woodland but in a savannah-like landscape with old scattered trees. Wood pasture seems not to have been significant in Blean in historic times.

Blean's speciality is that it was the woodland attached to a holy city. Most of its landowners were not secular lords but the great institution of Canterbury: the Archbishop (who seldom took a personal interest in his woodland), the Cathedral, the abbeys and lesser monasteries, hospitals and charities. This went back to the middle Anglo-Saxon times, when the magnificent kings of Kent gave much of their property to endow pious institutions

Institutional ownership resulted in centuries of well-organised management and conservation of woodlands. I have elswhere remarked how the woods of Bury St. Edmunds tend to survive within ten miles of the Abbey, but the more distant woods disappeared.[2] Something similar happened here. Timber from the Blean presumably contributed to the roofs of the great abbey churches and halls, and to the barns of their agricultural estates. Underwood was consumed in monastic kitchens, in the fires of all the inns in the city where pilgrims and travellers to France stayed, and in the kilns that made the bricks and tiles of east Kent. The institutions went to great trouble to protect their woods from encroachment and damage from browsing animals, hence the miles of banks and ditches defending the boundaries.

The Blean woods are mostly real woods. However much they have been managed, they consist of wild trees and are not plantations. Modern forestry coniferized some of them, but is now in retreat: there are better ways to occupy a forester's time than to get planted trees to grow in the face of competition from wild trees. Chestnut, so prominent here, was encouraged in an earlier and more successful period of alteration. It is still not fully clear how this happened, for chestnut - although a southern European tree from a very different climate - grows well from seed and once introduced and can spread into native woodland. One of the best-known places for medieval chestnut, before the main period of introduction, is ten miles west of Sittingbourne.

Blean is part of the great region of hornbeam-dominated woods. This covers south-east England and much of the Weald (where it has not been replaced by chestnut), Hertfordshire and South Essex, and far into France (where modern forestry has not replaced hornbeam by beech). Hornbeam, in turn probably replaced lime for some reason in late prehistory. Limewoods still survive in quantity north of the hornbeam region.

The closest parallel to the Blean is the woodland of south-east Essex. There is a geological similar sequence of acidic sands and gravels sitting on London Clay. There is a broadly similar sequence of woodland types, from ash-maple-hazel in fertile valleys and ravines, through hornbeam and chestnut types to birchwood and sessile oakwood on leached hilltops. The ownership history is very different, mostly private: a feature of south-east Essex is that some woods belonged to estates at a distance which had no local woodland.. Woods were much sub-divided into small ownerships; in consequence there is a dense network of woodbanks, sometimes layers of woodbanks superimposed on woodbanks. South-east Essex has no surviving beech and much more service than Blean. The woods survive well, despite (or because of) urbanisation. They have largely escaped modern forestry.

For fourteen years it has been my privilege to be associated with the Blean Research Group, a band of investigators, knowledgeable in their different ways, who have upheld and extended the English tradition of amateur natural historians. This book is the result of their labours.

It is now fashionable to emphasise the difference between sites and play down the differences, as the object of woodland ecology was to show that every wood was much the same as every other wood. The reality, as this book should show, is that every ancient wood is uniquely different, in much the same way as every medieval church is different from every other medieval church. (I am surprised at how readily the *National Vegetation Classifciation* gained acceptance in lowland England although it does less than justice to the rich variation of English woodland). This book should pick out the feature that makes Blean special, especially the relations between its ecological and anthropological peculiarities. When writing on Hatfield Forest I tried to answer the question: What difference did it make being a Forest? What difference did it make belonging for 65 years to the National Trust? Here the question is: What difference did it make being the wood of a holy city?

Oliver Rackham

References
1. O. Rackham (1989) - *The Last Forest; the story of Hatfield Forest (Essex)*. Dent, London
2. O. Rackham (1989) - *The Abbey Woods' Bury St Edmunds: medieval art, architecture, archaeology and economy.* Ed. A. Gransden, British Archaeological Association, London. p. 1349-160. Plates XXXIII - XXXIV
3. O. Rackham (1986*) - Ancient woodland of England: the Woods of South-East Essex.* Rochford District Council

INTRODUCTION

In 1987 the University of Kent at Canterbury invited adult students to study the ancient woodland of the Blean. Participants, mostly retired, had a wide range of interests and experience. Following an earlier course the subjects included history and archaeology but in addition, according to the University Prospectus, students were:

> *'to take account of vegetation as a third dimension in a historical and archaeological synthesis.'*

After over ten years of study, English Nature, whose staff have been consistently helpful, generously offered to sponsor the publication of a book about the woodland. It summarised the results of those investigations by what came to be known as The Blean Research Group. The book, *The Blean - The Woodlands of a Cathedral City* followed the lines of a report by Dr. Oliver Rackham, OBE entitled *The Woods of South East Essex*, published by Rochford District Council. That book, in the words of Councillor Derrick Wood, was intended to *'illuminate the history, the environment and the archaeology'* of the Essex woods so that the reader *'could draw lessons for the future'*.

It is the Canterbury Woods Research Group's hope that this revised and updated second edition of The Blean which contains original observations both from translations from the original medieval documents and from observations in the field, should be of value to all those who care for the woods and *'wish to base their care on accurate knowledge'*. This is particularly important because in the words of Sir Martin Doughty, Chairman of English Nature, *'the Blean woods'* extending over 7,000 acres, including over 80 individual woods, some exceptionally well documented over many centuries *'are a national treasure on a grand scale'*.

The members of the Blean group spent many hours simply walking the woods, becoming familiar with the distinctions and peculiarities of each small part and inevitably asking themselves just why things were there. This led to three distinct methods of enquiry: searching the *'Written Record'* in local archives (Canterbury Cathedral has some of the oldest historical documents in England); *'Field Walking'* in its broadest sense as well as the strict archaeological practice looking for artefacts and other man-made structures which would provide a clue to history, and finally *'Botanical Surveys'* which give a reasonably reliable record of just what is growing where it is.

Many other organisations have supported the research group over many years. The various contributions to the book have been prepared by members each in his or her own separate style, but all striving for unity in diversity.

The group was not indifferent to the fauna and members had their own special interests but these have been augmented by contributions from a number of local specialists. Their reports, for which we are most grateful, have shown that the Blean Woods form important habitats even for some of the microfauna, especially spiders - an area in which our own ignorance was profound! That chapter (VII) therefore rounds out the ecological survey of the Blean Woods.

Much more of what members discovered about the Blean is also recorded in twelve annual reports lodged in several libraries in Kent, in particular in that of the Dean and Chapter of Canterbury Cathedral and in the local studies room of the Beaney Institute in Canterbury. They include records of over 200 detailed botanical surveys and contain acknowledgements to the many who gave lectures, advice and help in several specialist fields.

It is essential that such knowledge should be discovered and publicised so that those who all too often are happy to cut down and *'develop'* what to them is a just a group of trees, do not destroy part of the local heritage.

Finally it has to be stressed that the natural world is not a static arena; change is the name of the game. There are probably as many theories of proper conservation as there are conservationists and there will never be complete agreement. Some of these changes are good, others well intended and yet more are plainly deleterious; some are man-made and others, such as climate change, beyond our immediate control. What is essential is that someone, somewhere should be constantly monitoring what is happening. We believe we have in some small way, done just that!

Robert E. Foster

THE BLEAN

Chapter I

Methods of Investigation

The area lying to the north of the city of Canterbury in East Kent, includes lands which had until recently been in the possession of the Church for at least one thousand years. It was therefore particularly well recorded and many of the records are still available, stored in the archives of Canterbury Cathedral, at Lambeth Palace, London, or in other libraries. Some were also stored until recently in the British Museum and are now in the British Library. These documents provide an impressive written record of the Blean, and indeed probably refer to one of the most comprehensively documented areas of England.

The earliest charters, which granted lands to the church, are stored as scrolls on parchment or vellum. Later medieval documents are in the form of books written on parchment or paper. The condition of many of the documents has deteriorated but an increasing number have been carefully restored by members of the archive staff. One batch of records on paper, which had been rescued in 1640 from a fire at the Cathedral and lain unattended, was restored only recently.

The Written Record

The Blean Research Group had access to these archival records and some members became highly skilled in tracing and deciphering the information recorded.

Included were charters, written in Latin, gifting lands to the church with records of boundaries. There were also reports and accounts, in medieval English, provided by beadles, foresters and monks of the Cathedral Priory, and by woodreeves who were responsible to the Dean for the management of the woodlands. Reports on income and expenditure in specific woods were available, not in entirety, but sufficient to give a picture of the extent of the lands and of their produce and annual sales. Although many of the records no longer existed in the original manuscripts they were still held in medieval registers and cartularies as copies of the original charters and other records.

Useful extracts from such documents are also to be found in books written in the seventeenth century.

Hasted, in his *History of Kent* (1778)[1] describes not only the parish of Blean itself but also refers to the dozen or so adjoining parishes which also include portions of the Blean Woods. But neither Hasted nor later writers have dealt with the Blean area as a whole, until the short account in *The Wild Woods* by Marren (1992).[2]

These archives also include early maps of lands possessed by the Church, dating from the 18th century. These maps were available both in the original or, on micro-fiche, for detailed study through a projector, and give quite detailed descriptions of some of the woods. The group also had access to later maps of the area, although some of these are of doubtful accuracy. They also inspected the maps first prepared at the end of the 18th century by the Ordnance Survey issued from 1801 and found the subsequent issues of 1870 and 1898 to be the most accurate and useful.

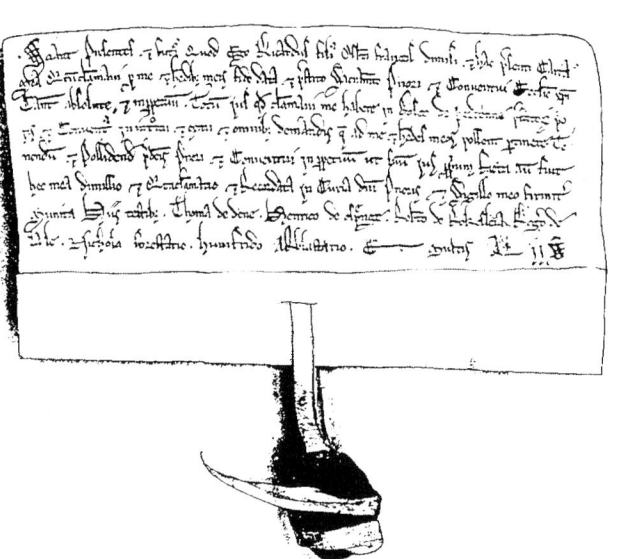

An example of a 13th Century Charter. It gave up rights in woodland to the monks of the Cathedral Priory and made early reference to Thornden Wood (in bosco de Thorndenne)

In these studies of records and other aspects of the work the group had help, not only from current members but also from earlier members who had not been able to continue. Many local people kindly shared their knowledge and several experts contributed lectures or demonstrations of their particular skills.

Field Studies

Much of the work was done in the field, an open-air aspect which had a particular appeal to several members of the group. In preparing for these the group were again indebted to many experts who described and demonstrated their techniques. Usually the first activity was to walk an area, noting its topography, the soils, the vegetation, the fauna, the presence of any earthworks and any other unusual or interesting features, bearing in mind, meanwhile, any information already discovered from local knowledge or from study of the written records.

A stream might be noted and then followed, while the bank sides were inspected for any signs of early man's activity, such as pot-boilers, charcoal, flints, or pieces of pottery. Similarly the soil exposed by an up-turned tree, a result of the 1987 or later storm, could reveal not only the soil type, but might also reveal artefacts. One such was the remains of a Roman funerary pot, dated to the 2nd century AD, which was found in 1999.

The dimensions of boundary banks and ditches were recorded and the direction of linear ditches was noted as a compass bearing. Where possible, straight linear ditches were followed for some distance to see whether, even if the ditch disappeared, it re-appeared further along the same line, a possible indication of Roman origin and of a grid system. In seeking the line of ditches, the time of year and the time of day were both crucially important. Mid afternoons in January or February were best since most of the vegetation had then died down and the low angle of the sun's rays threw shadow into any depression. A light covering of snow was also helpful!

Field walking in open areas and on recently tilled land often revealed artefacts. Worked flints and pieces of pottery were collected by sharp-eyed group members and items of archaeological interest passed to the Canterbury Archaeological Trust for assessment. Fragments of decorated floor tiles, presumably manufactured at Tyler Hill in the 13th century, were found on one field walk near Blean church. Their patterns matched examples on the floor of the Wax Chamber in Canterbury Cathedral and in the chancel of the church at Brook near Ashford.

Some of the group members had the ability to 'dowse' and an expert of the Society of Dowsers gave a demonstration. Dowsing refers to the ability possessed by some individuals to detect, by the reaction of hazel sticks or metal wands held in the hands, the presence below ground of water or of disturbed ground. For example, where a stretch of a linear ditch had been seen it was possible to infer by dowsing whether the disturbance of the ground continued on the same line, implying that the ditch had been filled in but its line continued underground. Dowsing was also used when an area of interest had been revealed from study of the records and an attempt was then made to confirm its presence on the ground. If dowsing suggested some disturbance of the soil, the soil profile could then be examined, quickly by the use of a soil auger, which extracts a core about 5cm in diameter, or, more laboriously, by digging a trench under archaeological supervision.

Botanical surveys

Ancient woodlands have been of considerable interest in recent years.[3,2,4,5,] Much effort was spent in assessing the botanical composition of woodland in various areas of the Blean. Groups of two or three people including at least one competent botanist, equipped with a hand lens and a good field handbook made the surveys. The procedure followed the method outlined by Rodwell[6] (1991) and adopted by the Nature Conservancy (now Natural England). Areas, considered to be representative of the particular wood and approximately 50m x 50m were walked, the species of trees and saplings were noted and estimates were made of the cover attributable to each species (out of 100 for trees and saplings separately). Then, within the sample area, five representative areas each of 5m x 5m were carefully examined and the percentage of each plant contributing to the ground cover was estimated for each. After a few trials it was obvious that some variation could occur between estimates. Accordingly two separate studies were made in which two or three teams each assessed one particular area and the resulting data were statistically analysed. These confirmed that considerable variation could occur (coefficients of variation were up to 50%) partly because of the inherent variability of woodland flora and partly because teams could differ in their estimates of numbers (Blean report 1992).[7] Any values shown are therefore indications of the plant cover rather than precise measurements. However these surveys were continued in all woods studied in detail since they ensured that an area was carefully inspected and they revealed the range of flora present, indeed the species list is almost as important as the numbers of species estimated to be present.

Unlike animals or birds, plants do not run or fly away but they do change by growth and decay over the season. The studies were nearly always made in the late winter when change is slow. This meant however that summer flowering species might not have been obvious and could be missed.

It is not always easy to identify plants especially from seedlings or immature saplings. Flowering plants are most easily identified from flower or seed pod but the general habit of growth, the size and shape of buds or leaves, the presence of hairs all help.

With trees in winter, patterns of bark, bud shape and branch form are useful clues but hybridisation can be a problem. For example the Pedunculate and the Sessile Oak hybridise as do the Service and the White Beam. Both of these occur in the Blean, the latter hybrid peculiar to only one other site in Britain.

In recognition of the difficulties in such assessments botanists have adopted more compact scales, e.g. the Domin number, which gives more emphasis to scarcer species. However initially the group used percentages. So long as it was accepted that differences less than 20 percentage points could occur by chance these gave a reasonable guide to the species composition of the wood. Occasionally quite large differences were recorded from different surveys of the same wood but this is not surprising since few woods are of uniform composition.

Frequency		Abundance		
%	Scale	%	Assessment	Domin No.
1-20	I	{	few	1
21-40	II	<4 {	several	2
41-60	III	{	many	3
61-80	IV	4-10		4
81-100	V	11-25		5
		26-33		6
		34-50		7
		51-75		8
		76-90		9
		91-100		10

Frequency indicates how often the plant is found in moving from one sample to the next, irrespective of how much of the species is present in one sample. It is summarised in Roman numerals. **Abundance** describes how much of the plant is present in the sample irrespective of how frequent or rare it is among the samples. Abundance is expressed either as a percentage or, preferably, by the Domin Scale shown above, which gives more weight to small numbers.

Figure 1.2 Recording Assessments in Botanical Surveys
[After Rodwell 1991]

The conversions from percentage to Domin are in Fig 1.2. Fig. 1.3 summarises five surveys of woods in the Blean; in these abundance is expressed on the Domin Scale.

The alternative method of taking transects on a compass bearing across the wood is very difficult in practice because some of the undergrowth which can develop after coppicing becomes almost impenetrable.

Hedges were also examined, both to assess their direction in relation to the direction of any ditches noted and also to estimate their age from application of Hooper's Rule (Pollard et al. 1974).[8] This was based on an initial study of 227 hedges of

	WOOD								
	Gt. Den Lees		Grimshill		Mincing		Church Wood		Ellenden	
Species	F	A	F	A	F	A	F	A	F	A
Oak [Both species]	V	0-4	V	6-10	V	5-8	V	4-7	V	4-10
Chestnut [Sweet]	III	0-4	III	6-10	V	4-5	V	2-8	III	1-7
Birch [Both species]	III	1-4	IV	1-4	III	2-5	IV	1-7	IV	1-5
Hazel	III	4-6	III	1-4	I	2-5	III	1-6	I	4-4
Beech	III	4-7	V	2-7	V	1-7	III	1-7	III	4-6
Holly	IV	1-2	IV	1-4	IV	1-4	I	1-1	I	1-1
Hornbeam	V	7-9	IV	5-10	III	1-9	III	1-5	0	0
Woodland Thorn	III	4-5	III	1-5	I	1-1	I	1-1	0	0
Service	III	1-1	II	1-5	I	2-2	I	1-1	0	0
Bramble	V	1-10	V	1-9	V	1-6	V	1-6	V	2-7
Honeysuckle	V	1-8	V	1-8	V	1-6	III	4-7	V	2-4
Wood Sage	II	1-4	II	1-8	III	1-2	III	1-3	II	1-1
Bluebell	IV	1-10	II	1-8	0	0	0	0	0	0
Bracken	0	0	III	1-8	IV	1-2	0	0	IV	4-4

Fig. 1.3 Summaries of Representative Botanical Surveys

Notes. 1. For an explanation of the symbols and numbers used above see Fig. 1.2
2. The abundance assessments are shown as the range found among the various samples used to determine the overall frequency.
3. The predominance of Oak, Sweet Chestnut and Birch can immedately be seen; Bluebell and bracken occur in only in some woods whilst the Bramble is universal.

known age. Age of the hedge is then estimated by assessing the number of distinct tree and shrub species in a representative 30 yard stretch of the hedge and assuming that each species indicates 100 years of age. Whilst not infallible as it can be frustrated by a modern trend to plant mixed hedges, it gives a useful indication which may often be confirmed by other information.

Minor interests

Several other interests were also followed, in particular wood ants and stream fauna. The influence of coppicing on the wood ant population was studied over a period of five years by recording the presence and activity of nests in areas which had recently been coppiced and in similar areas not coppiced. The small creatures in the main stream, the Fishbourne or Sarre Pen, running through Church Wood were examined, primarily to gain some information on the extent of water pollution. This showed that the water emerging from the Blean was relatively clean and free from pollution.

Recording of information

In order to help in providing records of value to other researchers in the future, annual reports on the activities of the Blean Research Group were produced. These have been deposited with several libraries including Canterbury Museum, The University of Kent, Canterbury, Wye College, University of London (now Imperial College at Wye), Natural England and other institutions, to be stored as a permanent record.

William Holmes

References
1. Hasted E. (1778 1st ed. 1801 2nd ed.) *The History and Topographical Survey of the County of Kent.* Blean Report (1992) App. F.
2. Marren P. (1992) *The Wild Woods*, David & Charles 89 ff.
3. English Nature, (1998) *Management Choices for Ancient Woodland.* Publicity and Marketing. English Nature, Peterborough PE 1 1 UA.
4. Peterken G. F. (1996) *Natural Woodland*, Cambridge University Press.
5. Rackham O. (1994) *The Illustrated History of the Countryside*, Weidenfeld & Nicholson, London.
6. Rodwell J. S. (1991) *British Plant Communities Vol. 1*, Cambridge University.
7. Blean Report
8. Pollard E., Hooper M.D., & Moore N.W. (1974) *Hedges*, New Naturalist Series, 58, Collins, London (Hoopers Rule).

Woodlands: Myth and Reality

Chapter II

Factoids and Facts

The present chapter follows a rather different direction from most in this book. For one thing, its scope is broader and more general, applying not just to the Blean but to woods at large. For another, it is as much about wrong thinking as right, and what lies behind and entrenches that wrong thinking.

Not all wrong thinking about historical and current ecology and wood management is entrenched or remotely seductive. Being wrong about the etymological significance of a place-name, the fifteenth-century ownership of a tract of woodland or the historical predominance of hornbeam over oak at a given site is likely to be just that and no more: being wrong about the facts of a particular and fairly unexciting matter.[1] The kind of wrong thinking in mind, however, is unlike discrete, and usually easily corrected, mistakes such as these. It is the kind that Oliver Rackham has recently drawn attention to in several of his works, albeit in scattered fashion.

Rackham's most striking identification, and indictment, of this wrong thinking is to be found in his *Trees and Woodland in the British Landscape*.

> 'A fascinating aspect of anything to do with trees and woods is that there is a rival version. I do not refer to conflicts of evidences and differences of scholarly opinion ... [but to] a consistent, logical, and widely accepted story - which, however, cannot be sustained from the records of actual woods or forests. It is a pseudo-history which has no connexion with the real world, and is made up of <u>factoids</u>. A factoid looks like a fact, is respected as a fact, and has all the properties of a fact except that it is not true.
>
> Pseudo-history is not killed by publishing real history ... [It] is not static but alive and growing,

[and] new factoids are even now being devised and added to the temple of Unreason. It wins ground at the expense of real history.'[2]

To the lover of woods, they serve, as we shall see, as a warning against supposing, however great the temptation, that the countryside is an artefact as man-made as a suburban garden. In what follows I shall examine selectively, but not always hold distinct, a number of questions inspired by Rackham's claims, adding a few of my own for good measure.

First, which are the most commonly accepted factoids, and to what pseudo-vision are they taken to point?

Secondly, are they really as prevalent in thinking, both popular and expert, about woods and their management as Rackham believes?

Thirdly, are they as obviously misconceptions as he claims?

Fourthly, what bearing does all this have upon our understanding of the Blean?

The Myths

I list below a selection of inter-connected factoids gleaned for the most part from Rackham's writings. The list is not of course exhaustive.

1 - Medieval England, and arguably Britain, was still very largely wooded; and it was only in times subsequent to the Norman Conquest that the land was dramatically, and perhaps disastrously, cleared and worked.

2 - Until post-Medieval times the British Isles was largely impenetrable, except for trackways and the neglected vestiges of a handful of Roman roads.

3 - Travel within the country was rare, dangerous and laborious. Effective communication between regional centres is a fairly recent achievement, dating from no earlier than the late seventeenth century.

4 - The countryside as we now know it is discontinuous with its past, and would be unrecognisable to anyone born before about 1500.

5 - The densely wooded countryside of early and even late Medieval Britain was transformed in a remarkably short space of time into the predominantly denuded land we now know. Post-Medieval England was hungry for limitless supplies of wood for

its new iron and glass works, with the consequence that much of South and South-East England was laid waste.

6 - The remaining timber went to make ships; and by the early eighteenth century the country was starved of woods.

7 - Land reclamation is a post-Medieval invention. For instance, it was not until the seventeenth century that, with the expert help of the Dutch, fenland and wetland were drained and became habitable.

8 - The hedges which have been grubbed up so industriously since the late 1940s a peculiarity of the English (and to some extent the British) countryside, for the most part the artificial creation of the late eighteenth century Enclosure Acts and their subsequent impact. So those hedges which are left are never really old.

9 - Trees normally die when felled (or pollarded, or coppiced!) and so woodmen have always spent much of their time planting new ones. Furthermore, several species of tree which are so much a feature of our countryside are comparatively recent imports. For example, the chestnut was (along with rabbits) introduced by the Normans.

10 - Until fairly recently the countryside was a desperate and barbaric place in which to live: punishment for poaching and trespass was savage and immoderate, and those who either owned or managed the land were cruel and uncivilized. This view owes much to a misunderstanding of what a medieval *'forest'* was and was not.

My list is undoubtedly incomplete, and there is considerable overlap between items. But this is just what we would expect; for taken together rather than individually the factoids suggest a certain sort of vision of our countryside and its past. The vision has sometimes been labelled "romantic", largely by virtue of the nostalgia which both generates and permeates it, but partly, too, because it emphasises a discontinuity between the thought and activity of modern and medieval and, indeed, pre-medieval people, aggrandising the achievements, skills and know-how of the former, and depreciating (and misinterpreting) those of the latter. It is a vision of **our** countryside as for the most part a pretty recent artefact, and of theirs as a world we have lost. This, precisely, is what makes it so attractive: we can enjoy the countryside as an unthreatening amenity we have constructed and at the same time relish the idea of what it once was. So I prefer to call the vision primitivist.

Sources of the myths

To what extent do experts as well as laymen believe in the vision I have sketched? What evidence can be found?

As a child growing up in the 'forties in North-East Essex and even then taking a juvenile interest in the countryside and woodland around I read and re-read with delight Margaret and Alexander Potter's little book called *A History of the Countryside*.[3] The authors describe their book as:

> *'the story of how man made the English countryside [and] its gradual development into the countryside that we know today'.*

We may feel uneasy with the unqualified statement that man made the countryside; but what is far more interesting is their more promising claim to show its gradual development. For it emerges that they think it to have been anything but gradual. *'Man had not left any great mark on the natural landscape until the Romans came'*, they write. Although the Romans *'cut trees down round their towns so as to grow crops'*, and the Saxons cleared some forest land, at the time of the Domesday survey the country, particularly in the north, *'was still largely forest'*.

The Norman Conquest, they tell us, *'did not change the face of England very much'*, and following the Black Death in the mid-fourteenth century much of the land that had been cleared reverted to forest. It was not until the two succeeding centuries that *'the forests were ... rapidly cleared'*, and even then there *'were no hedges as in our day'*. The clearance must have been extraordinarily rapid for:

> *'by the middle of the seventeenth century England had become almost bare of trees and the rulers of the country were afraid we should not have enough timber for ships.'*

And so it continues.

This enchanting book has redeeming features, in particular its awareness of early land reclamation. But the reader is left with a conviction not of gradual development but of very recent, dramatic transformation. The pattern of the countryside today, with its fields, woods and hedges, is the result of an early eighteenth century *'plan'* - the Enclosure Acts - to make *'farming efficient and prosperous'*. It will be obvious how closely - though simplistically, to be sure - this account corresponds to, and nourishes, the vision described above. I do not mean by this that it reproduces each and every factoid on my list, but rather that it communicates their collective atmosphere. And much the same is true of other, less juvenile works.

Thus, a not dissimilar overall picture is to be found in the far more detailed *Story of Britain* by Jacquetta Hawkes.[4] Again, we are asked to believe that changes took place much more recently and rapidly and totally than seems possible. The Saxons began *'forest clearance and the reclaiming of waste'*, and the later Medievals continued, not to say completed, these tasks with reckless enthusiasm:

> *'By Tudor times a country that had once been choked with trees was growing short of timber ... already in some regions the shortage was so severe that families were deprived of the fire on the hearth that had burned without thought or question since the beginning of human history.'* [5]

The vision captured in less and more complex ways by the Potters and the Hawkes emerges, too, in Edward Hyams's *The Changing Face of Britain*, although he was writing as recently as the mid 1970's.[6] At the time of the Domesday survey, he writes:

> *'the communities of England were like small colonial settlements of a few hundred stockaded acres, islanded in a land of primeval forest, marsh and moor ... England, like most of Wales and Scotland ... was a jungle ... in which settlement ... had not yet 'taken' very well.'* [7]

Hyams's summary description of what he takes to be the transformation brought about by *'countrymen'* between the Norman Conquest and Tudor times is elegant and revealing enough to merit quoting in full:

> *'Suppose that you had a film shot with a movie camera mounted on the platform of a satellite in orbit high above any of the great forest regions of Britain, a film which had been exposed at the rate of one frame every midsummer day every year for 500 years from 1066 to 1566; and that you projected it on to a screen. At first you would see a great expanse of green fabric - treetops - with little*

rents or holes in it, few and small to begin with, growing steadily larger as the film progressed, and more numerous too. As the rents enlarged they would join to make large holes, and meanwhile at the edges, the green foliage fabric would be contracting towards the middle of the picture, not in a regular shrinking, but irregularly, in capes and bays, like the map of a coast. At last there would be more hole than fabric, the fabric would be seen reduced to a ragged vestige, with some large pieces still, and many small pieces islanded by the process of clearance all round them. As for the great clearance now occupying most of the picture, part of it would appear as the familiar patchwork pattern of the open field, part of it as a reticulated pattern of hedges round irregular fields, the hedges looking like threads connecting the rags and tatters of remaining woodland.' [8]

At roughly the time Hyams wrote *The Changing Face of Britain* some historical ecologists were beginning to question elements in the composite vision we have explored. Hoskins, most notably, treads more cautiously, no longer writing of transformation but rather of evolution, of change as a complex of continuous processes stretching back to at least mesolithic times.[9] He allows the dramatic to give way to the gradual, and along with this hints at new perceptions of the country's past - and, of course, of the very idea of *'pastness'*. Even so, the shell of the old vision seems to me to remain, coexisting uncomfortably with the new perceptions. He writes that the map of, for example, Devon in the eleventh century would have looked very like the Ordnance map of today - and, indeed, that it would have been much the same for other parts of the country. At the same time he can write:

'Our villages, hamlets and farmsteads were mere islands - large or small - in a great sea of waste ... Many millions of acres remained to be rescued from their natural state and colonised. This vast area was under wood '..[10]

Lastly, some brief comments on the rather diffuse bundle of erroneous beliefs grouped together as factoid number 9. They should not need making; that they do is a sign that despite tremendous popular enthusiasm for trees and woods little has been learned and much forgotten since woodland management as this traditional expertise ceased to be a general practice. In its place we find misconceptions, all making their contribution to the vision described - which would have stunned our forbears.

Over the last decade or so pollarding and, very recently, coppicing has once again[11] been carried out on what little woodland remains on the southern slopes of the campus of the University of Kent. Half-hearted as this undertaking was it represents a genuine attempt at decent woodland management. Many, however, perceived it otherwise. The then Estates and Buildings Department was flooded with angry letters accusing it of killing trees, almost always assumed to be ancient oaks! The idea of timber as an indefinitely renewable resource, taken for granted by earlier generations, had simply vanished, leaving only a well-intentioned but ignorant enthusiasm for trees. A similar outcry attended the felling of half-a-dozen rather decrepit oaks to make way for Becket Court, a new annexe to Eliot College.

Just as most trees and their surrounds benefit immeasurably from managed coppicing so, typically, they reproduce themselves if given the opportunity. The passion for planting trees goes hand-in-hand with the fear of destroying them. It is not a new passion exactly, but one the medievals would have made little sense of. Yet in every book referred to above the benefits of tree planting are extolled as the appropriate means to replace trees which are dying or have died, or have been damaged or uprooted by storms and gales.

Oliver Rackham regularly draws attention to the misconceptions which drive people, including conservation bodies, to plant trees, and inclines to see this obsession not as conservation but as an admission that conservation has failed. His latest thoughts are to be found in an issue of *Tree News*, where he writes that the passion to plant trees:

> ... *'began at the time of the 'Plant a Tree in 1973' campaign, when somebody got the idea that the landscape was short of young trees, and set about a public campaign to encourage people to plant trees. I think this was, at that time, without any great thought as to what sort of trees, where they should be, or how they were to be maintained.*
>
> *I've never seen any sort of inquest into the*

> *results of the 1973 campaign or, for example, how many of the planted trees survived the hot summers of '75 and '76. It's something which began being applied indiscriminately and unintelligently. I think it has got somewhat better over the years and it has been realised that there is more to conserving trees than planting them. More effort should go into looking after the young wild trees that are already there, rather than planting new trees.'* [12]

A case which illustrates all these confusions about the life, propagation and death of trees comes from East Lothian rather than the Blean. Even so, it is too instructive to omit.

The owner of a decaying 25 acre oak wood intended to revitalise it using the expertise of a reputable forest management company. He hoped that the timber felled would cover much of the cost. His project excited a lively protest from a variety of quarters: East Lothian Council, Scottish National Heritage, the Dunbar John Muir Association, Scottish Wildlife Trust, and numerous other groups and individuals. Many of these opposed any change at all, some protesters claiming, and presumably believing, that the oaks on the site were thousands of years old when in fact they had been planted some two centuries before and managed for coppice before falling into neglect. Responding to the protest, the East Lothian Council clapped a tree preservation order on the whole site, and the regeneration plans, enlightened as they were, were postponed indefinitely.

The point, of course, is to draw attention to profound and widespread misunderstandings on both sides, of the nature and history of woodland management. Others may know of similar cases much closer to home.[13]

The Reality

The foregoing tries to describe and illustrate in a fairly general way a number of what are arguably deep and diffuse misconceptions about this country's woodlands, both past and present, and to account for the persistence and attraction of these misconceptions, and of the vision of the countryside which they help to form. I have suggested that they, rather like strongly held beliefs in other fields, survive and flourish in the face of much contrary evidence which often stares us in the face. The Blean is no exception; and from one point of view this book may be seen as itself a detailed examination of such evidence drawn from one particular area. For the recording of research into the Blean enables us not only to apply conclusions of historical ecology but also to disseminate those conclusions in the hope of driving out questionable beliefs and assumptions. So I shall end with some thoughts about the bearing of Blean studies upon the erroneous beliefs I listed at the beginning.

It will already be apparent from Rackham's introduction that the Blean is not a microcosm of the history of English, let alone British, woodland in the same way in which, for instance, Hatfield Forest in Essex is. Managed for its woods by a series of -predominantly ecclesiastical, institutional owners - it was never a forest, had no deer parks and lacked any substantial wood-pasture so far as we can tell. What it strongly suggests, however, is the dubiousness of the vision, and its component parts, which have been the subject of this chapter. And in this respect it is not unrepresentative of other sorts of woodland.

The first five pseudo-facts, different though their emphases are, all developed from the idea that the countryside we are familiar with today is a very recent invention, profoundly different from that which our Saxon and even medieval forbears knew, and scarcely recognisable to them. Historical study of the Blean, with its written records, gives the lie to this notion. Although we cannot say precisely when Blean woods ceased to extend to the coast, we know that it was long before the Norman Conquest. Certainly by the time of the Domesday Book, the outlines and conformation of the woods were very much as today. To be sure, there was still clearance to be done; but this waxed and waned, and made little if any substantial difference to the overall profile of the woods. The great clearance work had already been done not centuries but millennia before; and the stripping of Kent's wildwood was a gradual but steady undertaking all but complete by the time the Romans arrived.[14] This is a far cry from the idea that major clearances took place swiftly in the later Middle Ages. A Blean resident of 1100 would not find Blean woods very different in essentials now; indeed, what would probably strike him most - apart, that is, from current neglect and change of use, or indeed disuse - would be the density rather than the absence of woodland across certain areas of the Blean nowadays.

This, of course, puts paid to the belief that until modern times large tracts of the Blean were impenetrable, and where not impenetrable hazardous to travel through. It is truer to say that the Blean was more extensively habited, I do not say more populous, a thousand years ago than at any time since. For this we have much evidence of archaeological, written and topographical kinds considered in detail in later chapters, ranging from a wealth of Mesolithic tools[15] to Domesday records of wood management and land use. Above all, there is evidence <u>on</u> the ground of woodbanks and ditches, field patterns and boundaries, trackways and path ways. It is possible that some at least of these are of Roman origin. What seems more certain is that the Blean is crossed with ancient ways used to move animals from one grazing area to another. As noted in Chapter VIII, the most obvious, and perhaps the most important, is what is nowadays The Radfall Road.[16]

I shall deal more briskly with the five remaining pseudo-facts. The seventh, about land reclamation, does not apply in any significant way to the Blean; and this is not the place to explore Romney Marsh or the East Anglian fen lands. The others are, to varying degrees, of local importance. The much repeated claim that the country, and in particular its southern parts, were stripped of woodland because of an unremitting demand for wood to burn in its iron and steel works and for use in its ship-building yards is unpersuasive in general and plainly false with respect to the Blean. For one thing, iron working is associated with the Weald of Kent rather than with Canterbury and the Thanet area. For another, the mediocre soil of the Blean did not, and does not, yield any sizeable stock of large timber to exploit and exhaust. The quality of timbers characteristic of the Blean in those dwellings and barns surviving from the later Middle Ages is, typically, twisted, gnarled and undersized. So if there was a shortage it was of this selective kind; and it must have been a chronic natural phenomenon rather than the result of greed and over-exploitation in the seventeenth and eighteenth centuries. A further and less precise ground for the belief that man exhausted England's wood resources has already been noted: the idea that wood is worth having only when it comes in the form of large standard trees, and once they're gone they're gone forever.

The suggestion that hedges are a recent contrivance dating no further back than the late eighteenth century Enclosure Acts is, likewise, misleading in general and false of the Blean. A number of hedges greatly antedate the Enclosure movement in several of the Blean's woods. Old, not to say ancient, hedges may be detected next to Church Wood, and in Short Tenement and Ellenden Woods. And there is reason to think that some of the Blean woodbanks were originally hedged on top. It is worth adding, too, that by no means all hedges are human-made. Not all hedges were made to enclose fields as such. If a line of scrub grew up to the edge of your cultivations - and you found it convenient to drive your stock along that scrub line, out to their pasture in the morning and back to the fold yard in the evening, a "hedge" would be created in a matter of a few years.[17]

Earlier I discussed the enthusiasm for planting new trees. This is one area of a vast topic, and it is possible to do little more than diagnose one well-intentioned but misguided motive: the idea that interfering, no matter how expertly, with trees destroys them so that unless we replace them none will eventually be left. Quite apart from the risk of planting the wrong kinds of trees (rather like the nineteenth century introduction of red foxes and rabbits into Australia), replanting is often born of alarm and misunderstanding which drive out more appropriate methods of conservation. After all, woods have been around a long time and are still there largely by courtesy of nature; and nature is ill served by attempts to usurp it. The alarm and misunderstanding are a part of a fashionable global panic about, amongst much else, alleged deforestation worldwide. For example, the Worldwatch Institute claims that *'deforestation has been accelerating over the last 30 years'*, and that now is the eleventh hour for saving the world's forest. By contrast, Bjørn Lomborg has recently argued that this is far too alarmist: Although the world has lost about 20% of its forest cover since farming began, depletion has come to a halt and temperate forests are in fact expanding.[18] And surveys do indeed suggest that Britain has more woodland cover than it had 200 years ago. But this is another broader story.

Christopher Cherry

References:
1. Even errors of this sort may contribute to some grander misconception. But it is not typically so. Grand misconceptions about woods as about other things are not collections of individual muddles and mistakes but visions we cling to because *we want and need to*, irrespective of their authenticity.
2. Revised edition, J.M. Dent & Sons Ltd. (London), 1983, pp. 23-24 (excerpted). Slightly different formulations of pseudo-history and its attractions are to be found in Rackham's *History of the Countryside*, and *The Lost Forest: the*

story of Hatfield Forest, J.M. Dent & Sons Ltd. (London), 1989; and in "Prospects for Landscape History and Historical Ecology", in *Landscapes*, Vol. 1, No. 2 (Oct. 2000); see especially pp. 9-10. See also *The Making of the Cretan Landscape*, by O .Rackham and Jennifer Moody, Manchester University Press (1996), Ch. 2 pp.9-11.

3. Puffin Picture Books, Penguin Books Ltd., Harmondsworth. My copy gives no date, but it cannot have been published later than 1948. Neither pages nor pictures are numbered so I give no further references.

4. *A Land*, Jacquetta Hawkes, Cresset Press, 1951; and Penguin Books Ltd., (Harmondsworth), 1959.

. Op. Cit., p.171. Hawkes however recognises that "Mesolithic hunters" did sometimes fell trees!

6. Paladin (Frogmore), 1977. *The Changing Face of Britain* was first published ion 1974 by Kestrel Books.

7. Op.cit., p.74.

8. Op.cit., p.75. The whole of Hyam's chapter 5 - Deforestation and Building - is a joy for the student of factoids. It becomes clear that Hyams himself finds it hard to believe in the improbable time-span he allows for the transformation of the countryside. Speaking of what he supposed happened between 1100 and 1550, he remarks that "it must have seemed that no effort made by a few thousand men could ever make more than a marginal impression on the trees, (but) such was their energy that by Tudor times England was growing seriously short of timber …. And men of vision were not felling oaks but planting them". (Op.cit., pp75-77)

9. I have in mind W.G. Hoskin's *English Landscapes*, published in 1973 by the BBC.

10. Op.cit., p.23. Nonetheless it must be emphasised that time and again Hoskins challenges the prevailing vision. Thus: "there might have been as much land under the plough in 1086 as in the year 1914" (ibid.)

11. Brotherhood Farm, the University's site, was demolished in the Summer of 1964. Previous hedging, coppicing and ditching cannot date to after about 1950, which makes a gap of some fifty years. Since the University was established the old farmland to the South has been vigorously landscaped, orchards grubbed up, hedges demolished and trees planted. Many original standards remain, however.12. *Tree News*, the magazine of the Tree Council, Spring/ Summer 2001, pp.48-49.

13. The episode also shows that what until recently were regarded as the rights of a landowner have been eroded or over-ruled by legislation, public opinion or by a system of grants and subsidies which carry one or both an implicit right to public scrutiny and an explicit right of public access. [From a transcript of a talk by Anthony Waterson (12 July 1998).]

14. As Wheaten and others point out (see especially Chapter IV , page 35), one reason why the woods have remained much the same size and shape over the last two thousand years or so is that the soil tends to be poor for agricultural purposes. Land cleared from time to time was often subsequently abandoned and allowed to revert to woodland.

15. Prehistoric artefacts and 'pot boilers' may indicate transients rather than settled folk. But this is unlikely to always be the case. At the other end of the range we are on much safer ground, for the detailed records kept by the great Blean landowners, the Cathedral and other bodies provide a picture of life in the Blean unlike the earlier pseudo-picture.

16. Strictly speaking, there are two 'Radfall Roads', the more prominent being the one which appears to stretch from Chestfield (or Herne) to the north to Dunkirk and South Bishopsden Wood in the south-west, via Clowes Wood, Church Wood and Grimshill Wood.

17. Stringent new rules on hedgerows came into force on 1st June 1997, so there is hope that they will not disappear altogether. Even so, regulation 13 implies

that it makes good historical and ecological sense to "replace" a hedgerow rather as one might replace a lawnmower.

18. B. Lomborg, *The Skeptical Environmentalist*, Cambridge University Press, 2001. It needs to be said that Lomberg's work has already inspired considerable debate, and his claims are vigorously contested by some.

Geology and Soils

Chapter III

The Physical Background

The area covered by the Blean Woods lies in the north-east of Kent, between the Thames estuary and the valley of the River Stour and extends over the higher ground for about 11km from Boughton-under-Blean in the west to Herne and Hoath in the east. It encompasses over 3,000 hectare (about 8,000 acres) of woodland and scrub as well as some farm land, some of which was presumably reclaimed, or *'assarted'* from woodland in the middle ages.

Over recent years the area has been mostly dry with annual rainfall totals of 500-600 mm with most of the rain falling in autumn and winter. However at the time of writing [2001] there has been more than twice the average annual rainfall, extending over three months. This apparently follows the predictions of global warming which, if they are correct, may well change the nature of the woods over a long period of time. In any case when there is little evapo-transpiration it can become waterlogged for months in winter as much of the soil is heavy clay. Over the year, mid-day temperatures can range from -5° C in the winter to 30°C in summer. Occasionally nightly minima of five degrees or so below this have been recorded in winter with hotter summer days of 35°C or even more.

The area forms a gentle *'hog's back'* on a NE - SW axis sloping towards the Thames estuary in the north and the Stour valley in the south with a maximum height of about 80 metres above sea level. Small, mainly seasonal streams drain to north and south but the only permanent stream is the Fishbourne or Sarre Penn, which rises on the land of Forester's Lodge Farm near the boundary with the Brotherhood Woods at the western edge of the Blean woodlands, and eventually flows into the River Stour.

The whole area is surrounded by busy main roads (A2, A28 and A229) but the woodlands are relatively remote although readily accessible from minor roads and tracks. The atmosphere suffers rather severe pollution from the roads but more significantly from being south-east of London and east of the

Medway Towns. Attempts to reduce traffic and other forms of pollution can only be beneficial.

Overall control of land use is co-ordinated by English Nature although within the area separate parcels are managed, a large proportion by public bodies such as Canterbury City Council, Swale Borough Council, English Nature and the Royal Society for the Protection of Birds and some by private individuals and companies. In June 2001 an enlarged area was designated as Blean Woods National Nature Reserve.

The Geology and Soils

The woodland of the Blean to the north and west of Canterbury lies almost exclusively on a basement of London Clay, which was laid down during the Eocene Period. (See Fig. 3.1)

Fig. 3.1 Geological Time Scale

Periods	*Epochs*	*Onset [Millions of years ago]*
Tertiary	Holocene	0.01
	Pleistocene	2
	Pliocene	7
	Miocene	26
	Oligocene	38
	Eocene	54
	Palaeocene	65
Cretaceous		135

The Geological Survey for this region includes a few relatively small areas covered with either *'head gravel'* or *'head brickearth'* in which silts and fine sands predominate rather than clay. This is somewhat misleading as these maps show only areas where such *'drift'* is more than a metre deep. Other areas in the Blean have been found to have a sand-silt cover of up to a metre, e.g. 88cm in Grimshill Wood whilst at others the clay is covered by a thin soil of only a few cm e.g. Blean Wood itself. Extensively in the Blean area there are varying amounts of sub-sub-mature flint-pebbles.[1]

What has not yet been determined is the extent to which this sandy-loam capping affects the flora of the woodland. In a detailed study for the Nature Conservancy in 1973 Stevens[2] found Chestnut and Birch absent from the solid clay areas but the number of sites surveyed, seven in all, are too few for statistical reliability. No other studies are available. Kirby in 1985[3] made a more extensive study of the vegetation of the Blean Woods but made no soil analyses and our own work seldom involved soil study, or no proper survey of the flora accompanied it.

Fig. 3.2a: Section through the Weald: West Kent - East Sussex

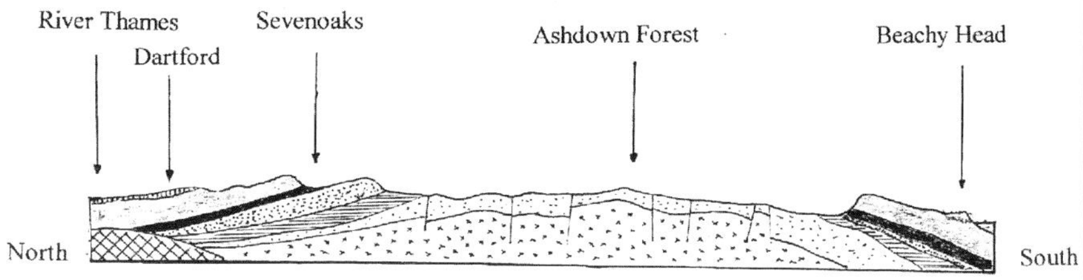
River Thames
Dartford
Sevenoaks
Ashdown Forest
Beachy Head
North
South

Fig. 3. 2a Section through the Weald: West Kent - East Sussex
[After A. E. Trueman]

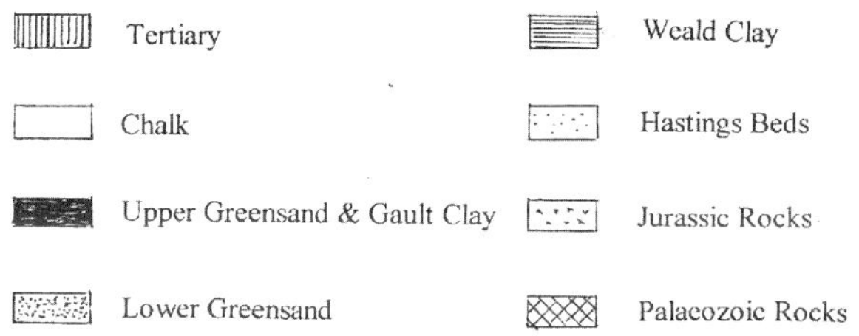
Tertiary
Weald Clay
Chalk
Hastings Beds
Upper Greensand & Gault Clay
Jurassic Rocks
Lower Greensand
Palaeozoic Rocks

Before considering the soil structure of the Blean Woods in more detail, the geological history is of interest. During Cretaceous times most of England was covered by a sea which deposited a chalk *'mud'* - made from the remains of vast numbers of microscopic organisms with a calcareous skeleton. Towards the end of this period earth movements, due in particular to the collision of the African Plate with the Eurasian Plate, caused the sea floor to buckle and in south-east England it rose forming a somewhat fragmented dome of land which is now the Weald (Fig.3.2a). Subsequently, the sea level has risen and fallen a number of times eroding the uplifted land and in north Kent some of this eroded material was re-deposited on the sea floor to form a number of soft rock strata which now underlie the Blean area (see Figs. 3.2b & 3.3) some of which, as in Ellenden Wood, show evidence of slumping.

Fig. 3.2b: Geological Section through the Blean Area to show Tertiary Deposits

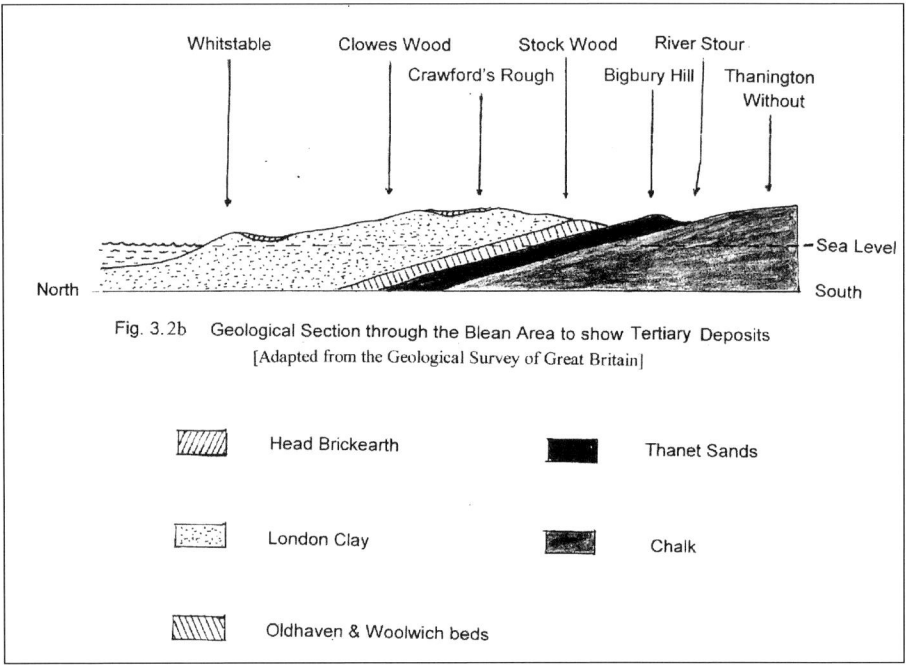

Fig. 3.2b Geological Section through the Blean Area to show Tertiary Deposits
[Adapted from the Geological Survey of Great Britain]

Since London Clay times (about 47 million years ago) there has been much erosion, particularly by the Stour and Thames but the London Clay itself is quite resistant so that hills of this deposit remain on the Isle of Sheppey and between Canterbury and Whitstable. The Blean Woods exist here almost certainly because the unforgiving nature of the clay has rendered the area unsuitable for agriculture.

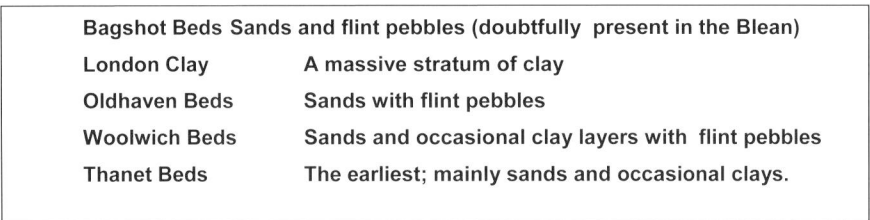

Fig. 3.3: Ecocene Deposits in North Kent

The origin of the *'head'* deposits capping the London Clay mentioned above is still in dispute. They are likely to be Late Glacial to Post-Glacial and probably formed by solifluxion (the slow downhill movement of soil as a result of the alternate freezing and thawing of the contained water); windblown loss from the north-west during Pleistocene times has been suggested for some areas. Neither theory accounts for the flint pebbles found extensively in the Blean and in Essex as well. It seems likely that at some time, probably during an inter-glacial period during the Ice ages, the entire area was flooded by the sea, and shingle deposited by longshore drift. Gallois[4] states that that chert pebbles deriving from the Lower Greensand are to be found in deposits dating from late Eocene time onwards. It is also possible that they could be remnants of the Bagshot Beds which have been recorded on the nearby Isle of Sheppey.

Moving from a general geological history to a more detailed consideration of the soils of the Blean Woods, we have a variable pattern ranging from heavy clays just below the surface to substantial depths of sandy loam with differing amounts of silt. Stevens[5] states:

> *'Soils on the London Clay are gleys (= bluish-grey sticky clays found under some types of clay soil) with poor drainage and heavy texture'* and later *'The (National Nature) Reserve is almost entirely wooded, the complete canopy permitting only sparse shrub and ground flora. However recently exposed coppiced areas on the London Clay have a dense shrub population and an abundance of herb species. The Plateau Gravel supports some woodland of a similar nature to that of the London Clay, but a heath type of vegetation is more extensive on the gravel, especially in the north of Crawford's Rough and extreme north of Mincing Wood.'*

Stevens was concerned only with the area of the National Nature Reserve which is only a small part of the Blean Woods, but it is likely that his conclusions would apply to most of the rest the area unsuitable for agriculture since the soils are similar. He found them to be universally acid, averaging about pH 4.5. The exception is the southern part of Stock Wood where a small stream, a tributary of the Stour has succeeded in cutting right down through the London Clay and exposes the Oldhaven and Woolwich beds; these are much sandier and better drained. We have yet to survey the vegetation in this area nor have we any detailed analysis of the mineral content but it would be interesting to compare it with those on heavier soils. And of course woodlands on quite different types of soil exist to the south of

Canterbury. A table of soil particle analysis is in Figs. 3.4 and Fig. 3.5 gives their location. These show the range of texture from the London Clay in Blean Wood to the sandy loam Woolwich Beds in Stock Wood. An even sandier sample taken from Hunstead Woods on the Thanet Beds to the south-west of Canterbury is out of our area but it serves to put the nature of the Stock Wood soil into perspective. A sample taken from the Moated Site in North Bishopsden Wood is so much out of character, almost pure sand, that it may be the result of human intervention although such sand-bases are known to occur on a similar geological profile in eastern England.

Further research in the Blean Woods needs to be done to establish precisely what, if any, effect the varying soil profiles have on the vegetation. However the situation is further compounded by the extensive human intervention which has occurred over the years.

Robert Foster

References:
1. *Soils of the Blean Wood National Nature Reserve, Kent*, P.A. Stevens, Pedology Section, Bangor, 1973
2. Ibid.
3. *A Survey of the Blean Woodlands (Kent)*, K. J. Kirby, 1985.
4. *British Regional Geology: The Wealden District*, R. W. Gallois, London: HMSO 1965.
5. Ibid., p.29.

Site	Stock Wood	Blean	Church Wood	N Bishopsden Wd	Grimshill Wood	Crawford's Rough	Hunstead Woods
	1m east of stream	Short Tenement		Moated Site	(After Stevens)*		
Parent Rock [Brit. Geol.Survey 1938]	London Clay	London Clay	London Clay	London Clay	London Clay	Head Gravel	Thanet Beds
Map Ref. [National Grid]	TR122590	TR120602	TR123595	TR094600	TR107607	TR117608	TR093565
Height above Mean Sea Level	50m	70m	78m	85m	67m	80m	96m
Sample Depth	45cm	30cm	70cm	30cm	30cm	30cm	30cm
Particle Size Range							
Pebble 64 - 4 mm	0	0	0	0	?	?	40%
Gravel 4 - 2 mm	0	0	0	0	?	?	15%
Coarse Sand 2000 - 200 μm	0	0	0	0	}	}	9%
fine Sand 200 - 20 μm	5%	0	20%	95%	65%	55%	18%
Silt 20 - 2 μm	10%	10%	30%	4%	23%	25%	17%
Clay < 2 μm	85%	90%	50%	1%	3%	10%	1%
Soil Type [UK Classification, 1976]	clay	clay	clay	sand	sandy loam	sandy-loam	sandy loam
Particle type	sub-mature	?	?	?	sub-mature	sub-mature	sub-mature

Notes.

1. The clay particle content in the top 80 cms of soil from areas all designated "London Clay" by the Geological Survey shows the extreme variation found.
2. The sample from the Moated Site suggests that human agency may be responsible here. More samples from this locality would be needed for confirmation.
3. The samples from Grimshill Wood and Crawford's Rough may have ignored gravel content and analysed only soil.
4. The sample from Hunstead Woods [to the south-west of Canterbury] where the parent rock is Thanetian gives a contrast to the Blean Woods.
5. That the soil particles were sub-mature suggests that they were orignally subject to river wash.
6. The samples were made by a member of the group except for one (marked *where the data was obtained from *Soils of the Blean Woods National Nature Reserve, Kent* , P.A. Stevens, Bangor, 1973).

Fig. 3.4: Soil Particle Analysis of Samples from the Blean Woods

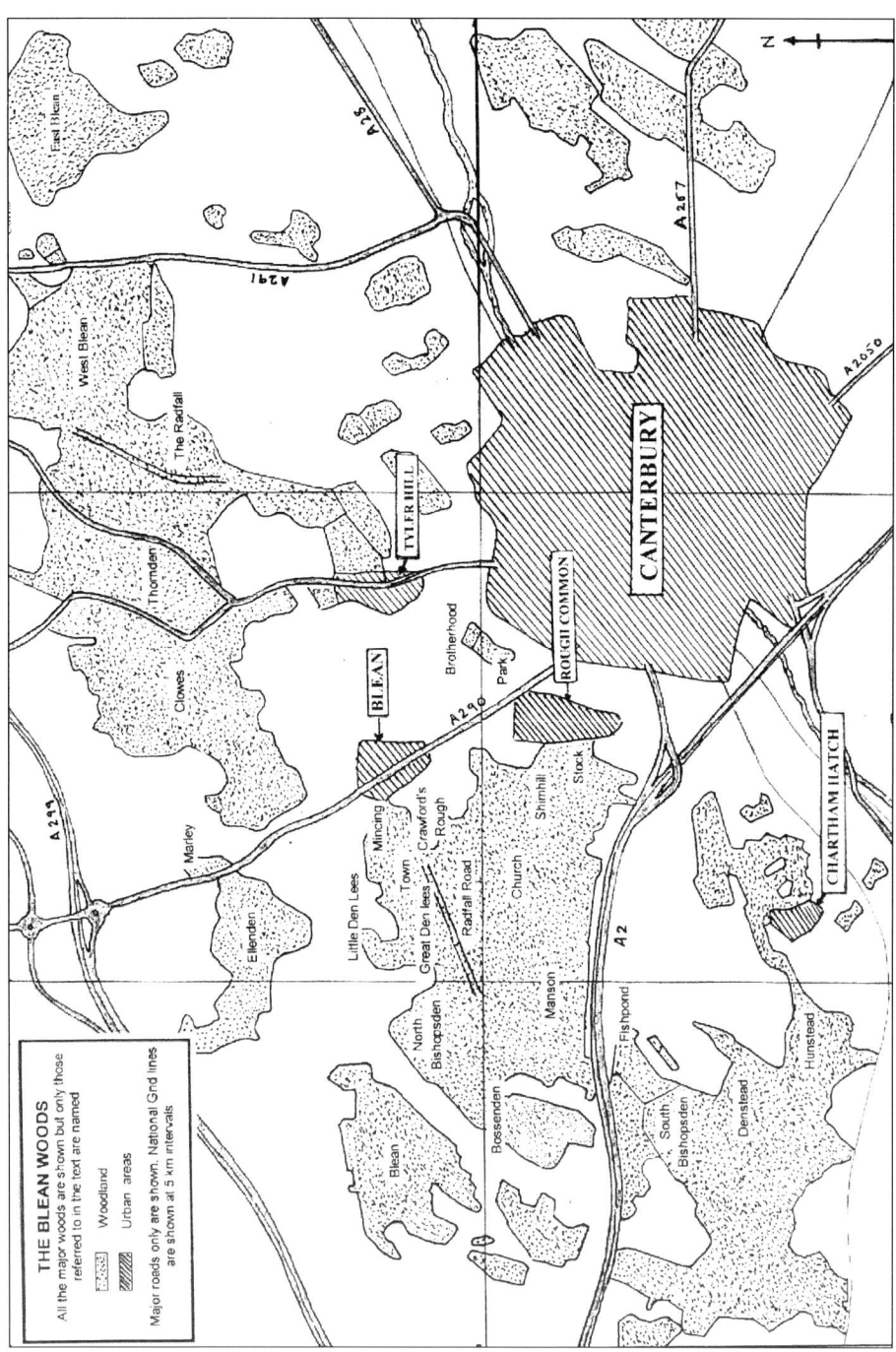

Fig. 3.5: The Various Woods which make up the Blean

Archaeology and History
Chapter IV
Artefacts as Evidence

Flints from Palaeolithic times, before the last Ice Age, have been found, often in spectacular quantities, in Kent. Some of the most dramatic finds were made in the nineteenth-century gravel workings at Swanscombe. Flint artefacts found on or near the surface in woods or open fields by walkers in the Blean are usually of the Mesolithic (Middle Stone Age) or Neolithic (Late Stone Age) periods.

As the last ice-cap receded about 10,000 years ago the tundra-like conditions in the south-east of England gave way to forests of pine, birch and hazel. As a warmer Atlantic climate evolved a more varied deciduous forest developed. Pollen counts show that lime, hazel, oak, and alder made up the 'wildwood' of southern Britain. At this time eastern England was still connected to the European mainland from Denmark to the Low Countries, the Thames joined the Rhine and they flowed into the North Sea. The slowly increasing range of vegetation sustained animal life which steadily attracted the hunting and fishing communities of the northern European forests as they sought new foraging opportunities. The Blean Woods, on the light sandy soil through which the Fishbourne-Sarre Penn stream flows, made an hospitable environment for nomadic communities to camp in. Their flint artefacts have been numerous and interesting in the limited areas of the Blean that have been cleared, cultivated and opened up for archaeological survey.

Below Tyler Hill in the exposed banks and stream-bed of the Sarre Penn several horizons of dense calcinated flint, often mixed with black ash and charcoal, suggest possible settlement sites.[1] Along the upper stream small 'pot boilers' have been found in the banks at a consistent longitudinal level of about 1.5 metres. These pot-boilers are stones that have crazed surfaces caused by exposure to heating and to cooling. As an early method of cooking, flints were apparently heated in the fire and then dropped into a lined pit, or later a clay bowl, containing food in water. Repetition of this process resulted in the water being heated until the food was cooked. The rapid changes of temperature caused a distinctive crazing on the flints. Flints with this characteristic crazing occur frequently on later prehistoric sites.

Fig. 4.1 - Scrapes and Flints found in 1994/95 (not original size)

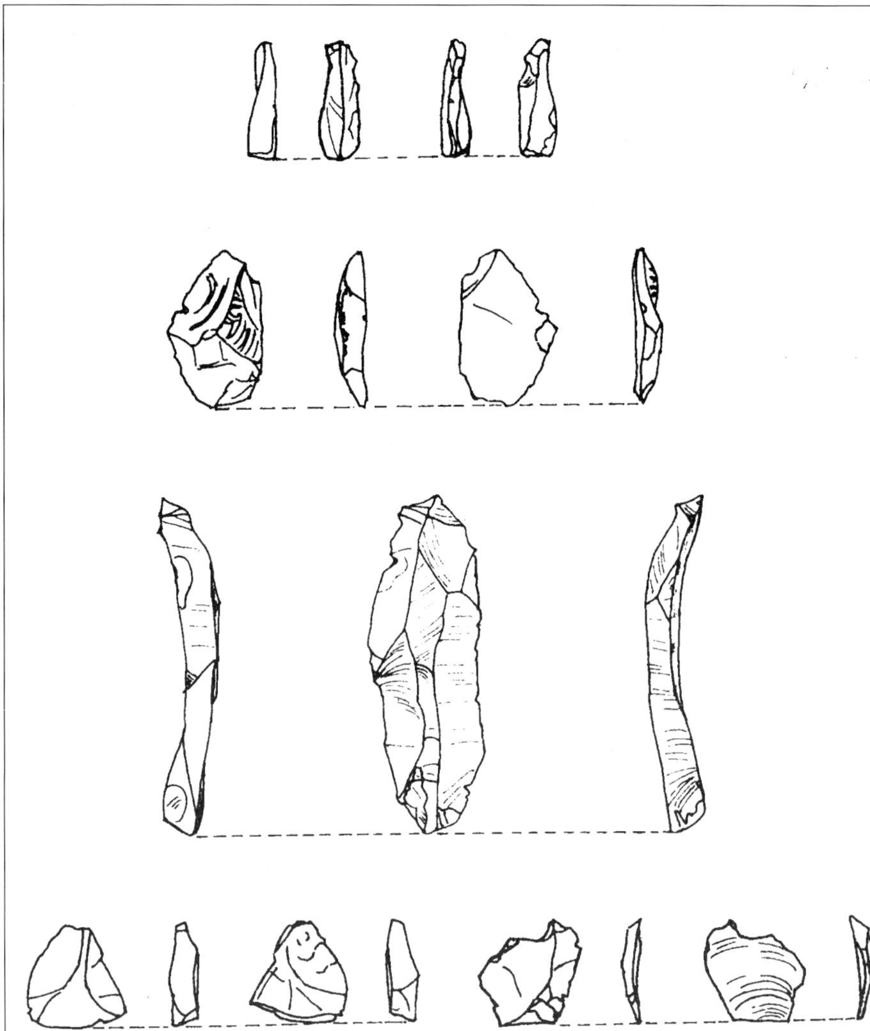

Field walking almost anywhere in the Blean can produce occasional finds of worked flint, but two areas which have recently been under the plough became of particular interest and provided an abundant quantity of worked material.

Along the stream above Tyler Hill, where it is called the Fishbourne, the Blean Research Group explored the three fields of Short Tenement which had been cleared in the sixteenth-century.

After a recent ploughing 350 worked, or re-worked, cores, blades, flakes, scrapers, piercers, were collected along with one tranchet axe, an awl and a large flint adze. The hunting communities which camped in the favourable conditions of the Blean and made their tools there could have found flint nodules on the coastal cliffs of Thanet, or in the Elham valley, or on the surface of the chalk uplands south of the Stour. Workable pebbles are also found in the gravel beds of many local streams. In a field which is known to have been cultivated for more than a thousand years, near Blean church and the site of the medieval Blean manor there is a spring known as 'Cosmus Well'. Plentiful worked flints, particularly cores and flakes were found.

The arrival of Neolithic peoples and ideas around 6000 years ago eventually brought changes to the Blean. The incomers introduced new knowledge of both agriculture and pastoralism and began the clearing, destruction even, of the 'wildwood'. Technology evolved in communities which were both larger and more sedentary than the foraging camps had been. The clearing of woodland for agriculture carried on steadily into the Iron Age, along the coastal lowlands of north Kent as well as the Isle of Thanet, the Stour valley and the Faversham farming parish of 'Boughton-under-Blean'. Many of the eighty or so individual woods within the Blean have smaller or larger signs of occupation, or even fortification, the largest prehistoric fort being at Bigbury, immediately west of Canterbury. Clowes Wood not only has burial tumuli but also pot sherds belonging to the transition from the Bronze Age to the Iron Age while Chestfield has its own Iron Age settlement.[2] The woods, however, were on the margin of the more actively inhabited coastlands of Kent and it has even been suggested that the name Blean might be derived from *blaen*, a Welsh term for an upland country of poor fertility.[3] The abandoning of land that had once been cleared but had later proved to be of mediocre fertility happened regularly in the Blean from early times. This partly explains why the woods remain so extensive to-day while other southern woodlands have shrunk dramatically.

By the time Julius Caesar passed though eastern Kent in 54 BC most of the lowland had been cleared of its 'primaeval' wildwood.[4] Land had been cultivated and roadways developed into a network leaving the woods largely confined to the higher ground. Caesar described Kent's inhabitants: *ex eis omnibus longe sunt humanissimi, qui Cantium incollunt* or the least backward of the people of south-east England. They were also, of course, those closest to Gaul and most open to new cultural influences.[5]

The Romans who arrived in force ninety years after Caesar's visit set about improving the old British road system which Caesar himself had used on his remarkable night march from the coast to Bigbury. The paved highway to London was named Watling Street and commercial roads linked Canterbury's northern gate to Reculver and its western gate to Seasalter.[6] To the west of the Seasalter road as it runs through the Blean a pattern of ditches which is independent of those associated with medieval wood banks have been recorded. Ditches which run parallel to the road may be of Roman origin and may indicate that areas which are now woodland were field systems in Roman times. A survey of these ditches in Mincing Wood suggested that the lengths of the ditches appear to be calibrated in multiples of the Roman *actus* of 39 yards and that field systems correlate to the Roman *jugera* of about one acre.

In addition to being surrounded by fertile countryside the Blean has an area in its midst where brickearth covers the London Clay and makes the land suitable for both ancient and modern farming. Evidence of a substantial Roman house has been found in what became the parish of St Cosmus and St Damian in the Blean. The extent of the farming household is demonstrated by the distribution of Roman potsherds, bricks, floor tiles and roof tiles of both the *imbrice* and *tegulae* styles.[7] Four fragments, in a fine sandy fabric similar to tiles excavated from kiln sites in Canterbury, have been dated to the first or second century. Two fragments of stone quern from the same site could be of Roman origin but may belong to the Anglo-Saxon period. Finds of a later period, thought to be from the site of the hall where a manorial court would have been convened, have been described as *'fragments of decorated glazed floor-tiles, largely featuring geometrical patterns with stylised flowers and heraldic beasts from panels of four to sixteen tiles'*.[8] Some of the local tile kilns which could have supplied such fine ware have recently been excavated.

Over the centuries sections of the Blean woods appear to have been only sparsely covered by trees. Where Thornden Wood slopes northward towards the sea, field walkers have found first or second century Roman potsherds in what is now woodland. Unusual shards of grog-tempered ware come from a large pot probably designed to contain the bones of a cremated body. The chance find of a Belgic gold coin in East Blean Wood, now in the Canterbury museum, may be less indicative of occupation than the Clowes Wood or Thornden Wood shards.

After the departure of the expatriate Romans in the fifth century early Anglo-Saxons of Jute affiliation began to settle in Kent. The less fertile fields in Church Wood, Mincing Wood and Crawfords's Rough were apparently allowed to revert to woodland fairly quickly. On the better soils such as those near the church of Blean farming continued to be practised and in 1995 Anglo-Saxon loom weights were found suggesting that further searches might be fruitful.

The Jutes probably used ancient drove-ways to move their animals seasonally from the low coastal grazing to the chalk upland further south. Drove-ways running from north-east to south-west have been plotted across the landscape from Ospringe in the east to Detling in the west and it seems logical to assume that similar drove-ways crossed the Blean to the east of Ospringe.[8] One prominent 'ancient lane with woodbanks' runs through the Blean on what is now the Swalecliffe road. Another, which is known in modern custom as a 'Radfall Road', follows the northern boundary of Church Wood and leads from Herne or Chestfield through Clowes Wood to Dunkirk and South Bishopsden.

The Written Record
In a charter of AD 850 the Blean is referred to as a 'wood', *silva que se dicitur Blean*.[9] At no time was it ever referred to as a 'royal forest'. Both Lambarde, writing in 1570, and Hasted, writing in 1778, state that there were no 'forests' of protected hunting land in Kent.[10]

The Anglo-Saxon period was a time when pannage or stock feeding on acorns and beech mast was important and when a number of the woods in the Blean appear to have acquired a name which includes the suffix 'den'. These names apply to some of the larger woods of the Blean lying near the two main drove-ways. Ellenden Wood, near Seasalter, lies north of North Bishopden Wood, Bossenden Wood and South Bishopden Wood. Thornden Wood is next to the Swalecliffe road. Other names suggestive of swine pasture include Denstroude, Great Den Lees and Little Den Lees, all near North Bishopden, and Denstead Wood further to the south. The right of pannage belonged to different manors and monastic houses. The pannage given in 724 to the nuns of Minster Abbey, in Thanet, might refer to the Mincing Wood which lies along the drove road from Thanet.[11] 'Mincing' derives from the old word *myncene*, meaning nuns, and occurs in the name of another Mincing Wood lying between Canterbury and Faversham Wood.[12]

By the end of the Anglo-Saxon period the importance of swine pasture, or pannage, had begun to decline. However in 1086 the compilers of the Domesday Book still chose to value woodland in Kent according to the number of swine that could be pastured there.[13] In the Blean they recorded the value of woodland attached to each of the manors. Chislet, a manor of St. Augustine's Abbey in Canterbury, was registered as a woodland *de pasnag cxxx porc*. The figure of 130 pigs represented one tenth of the swine herd that could be pastured there. The lord of the manor, the abbot, was nominally entitled to receive one tenth of the swine which his tenants grazed on the land. An attempt to speculate on the number of swine per acre, on the basis of a comparison with the Wealden woodlands of West Kent, has suggested that pannage was based on 'rather less than one pig for every three acres'.[14] Such a yardstick would suggest that the woodland of Chislet exceeded 3000 acres in extent. The Blean woods were apparently not dense, and the Domesday Book describes a woodland near Canterbury belonging to the king as 'mille acrae silvae infructuosae', a thousand acres of unfruitful woodland. On the scale of pannage suggested for Chislet the king's infertile soil may have only yielded fifty pigs in tax revenue. Overall the medieval Blean woods, listed in the table below, were distributed as they are to-day and had long since ceased to stretch towards the coast. Their monastic proprietors used them for feeding their swine herds but principally for coppicing to supply their considerable fuel requirements.

Each of the eleventh-century manors associated with the Blean possessed agricultural land as well as woodland. The column giving the number of ploughs registered by each enables an historian to estimate the land cultivated by each manor. It is assumed that more labour would be devoted to farming than to woodland occupations. The working population of most manors had access to a local church, as at Blean itself, though no record of a church has been found for Swalecliffe, Northgate or Bough-

Fig. 4.2 Manors with Woodland in the Blean Recorded in Domesday Book

Manor (old)	Manor (modern)	Lord of Manor	Swine Rent No.	Plough No.
CHISTELET	Chislet	St. Augustine's Abbey	130	2
FAVERSHANT	Faversham	King William	100	17
BLEHEM (unusual spelling)	Blean	Hamo, the Sherrif	60	4
ESTURSETTE	Westgate	Archbishop	60	-
NORTONE	Whitstable	Archbishop	50	37
BOLTUNE	Boughton under Blean	Archbishop	45	17
NORDEVEDE	Northgate	Cathedral Priory	30	3?
ESTURAI	Sturry	St Augustine's Abbey	30	14
SOANCLIVE	Swalecliffe	Odo, Earl of Kent	30	1?
ROCULF	Reculver	Archbishop	20	3
SESLTRE	Seasalter	Cathedral Priory	10	2
CERTEHAM	Chartham	Cathedral Priory	?	?

ton. The church-centred communities lie in a ring surrounding the woods and may have grown from manorial chapels. The only 'wilderness' church is that of St Cosmus and St Damian which lies at the heart of the Blean. It is not known whether the church had received its dedication before the Norman Conquest, but by 1220 it had become the Blean parish church.[15] By 1590 several additional churches had been added to those recorded in Domesday. A church, however, should not be taken as evidence for the existence of a village, some belonged to mere hamlets, manor, or even to single farms.

In the Blean it has been said that 'woodbanks' are sometimes a more eloquent record of medieval activity than any written record. Many of these woodbanks are fortunately still visible and, better still, can be linked to documentary evidence describing their construction and upkeep. In the thirteenth century the Kent population was rising and the demand for timber and fuel was increasing. The ecclesiastical institutions, hospitals and charity houses which owned the Blean woods underwent vigorous expansion. Beneath the high trees, or standards, grown for building timbers, a valuable underwood was coppiced for fuel. The new wealth of the woods meant that the old ownership boundaries needed to be further emphasised. The great boundary banks built up in the Middle Ages are still to be seen in many parts of the wood to-day. The massive woodbanks of the Blean were constructed with ditches on the outer side of the boundary. Many of them were topped with hedges to prevent cattle from straying and grazing the underwood. The compartments, or in Kent 'cants', were defined with a system of 'cant marks' which are short pollarded trees which were maintained along the boundaries. In certain locations the pollarded trees were much taller and formed distinctive boundary markers. Present-day cant marks rarely date from before the seventeenth century and even the heritage of the surviving ones is being lost since timber clearance is being abandoned in the twenty-first century. Although the earliest cant marks are no longer to be found, ancient layered beech hedges still remain on some of the woodbanks. For example on the southern boundary of 'Short Tenement.'

Place names, woodbanks and old boundaries can tell something about ancient woods and their management. More specific information is to be found in account books which describe the expenditures incurred by woodland owners. The most revealing archives are those of the Dean and Chapter of Canterbury Cathedral who took over the woodlands of Christchurch Priory.[16] By the late twelfth century the priory had become one of the largest woodland owners in the Blean, and from the thirteenth century accounts of the cash transactions relating to the woodland are preserved. These rather scant early records might be deemed to indicate that most woodland workers were paid in kind rather than in coin and that much of the timber and fuel extracted by priory labourers was for the priory's own use rather than for sale on the open market. The cash transactions do, however, include sums paid for the pannage of pigs and the pasturing of cattle. The composite accounts are listed under the heading *computus de bosco,* the accounts of the woodland. Timber from the Blean was probably less significant than fuel and its extraction is separately listed in the accounts of the monastery carpenter. For most building work local timber was quite inadequate, however, and by 1235 the records indicate that large sums were spent on importing timbers even from as far afield as

Ireland.[17] A century later, in 1341, timber was so scarce in the Blean that the priory was not even able to meet a request by the Prince of Wales for the supply of a dozen timber trees.[18]

One set of accounts relating to an individual Blean estate and its woodland concerns Amery Court. The estate, in the northern part of the parish of Blean, was managed by a monk who held the office of Almoner, hence the estate's later name of 'Amery'. In 1292 the overseer sold corn, cattle, fleeces, honey and faggots. In 1293 he spent one silver mark (13 shillings and 6 pence) to build a woodbank, *fossat faciend*, measuring 96 'old yards'. The old Anglo-Saxon yard, or verg, was measured with a 'gryd' stick cut from a coppice to resemble the latter-day measuring rod known as a pole or a perch. If the ancient yardstick measured 16½ modern feet the woodbank would have been 528 yards long, more than five times longer than 96 modern yards.[19] In addition to paying large sums for the building of long woodbanks, the estate also paid out a management fee to a 'beadle' of 13 shillings and 10 pence, a handsome salary compared to the wages of 2 shillings a year, *p'totum annum*, paid to working lads.[20]

Other Blean estates spent similar sums on their woodland management. In 1235 57 shillings and 6 pence was spent on a long woodbank around Thornden Wood, *in fassatis circa Thorndenn*, and sixteen years later a further 50 shillings and 3 pence had to be spent on woodbank construction or maintenance. The northern woodbank of Thornden Wood is large and was no doubt expensive to build, but small landowners also had to spend money on lesser banks around their properties. In Church Wood the bank which protects the priory's lands from cattle using the Radfall drove-road was higher than the one built on the other side of the fall by lesser landlords. Even after centuries of erosion on the banks and of silting in the ditches the priory woodbank is still five feet high while the opposing one is only three feet high. The width of the livestock roadway varies between eleven and twenty-one modern yards.

By the fifteenth century fuel was by far the most important source of income from the Blean. The pannage of pigs had virtually disappeared as an industry, either because pigs damaged the young shoots that had to be protected to make faggots or because the absence of mature oaks limited the supply of acorn fodder. When oak was harvested, however, the bark was highly prized for tanning. Some ash was also planted in the Blean to produce rods, stakes, poles, and hurdles. *Vynrodds* were used to support the monastery's vines. Both Short Wood and Thornden Wood appear to have hired 'foresters' to make faggots. *Ketchynfagots* were presumably prepared for the kitchen cooks and *Adventwode* was harvested at Christmastide. Logs for the hearth came as *ostwode, stumbyll* or *bilets*. The common small faggots were *Courtfagots* and large ones *Salefagots* or *Halfagots* as shown in the bill of sale drawn up at Michaelmas 1462 by John Smale, a forester of Short Wood (now Church Wood). He charged between 7 pence and 2 shillings per hundred for bundling up his faggots.[21]

> 44,500 courtfagots for the monastery (with the rest sold for 8s. 8d.)
> 500 ketchynfagots for the monastery
> 1,450 halfagots sold for 48. 4d.
> 950 salefagots sold for 63s. 4d.

It would seem that Short Wood did particularly specialise in faggot production and the annual accounts for 1462 totalled more than £21 of which 64 shillings were the salary of the forester and the wages of his assistants. The faggot industry continued for centuries thereafter, not only in the great woods of the priory but also in a dozen smaller undertakings owned by proprietors ranging from the rich abbey of St Augustine, with holdings in West Blean Wood, to the modest hospital of St Jacob with a property in Mincing Wood. Some titles of ownership survived the Reformation and were transferred to modern institutions such as the National Nature Conservancy and the University of Kent only during the twentieth century.

While some woodland was being more intensively used and protected in the thirteenth century, other areas were being cleared. The new pockets of cultivated arable land were known as 'assarts', one such being recorded in the village name of 'Smarden'. In the Blean assarts were relatively uncommon and were mostly located on the margins of the woods. Their outlines were marked by strips of wood known as 'shaws' such as the medieval one still visible on the northern edge of Thornden Wood.[22] A tenant who cleared and cultivated an assart in the woods could expect to pay appropriate rent to the landlord, as shown in thirteenth-century references to assarts in the charters referring to Blean church and manor. One very early reference to the practice of clearing assarts in the woods dates from the autumn of 1189. Shortly before Christmas Richard Coeur de Lion visited the Cathedral Priory at Canterbury when setting off to fight in the Third Crusade. Before leaving he gave the priory *totum boscum nostrum de Blean cum assartis omnibus eisdem bosci*, that is the whole of his wood in the Blean together with all the assarts in the same wood.[23] A Christchurch monk, Gervase, described one wood as *boscum de Blen quod Srutte cognominatur*, the wood in the Blean which is called Srutte, a word written as 'Sorotte' when applied to a woodland belonging to Harbledown hospital and later modified to 'Short' or 'Shoort'.[24] This type of assart was recognised as giving local people a right to work fields associated with woodland groves. Royal permission to assart woodland had to be given. In the case of the Harbledown hospital the necessary permission had been granted by Henry I for *de bosco de Blen x perticatas terrae ad exsartandum*, ten perches of land to be assarted in the wood of Blean It was hardly a generous plot of land.[25]

At the time of the Domesday survey the manor of Blean and its church and outlying settlements were held by Hamo, the Sheriff of Kent. His descendant, Hamo de Crevecoer, also known as Hamo de Blen, became lord of the manor in 1199 according to the Curia Regis Rolls. Towards the end of his life Hamo began to give his properties in the Blean to the newly-established Hospital of St Thomas, on the Canterbury East Bridge. The Eastbridge Hospital became such an important Blean landowner that it acquired the status of a sub-manor with the right to hold a court and receive hearing from its tenants, to the detriment of the diminished secular lord of the manor of Blean. Some of the hospital's new properties were later sold to the Cathedral priory. Meanwhile Hamo of the Blean gave other properties to St Gregory's Priory in Northgate and by the thirteenth century the family was no longer the title holder to the manor of Blean. In 1260, indeed, the fortifying walls around the church were demolished (possibly along with the manor its self) when the current tenant, the Earl of Gloucester, was suspected of being in league with Simon de Montfort during the Barons' Revolt against Henry III. De Montfort's mother is said to have lived in a neighbouring parish.[26] Some years later another illustrious tenant, the ill-fated Sir Bartholomew Baddlesmere, apparently fell foul of Edward II and was eventually hanged for treason at Blean manor. In 1358 the manorial right passed to the Eastbridge Hospital which, in good institutional style, preserved the woodland charters representing a very long record of continuity of ownership and manorial lordship, these are now held in the Cathedral library. There they complement the records of other charitable bodies which held woods in the Blean including the hospitals of Northgate and Harbledown, both founded in the eleventh century by Archbishop Lanfranc, and of the Poor Priests' Hospital which acquired Town Wood in the thirteenth century.[27]

A 'Moated' Site

The Archbishop of Canterbury had a very early title to woodland in the Blean. Ownership was established over a thousand years ago between 597 and 762 and related to land at Boughton-in-the-Blean in the manor of Westgate.[28] This ownership is reflected in the name 'Bishopden Wood', both north and south. The south wood was managed for Archbishop Chichele in 1435 by his keeper, Simon Morle, who held the life-long title of *officium custodie boscorum* with a weekly wage of 18 pence and responsibility for four of the archbishop's woods. The keeper of the northern *Byssypshoth* was Guy Elomaster who was also *forestar* of the Shurte Wood (now known as Church Wood).[29] Since North Bishopsden bore the name *hoth* it may have included open heathlan

A survey of North Bishopsden, made in 1988, revealed a medieval 'moated site' (Fig.4.3) in the middle of the wood about a mile off Watling Street. An inner platform measuring about 25 yards by 25 yards is surrounded by an outer moat 100 yards long by 50 yards wide. The six-inch ordnance survey maps of 1870 and 1898 show a well on the site where the lands begins to slope down towards the north. In 1382, a year after Archbishop Simon Sudbury had been murdered in the Peasant's Revolt, William Courtnay, the new archbishop, ordered that trespassers in his Blean woods should be excommunicated. The purpose of the enclosure was probably for the protection of the archbishop's men from lawlessness and violence as they tried to deter these trespassers. The archival text especially condemns those who *intrant et inibi arbores succiderunt* or in other words those who cut down trees, whether in woodland or in coppices, without first obtaining the consent of the prior.[30] Although the site has been carefully examined, both when thickly wooded and after it had

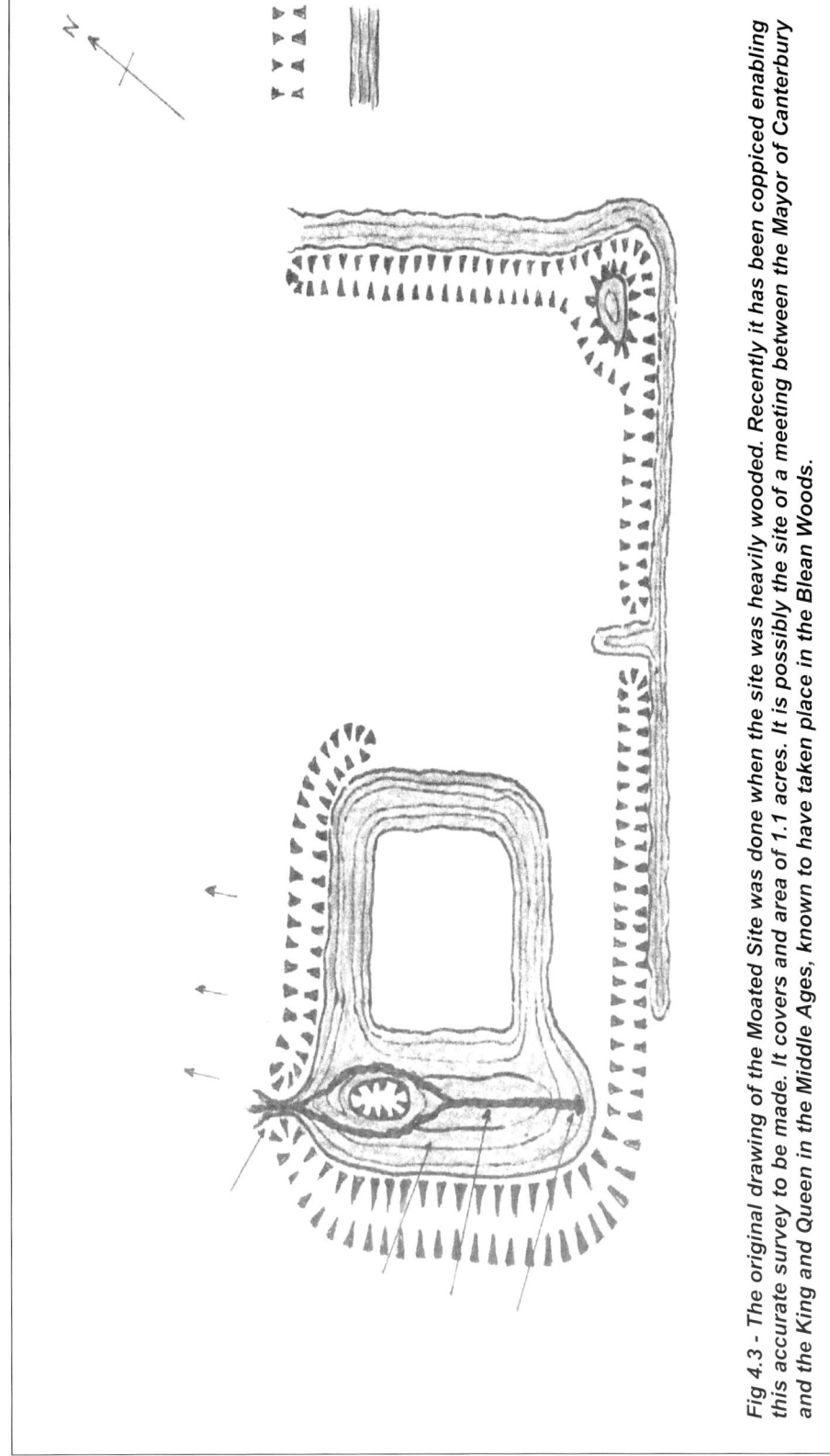

Fig 4.3 - The original drawing of the Moated Site was done when the site was heavily wooded. Recently it has been coppiced enabling this accurate survey to be made. It covers and area of 1.1 acres. It is possibly the site of a meeting between the Mayor of Canterbury and the King and Queen in the Middle Ages, known to have taken place in the Blean Woods.

been newly coppiced, no evidence of lengthy occupation was found. If policing activity was the main purpose of the enclosure any temporary buildings might have left few traces. It is also possible that the site might have been used as a caravan stop for passing royal cavalcades. Between 1445 and 1492 the city of Canterbury made lavish arrangements for provisioning passing royalty at *la Hale in le Blen*, the location of which is not defined.

A moated site with a water supply might appear a possible place for this 'Blean Hale' to have received travellers, being less than a mile from Watling Street and on high ground. The expenses attending the erection of this ' Blean Hale' caused all royal visits to be noted.[31] An officer went round with a wagon to the fuller for the cloth covering, and to the builders for the scaffolding poles and sandwich-cord, these materials being only hired and not bought. Another wagon collected bread, wine and beer from various retailers of such things, even hot rolls for His Majesty's breakfast. In 1479, when Margaret of Burgundy came to visit her brother the king, the floors of the tent were strewn with flowers in addition to the rushes usual on such occasions. When the 'Hall' was built, the process taking about two days, a couple of men well supplied with provisions were left in charge until the coming of the king. Oysters and eggs formed part of the watchmen's supplies whence it may be concluded that that at that time they were reckoned among the cheapest of victuals.

The 'Dissolution' of the Monasteries in 1538
Monasteries were among the largest landholders in the Blean and when the monks' houses were 'dissolved' regular churchmen took over many of their properties. Archbishop Cranmer added the woods of both East Blean and West Blean to his existing holdings to become the largest forest proprietor. The Lambeth Palace records suggest that once the inhabitants of the large monastic houses in Canterbury had been dispersed the demand for fuel was greatly reduced and timber became a more important crop. A survey of North Bishopden in 1611 shows that areas of high trees were being felled and that some of the underwood was being grubbed for cultivation leaving a landscape pattern very different from that of the medieval woodland. Later documents, loosely transcribed and abridged, give a flavour of the time in 1683 and 1687.

Falls left fair, the fences good and the springs

> *[coppices] in flourishing condition. Underwood (poor stuff made by the great number of small trees there growing) sold well from £2.15.0 to £3.10.0 per acre. The timber felled because standing so thick they hinder the growth of their neighbours for which it is difficult to get them out of the wood. We want chapmen to provide extra horses to help remove the timber there. Land so rushy and bad that we cannot get anybody to take it.*[32]
>
> ...
>
> *The timber being 33 batts [boles] containing 6 tun 3 foot we have sold for 32 shillings per tun. The underwood being 5 acres sold from 50 shillings to £3 per acre. The pound and the gates are out of repair and we have appointed Mr Janaway to fell 2 rugged batts such as shall never flaw to mend these defects. We were informed that a baker of Canterbury had made great incroachments upon that wood (he being the tenant of the adjoining wood) and had lopt Pollard Oaks which were made pollards on purpose to distinguish ye boundaries of those two woods according to the usage in all other parts of North Bishopden; the distinguishing pollards were always lopt by the Wood Reeves of North Bishopden.*[33]

Modern Forestry

The ninteenth century saw significant changes in the management of the Blean woodlands. In 1836 Parliament created an 'ecclesiastical commission' with powers to acquire properties belonging to bishoprics and cathedrals or to recommend improvements to land management. Although the Canterbury Dean and Chapter resisted interference, the commissioners asked Cluttons, their agents, to recommend improvements to the management of Shoort Wood (Church Wood). The agent's report is dated 26 July 1845:

> *We have surveyed the tract of ground called 'Huetts' belonging to the Dean and Chapter of Canterbury lying in the middle of their woods called Shoort Woods in the Vill of Dunkirk....The property is 2 miles from the city of Canterbury and is computed to comprise from 300 to 400 acres of*

rough and comparatively unproductive land...the remainder of the woods...are of slow growth but this we believe to be in great measure owing to want of sufficient drainage by open ditches...

No attempt appears to have been made at any time to convey from this Plain the surface water until Mr Austin, the present Woodreeve, became Agent of the Dean and Chapter; he has recently had a few open ditches made at intervals of 30 poles; immediately adjoining these ditches the Underwood and Furzes show that it is only necessary to convey the water effectually away to render the land more productive.

The outcome was a proposal that the Dean and Chapter grant a ninety-nine year lease on some of the land in need of draining to Mr Austin who offered to bring it into cultivation as a farm and pay a rent of one shilling per acre. By 1898 the ordnance survey map showed the farm as Church Wood Farm and Shoort Wood as 'Church Wood'. Ditches were opened up there and also in other parts of the Blean. Elsewhere woodland continued to be the economic mainstay of the Blean. Oak, yielding heavy timbers and a coppiced underwood, produced valuable quantities of bark for the tanning industry and from the eighteenth century hornbeam was planted to provide high-grade charcoal for the Faversham gunpowder mills. A new source of revenue was tapped in the nineteenth century through the rising demand for hop poles of coppiced chestnut for the Kentish hop gardens. But meeting the market was not straightforward, as a report of 1815 to the archbishop made clear when it stated that in his thousand acres 'the only part of the coppice wood that is saleable are the hop poles but the hop planters, having discovered that they have injured themselves by buying large poles, the present demand is only for ash and willow'. The hop growers did eventually adapt to chestnut hop poles and Stock Wood near Harbledown was found to have soils on which chestnut thrived and planting was encouraged both by Cluttons and by the Dean and Chapter. It was estimated that permanent chesnut stools, suitable for coppicing, would give a rental of 40 shillings per acre per annum. In 1864 Cluttons were also recommending that larch be planted in Thornden Wood with costs of £15 per acre for clearing and trenching, £10 per acre for nursery seedlings and a promised revenue on twelve-year-old larch trees of £30-40 per acre.[34]   By the end of the century so much chestnut, and also some ash, alder and even a little maple and pine, was being planted that traditional oak was disappearing from parts of the Blean. Further transformations were brought by the twentieth century demand for fast-growing conifers but by 1991 the lobbying of conservationists brought protection to the Blean. The conifers are being replaced following appeals from the Royal Society for the Protection of Birds, who with the local authorities of Kent, Canterbury and Swale, together with the Woodland Trust and the owner of Bossenden Wood co-ordinated by English Nature brought a measure of reserved status to southern England's largest surviving woodland.

Maps

Maps, carefully interpreted, tell much about the past and some place names are very old indeed.   When older maps are compared with those of the nineteenth century, and later, changes in the wood cover can sometimes be discerned.   Many of the oldest and most interesting maps are held by the library at Canterbury Cathedral. Among more recent ones Jared Hill's map of Christchurch Wood (now Church Wood) shows the areas of unproductive land as they were in 1718 and indicates that some woodland had already been grubbed by the late sixteenth or early seventeenth century before the plots were expanded.   A map of Thornden Wood drawn in 1752 shows that the boundaries marked by woodbanks had not changed since 1250.   By the beginning of the nineteenth century the first ordnance surveys indicate the marked degree of continuity in the boundaries of the woods as they stretch across East Kent from Chislet to Boughton in much the same way as they do to-day and as they did in the days of Hasted and his map-making contemporaries.

**Alexander Wheaten
& Elizabeth Birmingham**

References1
1. Cross R 1990 - 91 pp2-6 and 1992 pp 42-44 *Canterbuy Archaeological Trust Annual Reports*
2. Allen T et al 1997 *Recent Archaeological Surveys. CAT 20th Ann. Rep.*
3. Evans R.J.O.1943 Glamorgan, Cardiff pp 6-68.
4. Rackham O. 1986 *The Woods of SouthEast Essex*
5. Caesar Julius, *1st century BC De Bello Gallico Book V* Chapter 14

6. Harrison L. *1998 CAT Report*
7. Pellett, I. 1996 Tyler Hill Tiles from Blean.
8. Everitt A 1986 *Continuity and Colonization, The Evolution of Kentish Settlement*. Leicester U.P
9. Birch W (ed) 1885 – 93 *Cartularium Saxonicum* (BCS) 459
10. Lambarde W. 1570 *A Perambulation of Kent.* Hasted E. *1797 History of Kent*
11. Birch W. 0p. cit. BCS 869
12. Somner W. 1703 *Antiquities of Canterbury*
13. Morgan P. (ed) 1985 *Domesday Book, Kent* - Phillimore.
14. Witney K.P. 1990 *The Woodland Economy of Kent* 1066 – 1348
15. Bacon R.*1897 Works Vol 2* Oxford
16. Accounts of the Treasurer, Almoner and others 13th to 16th centuries.
17. *Assissae Scaccarii* 4,5 et al
18. HMSO 1888 *Literae Cantuarensis* II para 715
19. Witney K. 1991 *Kentish Land Measurements of the Thirteenth Century. Arch. Cantiana Vol CIX*
20. Canterbury Cathedral, Library of the Dean and Chapter (Archives) MSS Blean Beadle's Account Rolls.
21. Canterbury Rural Economy 114 E
22. Everitt A.op. cit p 27
23. *Canterbury Chartae Antiquae* B318.
24. *Gervase's Chronicles* Rolls Series *1879 Vol 1* pp502 – 3
25. Somner W. 1703 Appendix XIV b
26. *Close Rolls 1259 – 1260*
27. Somner 1703 p37 Canterbury Bunce's Register of Charities, Poor Priest's Hospital. Cotton C.ed 1934 The Canterbury Charities and Hospitals – in 1546 Kent Arch. Soc. p23.
28. Brooks N 1984 *The Early History of the Church of Canterbury*. p106
29. Canterbury RE 114 E
30. Canterbury, *Chartae Antiquae* B334
31. *Historical Manuscripts Commission Report Vol 9*
32. Lambeth T S 2 fo. 41
33. Lambeth T S 2 fo 82
34. Church Commissioners, Records Section. File 28417

Addendum - The Trench along Watling Street

Er we had ridden fully fyve myle,
At Boghton under Blee us gan atake
A man, that clothed was in clothes black ...
                Chaucer *-The Canon's Yeoman's Prologue*

Chaucer's pilgrims coming from the west, on seeing the wooded heights of Blean rising behind Boughton-under-Blean, would know that another hour and a half's riding would take them to end of their journey. This large and armed party was telling merry tales, but a solitary traveller might be less high-spirited. Having escaped Dick Turpin's predecessors at

Shooter's Hill, Oxleas Wood or Bexley Heath near London, he would have passed through a long stretch of safe country, but now on this last stage of the journey he would be apprehensive of muggers lurking in the underwood.

Travellers' fears were not unfounded. In 1261 two French travellers, Brother Matthew and Brother Ralph, Premonstratensian canons of Séry-aux-Prés in Normandy, were robbed in Blean (La Ble, le Blen) of £27. 12s. 1d and a horse loaded with cloth and other goods. The matter was taken very seriously; King Henry III ordered a court of inquiry to be held, the people held responsible for travellers' safety were punished and the canons compensated out of the fines[1].

To reassure travellers, clearings called *trenches* were often made where main roads passed through woods. A good example is where Watling Street, the pilgrim's route, now the A2, passes through the Blean. The road went through the middle of a clearing about 100 yards wide. In later centuries much of this reverted to woodland or was used as orchards and some of the evidence has been destroyed by alterations to the road, but some stretches are still visible.

The clearing was evidently made piecemeal; it is not constant in width, and the banks made by adjacent owners are not continuous either in character or alignment. Alongside Church Wood, for example, the wood is separated from the road by a field 50 yards wide, bounded by a prominent woodbank lined with beech and hornbeam stools. This feature was made to give people like Chaucer a sense of security against highwaymen. Then as now it did not greatly matter whether the security was real or false; at least it would have been difficult for an archer hidden in the bushes to pick off passers-by.

When were the trenches made? They were legalised by the Statute of Westminster, 1285:

> *Commanded… that the high roads from merchant towns to other merchant towns be widened, where there are woods, or hedges, or underwood, so that there be no bank, underwood or bushes, where a man can lurk to do harm near the road, for two hundred feet on one side and for two hundred feet on the other side. So that this statute shall not ex-*

tend to oaks, nor to great trees, under which it clear beneath. And if by default of the Lord, who does not wish the banks, underwood, or bushes to be felled in the manner aforesaid, and robberies are done, the Lord is responsible; and if there is murder, let the Lord be fined at the will of the King.

However, let it not be thought that all owners of woods along side roads hastened to cut trenches just because the statute told them to: that was not how medieval legislation worked. The statute seems to mark the end, not the beginning, of making roadside trenches. That through the Blean, alongside the pilgrim route on which Canterbury's reputation depended, and through woods owned by Canterbury institutions, is likely to have been made long before Chaucer's time. The 1261 incident would have reminded landowners that failing to maintain trenches could result in heavy compensation if valuable consignments were delayed.

Oliver Rackham

Reference:

1. Calendar of Patent Rolls, 46-47 Henry III, p.229; Cal. Close Rolls, 47 HIII, p.182; Cal. Liberate Rolls, 46 HIII, 20 Jan. 1262. [References found by Alexander Wheaten]

TREES & WOODLAND PRODUCTS
Chapter V

Faggots, Charcoal, Tanning & Thatching

The woods of the Blean have seen many changes over the centuries as the demand for products and the corresponding woodland management changed. There is evidence that before and during the medieval period the major demand was for the products of coppice for faggots, charcoal and tanning and depended mainly on the indigenous species of trees such as oak, hornbeam, beech and hazel. Brewing industries developed locally and the demand for timber increased. At the end of the 18th century more timber for ship-building was needed and in the 1870's the widespread restoration of church buildings and the development of the London Underground increased demand for timber, although the quality of timber from Blean was lower than from the Medway area. In recent years the demand for coppice products has fallen particularly after the North Kent paper industry's rejection of its use of mixed coppice wood. This dealt a major blow to local woodmanship.

Carpinus betulus - Hornbeam

The timber and coppice grown was primarily from Oak, Chestnut, Hornbeam, Beech and Hazel. Species of lesser importance included Ash, Birch, Elm and Holly. Species of minor importance in the area like Lime, Service, Thorn, and Alder Buckthorn, planted in a few areas, served specialist uses.

Trees in the Blean - Habitats and Uses
OAK: Pedunculate Oak (*Quercus robur*) & Sessile Oak (*Quercus petraea*)

Both Pedunculate and Sessile Oak trees occur in the Blean, the former favouring the heavier clay soils while the sessile species is on the lighter sands or gravels. Hybrid forms also occur which confuses identification. While the acorns of the Pedunculate Oak are suspended on short stems or peduncles, the leaves of that form have very short petioles (short stalk from twig to leaf), while the reverse occurs in the Sessile Oak, where the acorns are held close to the stem and the leaves have quite long petioles.

Oaks also differ in type between the fastigiated, tending to upright growth, and those of the horizontalis form with more spreading branches. This variation yielded many trees with branched timber useful in building and construction work. It is probable that the root systems vary correspondingly.

Traditional planting methods may also have modified growth. Until recently, when young oaks were lifted from the seed bed at two years of age, the initial tap-root was cut about four inches below the collar. This probably restricted the depth of the root system. Some two years later the main shoot was cut and the best stem was selected from the re-grown tillers. A curious practice noted from an early woodreeves manuscript was: '*For the planting of Oak every sixth will be planted for keel and corner*'.

During the early 1970's I would collect many acorns from an elite tree (a tree sound in bole, free from epicormic growth and with an even canopy of branches). These acorns were packed and sent to a nursery to be grown into saplings two or three years old. They would then be used to plant up poorly stocked areas in Blean Woods. To plant these oaks it was customary to cut the tap-root off four inches below the collar (collar being at the point of ground level). This encouraged a bushy root growth and ease of planting. Every sixth sapling planted was set at an angle and not upright, almost parallel to the ground. This was to encourage the young tree to grow up with a curve in its trunk (*buttsweep*), and the wood provided the keel, boat wood and corners for construction of houses and barns.

There are a significant number of oak trees of similar age in Mincing Wood, Great Den Lees and Crawfords Rough with 76 trees cored with a Prestler's Borer and dated between 1915 and 1922. A lot of these oaks appear to follow straight lines and have similar generic characteristics, such as epicormic growth giving the impression these trees have been planted from a similar genetic source.

Large straight oak trees are only rarely produced in the Blean although some can be found in areas such as the deeper more fertile areas along the Fishbourne stream.

Most of the timber from the Blean indicates that the produce from the woods was used for small and light construction work. Few records exist for larger timber although a number of large trees from the Blean can be found in places like the Littlebourne Barn. These trees were planted at 60 – 70 per acre and harvested usually less than 11 inches diameter. These oaks from the Blean were generally short in the bole with close ring counts and dense heart wood reflecting the poor soils of high acidic nature (Stevens 1973). Extraction of these in the winter after felling was often difficult on the Blean clays and the woodmen sometimes had *'to call a chapman'*, a person who provided an additional horse not as large as a shire but bigger than a cob, to help pull the timber out of the wood (Somner 1784).

One of the important uses of coppice was to provide tannin. Ellenden Wood was much used for tannin which was supplied to three tanneries in Canterbury until the trade ceased in 1953. For this purpose the coppice was cut in April-June, the bark was stripped from the wood, or *'cord'* (upper branched wood deemed useful other than for faggot material) and stacked upright to dry. One of the Canterbury tanneries required a wagon load of bark per week.

SWEET CHESTNUT: (*Castanea sativa*)

Chestnut is now one of the most common trees in the Blean but there is little evidence of it before the 17th century, although a couple of notable stools in Mincing Wood and possibly the woods near Chislet could be older. Big stools exist in several Blean woods although not in large numbers.

From 1720 onwards many thousands of chestnut trees were planted each year to make up the large area of chestnut coppice which now exists. Between 1720 and 1740 it is believed that annual planting of chestnut saplings of 24,000 – 32,000 occurred in areas on the lightly tree'd, poor heathy soils of Christchurch Wood (Church Wood), Crawfords Rough and the sparse woodland pastures of Great Den Lees.

Eighteenth century records of the Dean and Chapter refer to Christchurch Wood in the Blean as '*only 800 acres*' of the estimated 1200 –1400 acres which are described as '*an indifferent good soil'* with the rest described as *'generally very barren and poor soil and the wood thrives upon that part indifferently'*

Chestnut was an important source of wood in the 18th century for charcoal and for hop poles. Formerly hops were grown up two poles of Ash or Alder per plant, but Chestnut was preferred because it gave straight poles which were resistant to rot at ground level and a single pole per bine sufficed. Chestnut was planted about 9-12 foot apart and cut on a 10-12 year rotation yielding a pole about 14 feet high with a top diameter of one inch. Gaps in the coppice could be filled by layering a stem from an adjoining stool. (A young stem is bent over at coppice time and pegged to the ground to take root). In the early 1900's wire work was introduced to support the hops and poles up to 18 feet high with top diameters of two inches were then required and the poles were grown for a further 8-10 years. Sawn chestnut was the favoured wood for the coal mines at Chislet, Snowdown and Bettshanger. The miners preferred this wood as it gave warning by *'squeaking'* and *'groaning'* as it came under extreme pressures, giving the miners a chance to clear the area before possible collapse of tunnels.

The recent development of dwarf hops which reduce the need for expensive wire work has reduced the demand for long hop poles but chestnut still commands the best prices for poles, stakes and cleft chestnut fencing in estate, farm and garden use. It is also valued for charcoal.

HORNBEAM : *Carpinus betulus*)

Hornbeam occurs in the wetter areas of the Blean in the form of coppice stools, some as much as 24 feet in diameter - some of the biggest known anywhere. Most of them are about 200 years old and some very old stools, thought to be over 350 years of age, are in Grimshill Wood, Great Den Lees and Little Den Lees.

It is thought that most hornbeams were planted as even those which reflect great age form regular lines with regular spacing and are all of a similar age. Examples of this are in Great Den Lees and North Bishopsden. A 17th century survey refers to: '30 *acres of grubbed ground and planted wood on the same 10 acres'*. This area of North Bishopden has regular lines and spacings of hornbeam and the coppice stools have been estimated to be about 300 years old and could be related to these records.

Hornbeam would provide material for charcoal for gunpowder manufacture in Faversham, and also for a high grade faggot preferred for heating kilns and bakers' ovens. Larger pieces of wood were valued for their hardness and wear resistance which made them suitable for pulley blocks, cogs, wheel hubs and for pegs. However, it is susceptible to insect attack and if used at ground level is liable to rot within a few years.

Hornbeam also makes a fine hedge. It is present in many boundary woodbanks where it was often *'layered'* to make a stock proof fence, but since layering is laborious, many old layered hedges have now been allowed to re-grow. They then provide some dramatic forms.

BEECH: (*Fagus sylvatica*)

During the 1960's and 70's beech of 35 - 60 years of age was used extensively in the coalmines. *'Faced'* (cut flat on one side) and cut to approximately three feet long, they were taken to the Kent coalmines to be used for roof supports. Beech was also used for treenware (bowls and kitchen implements such as butter pats) because of its appearance, ease of carving and the clean soft texture of the wood.

Beech has been present in the Blean for a long time. There are some coppice stools deemed to be in excess of 700 - 800 years of age in North Mincing Wood and beech pollards on the banks of The Radfall Road, the boundaries of Blean Common, Denstroude, Great Den Lees and Little Den Lees. Just outside Mincing Wood and to the north of Blean Common are a series of medieval earthworks with the remains of beech stells (Beech stools cut as mini-pollards and then layered to form a circle of 20ft diameter) At least three can be found in Mincing Wood where the surviving beech coppice stools suggest they are at least 180 years old. These were to contain livestock, protect them from weather and make feeding them easy. Some lines of beech mini-pollards, the remnants of a beech hedge estimated to be about 250 years old, also occur here. It is thought that some of the beech about 160-180 years of age was planted to replace chestnut where it was not thriving. A good example of this is in Grimshill Wood near The Radfall Road where numbers of small dead chestnut stumps remain on the floor under a beech canopy.

HAZEL: (*Corylus avellana*)

A considerable amount of hazel can be found in the understorey of the moist areas in the Blean, either planted or of natural occurrence. This has been exploited over the years for many woodcraft industries such as basket making However it is not good as an understorey - it needs light to grow properly.

Hazel, if left to mature naturally, will throw out new shoots each year forming a stool of poles of uneven age. If coppiced a number of shoots will develop, retaining a uniform age of poles for 8-10 years, before starting once again to produce a stool of uneven age by throwing new shoots from the base.

The flexibility of hazel rods makes them valuable for many purposes. Hazel stems were used to make hurdles, fish traps on the north Kent coast, hoops for barrels, spars for thatching and wattle for *'wattle and daub'*, used as a filler for medieval walls. It was also used for walking sticks, shepherd crooks and toys. Where the stems were required to be pliable, they were cut in spring and early summer. There are no references of hazel being used in sea defences, but during the First World War, according to a Bilsington wattle worker, it was drawn in from a wide area to provide woven wall support for trenches in France.

A major use was for hazel hurdles which were widely used in the arable areas where sheep were confined or 'folded' on successive areas of green forage crops like turnips. The customary Kentish sheep hurdle was 4ft. 6in. long and 3ft. high, with 10 upright supports and a hand hold for ease of carrying. The so-called modern wattle hurdle is now 6ft. long, 4ft. high and still keeps the 10 upright supports, or flags as they have been known, but lacks the hand hold for carrying.

ASH: (*Fraxinus excelsior*)

Although Ash is one of the most important of British trees, few grow in the Blean although there may have been more in earlier times.

Ash timber is flexible, resilient, straight grained and cleaves well. When heated in steam or in hot sand it can be bent into useful shapes. It was used extensively for shafts and for the handles of spades, forks, axes and pick axes. Ash wood shrinks, and has to be seasoned before use. It can be used for furniture and was also used locally in the tile industry to make crates. It is too valuable to be widely used for firewood, but it is well recognised that ash wood burns well when dry, giving off very little smoke.

BIRCH: Silver Birch (*Betula pendula*) & Hairy Birch (*Betula pubescens*)

The acid soil conditions of the Blean favour birch and the two species and their hybrid are common.

Their timber is useful for turning and was used to make

broom heads and domestic utensils like spoons. Birch timber is also much used in plywood, but since it is liable to infestation by wood boring insects, it is generally suitable only for short term use. Essential oils in the wood make it flexible and the brush (feathery branches) was used to make besoms. Birch faggots also burn well.

ELM: English Elm (*Ulmus procera*), Wych Elm (*Ulmus glabra*) & Smooth Leaved Elm (*Ulmus carpinifolia*)

The last species was fairly common in East Kent, but suffered badly from elm disease caused by the fungus *Ceratocystis ulmi* (Mitchell 1991), and is not suited to the shallower poorer soils of the Blean area in general. Few remain in the Blean in areas of richer soil, including the Denstroude Wood boundary and Little Den Lees. Elm seed is not often viable and it usually reproduces clonally by suckering from the stump.

Elm timber is resistant to permanent water logging and was favoured for construction of ship keels and also piers, moorings, sea groynes (evidence of elm being used as sea groynes may be seen on some of the coastal defences at Seasalter) and especially water pipes. Since it resists splitting it was valued for wheelhubs. It also used in furniture making.

HOLLY: (*Ilex aquifolium*)

In the Blean holly often occurs on the leached soil of woodbanks and in shaded conditions it can become dominant. Its wood is highly prized for wood carvings and other wood crafts such as treen. The evergreen tree makes an attractive hedge plant which displays diversity of leaf form, the lower levels prickly, and more so, if grazed or pruned.

THORN: Hawthorn (*Crataegus monogyna*) & Woodland Thorn (*Crataegus oxyacantha*)

Hawthorn, *C. monogyna*, is the traditional living fence. In the 13th century when many of the wood banks were constructed, thorn would be used to support and consolidate the work. It could also provide hedging on bank tops with live and dead thorn. Much of the present hedge thorn was planted to form the enclosures of the remaining old open field systems in the early 19th century. Hawthorn was the main species used. The Woodland or Midland Thorn is a less vigorous plant, generally found only in the shady depths of woods. It is regarded as an indicator of ancient woodland.

SMALL LEAVED LIME: (*Tilia cordata*)

The Small Leaved Lime which was common in the south of England in early times is rare in the Blean with only two localised areas of about one quarter of an acre, one in Grimshill and the other in Church Wood. Approximately 26 plants are growing in Grimshill Wood and 15 plants in Church Wood. The oldest of the stems is about 90-100 years old with a surrounding number of younger aged trees of which some have been coppiced. It is possible these trees could have come from a single source. The soft white wood is prized for carving and the bark or bast was used as a coarse fibre.

MAPLE: (*Acer campestris*)

This tree occurs sparsely all over the Blean with one or two trees to be found in most compartments of mixed coppice, although no records have been found to show it as planted for timber. Heavier concentrations are found in old existing hedges and boundaries particularly around settlements and habitation. Its golden foliage in autumn make this a lovely tree to see.

The wood is used mainly for furniture making and is excellent for turning and carving; the creamy yellow-brown maple wood polishes to a deep lustre. Some older stools may be found on the Denstroude boundary of Mincing and Grimshill Woods.

CRAB APPLE: (*Malus sylvestris*)

Crab Apple trees occur in the Blean in many of the mixed coppiced compartments . They are often solitary although groups may be found in Clowes Wood and Crawfords Rough and on old hedge boundaries, but with no evidence of being planted. Never short of blossom, they seem to bear little fruit, but many locals return each year to harvest enough for home-made wines, leaving sufficient for the wildlife. It is a good timber for logs, giving off a lovely scent when burned. The wood is very hard and has a rich rosy-brown colour. It is used for carving (especially detailed work) and frequently for beetle (mallet or maul) heads and is also used for inlay and marquetry.

WILD SERVICE or CHECKERS: (*Sorbus torminalis*)

Only a few wild service trees occur in the Blean and most of them as rather fragile understorey plants. It is an indicator of ancient woodland. The berries were used for medicinal purposes and in wines and preserves. Timber from a well grown tree is most valuable for the manufacture of high quality furniture. The wonderful pink colour of the heart wood is prized for carving and cabinet making. In 1996 a bole 15ft x 28 in. diameter sold for £5,000.

The Blean is one of the few areas, with the Avon gorge in the West Country where a natural hybrid occurs between *S. aria* (Whitebeam) and *S. torminalis* (Wild Service) [*Sorbus vagensis* is the name given to the naturally occurring hybrid of Whitebeam, *Sorbus aria,* and Wild Service, *S. torminalis*, which occurs in the Blean. It was formerly known as *S. confusa.*]

Sorbus torminalis - Wild Service tree

ALDER BUCKTHORN: *(Frangula alnus)*

Alder Buckthorn is a common component in Mincing Wood in the coppice layer where it seems to be planted with regular spacings and straight lines. Much of it is around a charcoal kiln used about 180 years ago. It was particularly prized for making high quality charcoal for making cannon fuses. It is a valuable food plant for the Brimstone butterfly.

HEATHER: *(Calluna vulgaris)*

Little is left of the once extensive areas of heather in the Blean. Larger areas were present during the 13th century according to manuscripts in the Cathedral Library which indicate that it was then harvested to provide thatch for buildings, bedding for animals, packing for pottery and as a binding material for the construction of cob walls. Evidence of the sale of heather from the Blean is provided in the accounts of Amery Court. Only small areas of heather remain on the gravel caps in Church Wood and Mincing Wood. The intention is to encourage an increase of this habitat which is rare in East Kent.

Coppicing

Most of the produce of the Blean in the middle ages was from coppice Oak, cut in rotation with the growth interval between harvests ranging from 5 to 25 years depending on the product required.

In view of the value of the produce, much labour and expense was incurred in protecting this coppice woodland by defining boundaries and building ditches and banks to prevent ingress by livestock which could hamper re-growth by grazing the young growths or 'spring'.

Ditches which were dug to a depth of at least five feet were on the outside, while the banks constructed from the excavated soil and about three feet above ground level were inside the area to be protected. The bank was then surmounted by brushwood, predominantly thorn or placed on the bank like a dead hedge to protect it, a wooden palisade or eventually a hedge so that a barricade, impenetrable except at planned access points was formed.

The more varied flora developing on the top of the banks may be the result of the improved drainage. Holly, for example, can be seen on the old boundary of Blean common and on the lower end of the Radfall Road near the pond. Wild Service also occurs. Much of the surrounding boundary area included the hybrid *S. vagensis*.

Cant marks (a term used by Kentish woodmen but referred to as *'upstands'* by the Ordnance Survey) sometimes remain on the boundaries or within the woods. These marked boundaries or compartments within the wood. They were formed by selecting a strong stem from a sapling or a coppice stool and cutting it about 3ft above ground level. A low pollard developed which was a permanent marker. It was harvested with the surrounding coppice. An example is the Grimshill/Great Den Lees pollard oak which is considered to be about 500 years old.

Cant marks also defined old boundaries where the bank had slumped into the ditch and was not worth repairing if invasion by livestock was unlikely. Uniformly spaced cant marks are on the northern boundary of Mincing Wood although few now remain alive.

The map of Mincing Wood (Fig. 5.1) shows a mixture of former field systems, the result of previous management between 1740 and 1760. This area would have been hedged and the indications from the remaining stools suggest it was chestnut. These areas would have been short rotation coppice woodland or open wood pasture with relatively few standard trees. As the density of canopy increased with lengthening coppice rotation the hedges would be shaded and weakened.

Sometimes after enclosure of the original wood with ditch and bank, the wood expanded and a further ditch and bank was made to protect it. This can been seen in Crawford's Rough adjoining Rough Common.

Coppice was also used to provide fodder for livestock especially in times of drought. Ash, hazel, hornbeam and willow have all been used locally. Research by Phillips[1] has shown that coppicing with an axe results in fewer but stronger shoots in the initial regrowth, than cutting with a chain saw, although after about five years there was little difference in the number of shoots. The axe would, of course, have been used in the middle ages.

Faggots
The major produce of the coppice areas was underwood and also logs and billets, cut by axe or hand bill (or billhook) and then bundled in faggots for ease of measurement, valuation and transport. Several sizes were defined, from *'ketchyn fagots'* for stoking fires and oven to *'salefagots'* used to fuel large fires set around salt pans to evaporate the sea water and extract salt.

The size of faggot depended on its use, e.g. Rackham refers to an account book dated 1270[2] by a forest of Beaulieu Abbey which indicates a bundle of wood three feet in length containing five pieces of wood little less than the thickness of a lance (about 1½ inches). Thicker pieces would be cleft to provide the required thickness. These were then tied in a bundle. A four wheeled wagon drawn by two horses could carry 20 dozen of these bundles. Faggots could also be twigs and small branches, not worth splitting or too small for a bundle of rods. Not until 1542 was a faggot standardised by statute as 3ft. long and 3¼ft. in circumference. Later documented evidence is missing, perhaps because the trade declined with the increase in use of other fuels, however descriptions were passed on by word of mouth as in the following account from an old faggot maker on the Romney Marsh escarpment who gives further definitions:

'Faggots, approximately 5ft. 6 in. long and 12-18 in. in diameter used mainly for domestic and light

> *industry firing, e.g. bakehouse ovens, laundry coppers and some types of wood burning stoves. The faggots must have at least 20% of wood of 2-2½ in. diameter, these to be fastened with two bands made from hazel whiffs, (defined later) and always trimmed. The 'lord', the same size as a faggot contains more brush and not so much thick wood, again fastened with two bands and used as for faggots and also for sea defences. For this the faggots were dug in and then infilled with soil. The 'brush' faggot contained the thinner wood and larger trimmings from faggots and lords. They were fastened by one band and not trimmed. They were used mainly by the poor for domestic firing. Faggots from Birch were used to make besoms.'*

Maintenance of sea defences is important in low lying coastal areas and in the Romney Marsh, much of which is reclaimed land below sea level. The local saying went *'Serve God, honour the King, but first of all maintain the sea wall'*.

Production of faggots took place mainly when leaves had fallen but oak faggots for the tanyard were made in April – June when the tannin content is maximal and the bark is easily removed. There is little demand for faggots nowadays, perhaps the odd bundle of peasticks or beansticks but not enough to sustain the former thriving industry. One possible renewed use is for sea defences to delay erosion and stabilise salt marshes.

To make a compact easily transported faggot, woodmen developed several ingenious gadgets. One of the most favoured was *'the woodman's grip, the cradle and roll'* [3] Ties or bands were usually made from natural materials, hazel whiffs, bramble or lime bast, although later, string such as recycled binder twine was used. For Blean faggots, birch, hazel and bramble were used. The thorns of bramble were removed with a *'dolly,'* a small forked hazel stick with another clamped on top. The bramble was pulled through between these and thorns were removed. Bramble lengths were then made into bundles and soaked in water till required. The hazel *'whiff'* was of green hazel, cleft if it was thick, and twisted to make a strong band.

David Maylam

References:
1. Phillips B. (1971) *Forestry Journal*, Royal Forestry Society, printed by Geerings, Ashford
2. Rackham O. (1980) *Ancient Woodland*, Edward Arnold, 140
3. The woodman's 'grip' is two handles secured by rope at one end. The 'cradle'is where the brush is placed between the four sticks before tightening with the woodman's grip. The roll is where the brush is laid on the tie and the faggot is rolled with the knee and pulling the tie tight to secure. Brush refers to sticks or top wood trimmings.

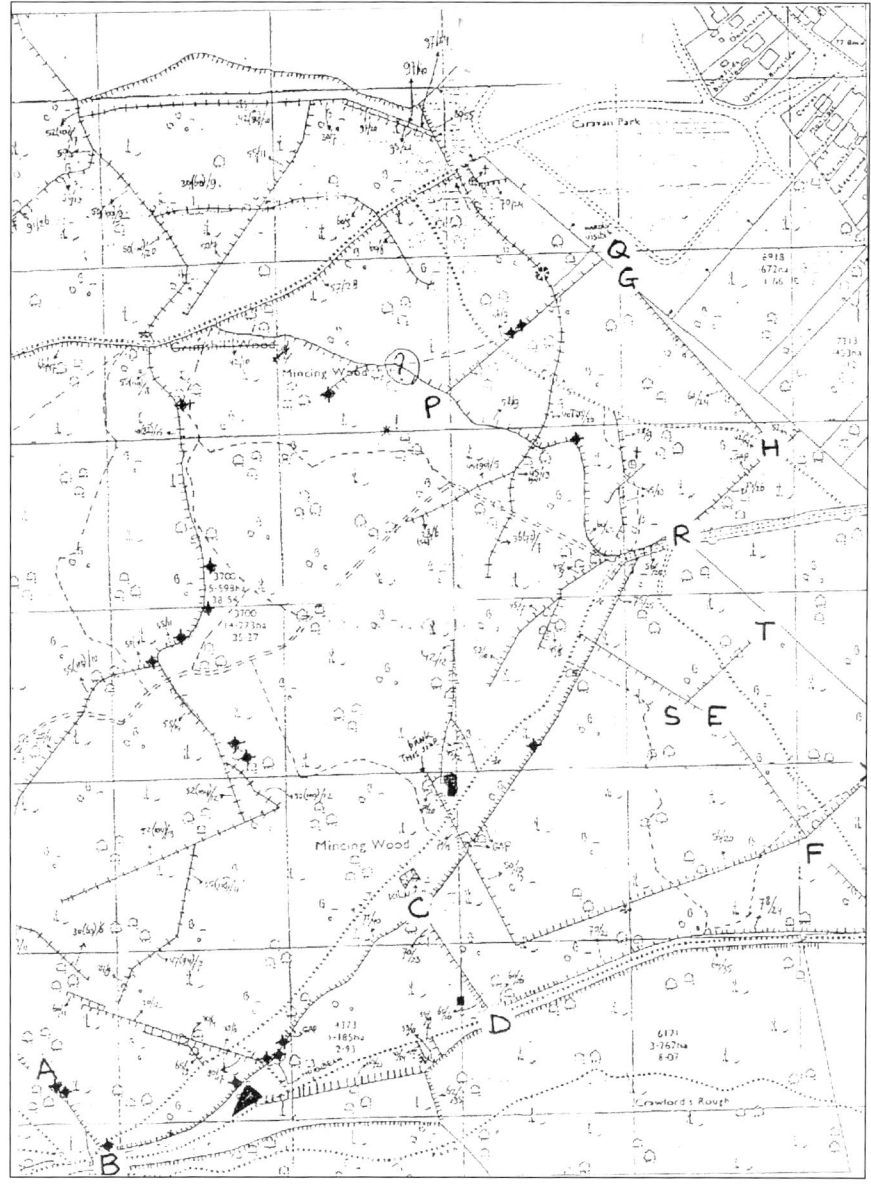

Fig. 5.1: David Maylam's survey in the mid 1990's of Mincing Wood Earthworks

BLEAN TIMBER-FRAMED BUILDINGS

Chapter VI

Wood Uses in Construction

Some of the trees from the Blean woods can still be seen in the timbers of ancient buildings. The Blean itself has only two surviving medieval timber structures but the area around has many timber-framed buildings and roofs from the middle ages onwards and there are many more in Canterbury city. This does not in itself imply a well-wooded area. There was a surprising variation in the amount of woodland per head of population in medieval England. Regions with a history of little or no woodland (e.g. the Breckland) can also have timber-framed buildings. Indeed the following study is probably the first to be done in a well-wooded region.

Producing timber-framed buildings was not the only or even the main function of the Blean. The woods also yielded underwood much of which contributed to buildings as fuel for burning tiles and bricks. Some underwood probably survives as the wattle-and-daub infill of timber-framed buildings. This might give valuable evidence especially on the history of chestnut, but it is not readily accessible, and I leave its investigation to our successors. There was, presumably, a huge consumption of underwood as fuel in the hearths and kitchens of Canterbury, its monasteries, inns, workshops and houses. Marshland coasts would have needed quantities of underwood as sea-defences. The salt boiling industry, of which the Red Hills on Seasalter levels are the remains, would also have been a big user of fuel.

Blean was not the only tree-land within reach of Canterbury. There were great woods to the south of the city; not far away was the Weald, the biggest woodland area in England. Some trees were doubtless harvested from hedges and fields. Nor were Canterbury and the local inhabitants the only consumers of timber and underwood. Dover and the Thanet towns, with no local woodland, needed supplies. If ever there was any difficulty in selling woodland products, it could be shipped to the hungry markets in London.

Nor must Calais be forgotten. For centuries this was an

English possession with very little land attached. It was forever threatened by the French and the sea (it was long doubtful which would get Calais first), and needed great quantities of timber and underwood for defences to keep both of them out.[1] The only supply within Calais territory was the Forêt de Guines, about one-third the extent of the Blean. Most of the known supplies, recorded in the archives of the king's works, came from Essex and other more distant places because the king owned very little land in south-east England. However there can be little doubt that the burghers of Calais got supplies from nearer sources, among which the Blean would have ranked highly.

Faversham Abbey Barns

Among the scanty remains of Faversham Abbey are two huge, stately but undecorated, 15th century barns of the home farm. The Great Barn measures 135 x 41ft, the Little Barn would have been 116 x 37½ ft, but has lost one end. Their size places them among the great barns of England, such as those of the Knights Templar at Cressing, Essex.

Each barn has 16 great posts (three are missing from the Little Barn), two to each bay and one at each end. These bear the high-roofs with their crown posts. The aisles, which are rather narrow, have timber-framed walls and lean-to roofs. The roofs were probably always tiled. These barns are peculiar in that the bays are of different lengths, the entrance bays being the shortest which would have been inconvenient for getting a cart in. This is probably not due to lack of long enough trees since the variations are repeated, on a larger scale, from the Little to the Great Barn.

In these barns, as in most structures down to c1580, the carpenter avoided lengthwise sawing. He would go to the wood and select the smallest trees suitable for the purpose, each timber being one tree. These were felled and '*scappled*' (hewn to the requisite square or rectangular section). Often they are left '*waney*', i.e. rounded at the corners through meeting the curved outside of the log. It is thus possible to count the trees that went into a building. The longer timbers also reveal something of the environment the tree grew in, whether it was allowed to branch low down or whether it was hemmed in by surrounding underwood, and whether the beam shows signs of running out of length where it reached up into the crown of the tree.

Each barn has (or had) about 160 rafters in its high roof. Those of the Great Barn are 18½ft. long, each hewn from a tree 8 to 9 inches in diameter at the base. They taper somewhat at the top. In one half of the barn they are straight, but in the other half they become crooked and waney, as if straight trees were scarce.

Those of the Little Barn resemble the straighter rafters of the Great Barn; despite its smaller size it is rather more heavily timbered. The other components are made out of trees not much bigger. The tie-beams of the Great Barn, for instance, each represent an oak about 14 inches in diameter and at 24 foot long show signs of not enough long trees.

The 32 great posts are anomalous. Those of the Great Barn are each a bigger oak set upside-down, so that its base forms the jowl or swelled head of the post. They are 20ft. long and come from trees about 2ft. in diameter. The trees however taper markedly so that the bases of the posts show branches coming out and reduce to no more than 15-20 inches in diameter; some of them are crooked and round at the base. The Little Barn posts are more remarkable still. Being of similar size they are from even shorter oaks; the posts taper at the bottom and three of them are forked from the bottom.

Fig. 6.1: Estimated sizes of original trees in the Faversham Abbey Barns

Basal diameter/inches	Great Barn	Little Barn
6 - 8	194	195
8 -10	317	362
10 -12	19	21
12 -14	62	72
14 -16	21	9
16 -18	6	8
18 -20	0	0
20 -22	0	0
22 -24	8	8
> 24	8	8
Total no. of trees	635	683

Were the two barns contemporary? They are so alike in detail as to suggest a common architect. The Little Barn, more heavily timbered, could have come first although its posts seem to be using up a very limited supply of suitable trees, leaving none for the Great Barn. Dendrochronology - matching the characteristic sequences of wide and narrow annual rings corresponding to good and bad years - indicates a felling date of c1475 for the Great Barn and c1426 for the Little Barn, which is an unexpectedly wide interval. These dates are a useful indication but should not be taken as absolute, since the technique is probably here being pushed to its limit.[2]

Each barn comprises about 650 oak trees.[3] (Fig. 6.1) The great majority were small oaks, probably grown as timber trees in woodland, in which they were drawn up straight by the competition of the surrounding underwood. Components such as tiebeams came from bigger trees representing the bigger or faster grown individuals in a varying population. The carpenter would have selected such trees from a copious supply, although there are signs of limitations on straightness for the smaller sizes and on length with the larger.

Faversham Abbey, although not among the biggest woodland owners on the Blean had extensive woods forming parts of Ellenden and Blean Woods. It had a tile works and therefore, presumably, coppice woods to provide fuel. It also had extensive hedgerows. Thomas Arden (the celebrated murder victim) bought at least 1,100 acres of abbey woodland at the Dissolution. I estimate that each Faversham barn would have represented the timber component of roughly 11 to 12 acres of woodland at 50 years growth. They would have been well within the Abbey's woodland resources; the monks should have been able to build two such barns every year if they had wished. The two together would have required only one oak per acre from the extent of the Abbey wood at the Dissolution (although much of these may have been acquired by the abbey after it built the barns).

The posts, however, tell quite a different story. Such oaks are common now but evidently were not then. They are probably hedgerow trees. The monks had to stretch their specifications to the limit to find two sets of 16 such trees.

Littlebourne Barn
This barn, lying to the south of the Blean, is attributed to St. Augustine's Abbey, the second biggest owner of Blean woodland. It is a huge structure, now of seven bays plus end aisles, but it has lost one bay like Faversham Little Barn. It would originally have measured 200 x 39ft. It is a more workaday building than the Faversham barns and has been much more altered and repaired. The high-roof is a later medieval replacement.

The original timbers are rather smaller than the corresponding members of the Faversham barns, and much more crooked and waney. This is conspicuous with the tiebeams and the curved braces, but extends to the low-roof rafters. The roof has always been thatched for which there is less need for straight rafters than if it were tiled. The great posts (16 survive out of the original 22) are snake-like, sinuous and waney, from trees between 14 and 20 inches in diameter. Some of them lack jowls.

This building would have required rather more trees (over and above its larger size) than the Faversham barns - probably more than a thousand oaks - but they would have been smaller still than those at Faversham. The disparity between the posts and the other timbers is not so apparent here. The carpenter had to make up by his skill for the poor quality of the material. This barn is very surprising from one of the largest woodland owners on the Blean; the Abbey could choose trees from many acres of woodland, but could still not find enough straight ones. There was evidently less competition between timber trees and underwood than in the Faversham woods a century and half later.

The replaced high-roofs, roughly contemporary with those at Faversham, tell a different story. The rafters are sawn, several per tree, from much larger and straighter oaks, which by this time St. Augustine's Abbey had at its disposal.

St. Augustine's Abbey
Probably the only surviving timber structure is the Great Guest Hall next the gatehouse: a building probably of the 13th century with an upstairs hall and an original, very complete, roof. It is now a refectory of King's School. The remarkable crown-post roof is nearly 40 foot wide, including the width of the walls - wider than the roofs of many cathedrals. The tiebeams, most unusually, are raised and thus shorter than the span of the roof. The rafters, about 35 foot. long, are small, waney, rather crooked oak poles. The tiebeams are a little bigger and seem not to run out of length.

Blean Church
This is one of two medieval structures actually on the Blean. The nave and chancel each has a crown-post roof whose rafters, about five inches wide, may have been made out of half trees sawn lengthwise. They are not waney and perhaps imply oaks

about 12 in. in diameter. The nave roof could be of the later 13th century and the chancel perhaps of the 14th. The two roofs meet, rather incongruously, where other churches have a chancel arch. The nave roof tiebeam has a number of mortices, evidently for fixing the Rood and its background. Although an important timber, it is hewn from a crooked, knotty oak barely long enough.

Chestfield Barn
Also on Blean, this is an aisled barn (now a restaurant) of four bays, originally of at least five mainly of the 17th century, but containing a fragment (with five posts) of a barn attributed to the 14th century. Although it is quite a big barn (22ft. span), both phases are of smaller timbers than Littlebourne or Faversham; the posts were hewn from oaks only 1foot in diameter.

St. Martin's Church, Canterbury
The roof is similar to the others but lacks crown-posts. The rafters are mostly two per tree, from slender oaks.

Poor Priests' Hospital, Canterbury
This building contains four late-medieval crown-post roofs, some of which may date from a rebuilding attributed to Thomas Wyke, 1373. The most impressive is the hall roof, about 30 foot wide - much wider than the high-roofs of the barns, though less than St. Augustine's. It involves 46 rafters some 30 feet long, comparatively slender (5 x 4in.) each one representing an oak only about seven inches in diameter. They are remarkably straight and free of branches. They taper but do not run out of length. They evidently grew up in intense competition. Similar timbers were needed for the two collars, the crown-purlin, base-triangle etc. The one tiebeam is about 12 inches square. Other roofs in the hospital are similar but of less span, and involved slightly heavier trees. All this roofing would have required about 220 oaks nearly all of nine inches in diameter or less and a few up to 22 inches for tiebeams. There is also a medieval floor, including the heaviest timber in the building, a principal joist from a tree about 2ft. 4in. in diameter.

Conclusions
Medieval buildings in general are made of what by 20th century standards are very poor quality trees. Usually they include hundreds of small oaks and a few middle-sized ones. They imply a woodland ecology very different from the present,

with a rapid turnover of small oaks and no problem with replacement. Carpenters could, for particular reasons, saw up big oaks, but these were rare and usually reserved for special purposes.

This generality, originally derived mainly from parts of eastern England with relatively little woodland, is especially true of the Canterbury area. It applies to all the buildings mentioned here, whether or not they derived their timber from the Blean. Their timber sources were managed to produce large quantities of oaks of small diameter. This is not confined to this part of Kent; the church roof at Wingham, with about 200 slender rafters, is another good example. A feature of some roofs (St. Augustine's, Poor Priests') is the unusual usable length. The shape of the trees varied, doubtless with the density and vigour of the surrounding underwood. Even the possession of about a thousand acres of woodland (St. Augustine's Abbey) did not guarantee a supply of straight trees.

There is no sign of any change during the 200 years or more which these buildings span. At a rough estimate, if there were 9,000 acres of woods in the Blean, they could have produced something like 15 great barns a year for ever, except for the posts, or the equivalent in other buildings.

How does this compare with the Blean today? These woods are renowned for poor-quality oaks. In some of them, however, such as North Bishopsden, there are still fast-grown *Quercus petraea* oaks of great length, which might make rafters like those of the Poor Priests' Hospital. This is one of the few parts of England where oak still grows readily from seed inside existing woods: the pine plantations in Thornden Wood are rapidly turning into oakwoods. Before 1900, when oak in general regenerated more freely, there should have been no difficulty in securing a continuous supply.

A consistent feature of these buildings is that middle-sized oaks - what modern writers call 'mature' - are almost absent, and when they do occur show every sign of getting the utmost from a tree that was not really big enough. It would seem that in the woods no tree was allowed to get much beyond 1½ft. in diameter, despite the greater value per cubic foot which would be expected from big trees. But 9,000 acres of woodland could probably not have produced the 250 posts a year that 15 barns would have called for; these would have to be gleaned from hedges.

This study is only a beginning. The subject of underwood needs exploring. Work is needed on earlier and later buildings and on the many timber-framed houses in Canterbury. Are there any structures extant for which the source of timber is known from the building accounts? Where did the timber come from for really big structures like the Cathedral and St. Augustine's Abbey Church?

Oliver Rackham

References:

1. History of the King's works.
2. *Nottingham Dendrochronology Laboratory, Vernacular Architecture 30* (1999) 93f. The first date is of the latest tree-ring represented in 11 timbers including great posts; there is an uncomfortably large amount of variation between different timbers. The Little Barn date is based on only five timbers, mostly common rafters. Coppicing could be a disturbing factor, not mentioned in the publication.
3. This leaves out the trees needed for tile-battens, doors and wall-planking.
4. Alas, it seems that very little medieval timber survives there.

FLORA AND FAUNA

Chapter VII

Aspects of Natural History

The woods of the Blean are mainly of chestnut, hornbeam and birch reflecting the infertile acid London Clay on which they grow. The mix varies. On the plateaux, oak, sweet chestnut and birch are frequent, whilst on north-facing slopes chestnut and beech are less prominent and give way to hornbeam. The valley slopes tend to support the best-grown trees. Great coppice stools of oak, hornbeam, beech and maple eight foot and more across are evidence of centuries of coppicing and regrowth. As elsewhere the majority of standards are oaks. Hazel and holly also occur frequently. Fig. 7.1 gives a list of trees in the Blean.

Deciduous Trees

Most of the oaks of the Blean are in late youth to early middle-age (80-100 years old) and slow growing on the heavy acidic clay, which often lies waterlogged for long periods. Many are variable in outline, with their twisted boughs giving a somewhat rakish appearance. In places even trees growing side by side tend to come into leaf at different times, differ in leaf colour and show different autumn tints. This variability, natural and characteristic of a wild species, is known to have existed down the centuries from prehistoric times[1]. It is in marked contrast to the uniformity of planted trees which have been grown in nurseries. There was a great deal of planting of oak in the nineteenth century in parts of Church Wood and elsewhere in the Blean. In general, large straight timbers are only rarely produced.

Both species of native oak, sessile and pedunculate, occur in the Blean with sessile the dominant species in many places. Sessile oak is characterised by acorns sitting directly on the twig with no stalk, while pedunculate oak has larger acorns growing on a stalk. The leaves of each also differ. Hybridisation occurs between the two species. Pedunculate oak tends to occur in valley bottoms where the soil is more fertile.

Though there are no impressive ancient oaks, oak pollards of great age can be found with healthy branches growing from the tops of their deeply fissured trunks. Until the eighteenth century these were used as boundary markers and a notable example is to be found on the boundary of Grimshill Wood and Great Den Lees. There are also ancient oak stools.

In some years there are huge crops of acorns, and in others very few. After good acorn years thousands of seedlings spring up but only a few, if any, survive to maturity, being eaten by birds and animals or shaded out by the tree canopy. Sessile oak seedlings can tolerate some shading, unlike those of pedunculate oak.

Oak is usually grown as a timber tree but in the Blean oak coppice occurs very widely, notably in Ellenden Wood. Oak bark from this wood was used for tanning in Canterbury until the early 1950s. The foliage of newly coppiced oak seems particularly susceptible to oak mildew.

Many parts of the ancient coppice woods of the Blean were replaced in the nineteenth century or before by sweet chestnut, a non-native which has been in this country from the time of the Romans and now behaves like a native. Its young foliage is sometimes damaged by late frosts while that of native trees is largely unscathed. It occurs in the Blean as coppice, with no stools of really great size dating from medieval or earlier times such as are found in some woods in Essex and Suffolk. In summer the creamy male catkins are noticeable even from a distance among the shiny spear-shaped leaves. It grows from seed and a crop of reasonable size is produced in most years. The very high rainfall of the winter of 2000/2001 resulted in the germination of an unprecedented number of chestnut seedlings. Very large trees are uncommon in the Blean, although they can be found in Stock Wood and on the Dunkirk/Harbledown boundary.

Beech is a welcome member of the woodland community - stately, beautiful in spring when the silky leaves emerge from the tightly-furled pointed buds, and with glorious autumn colour. Afterwards fallen leaves carpet the ground, a reminder of this glory well into the winter. Particularly heavy crops of nuts (beech-mast) are produced every four or five years while in some years the crop is sparse, with the masts usually all empty. Native to southern England, beech has been present in the Blean for many centuries, as evidenced by a number of very large coppice stools in Mincing Wood and elsewhere. Beech is found in what is left of a number of very old hedges, e.g. on the boundaries of Church Wood. With the disappearance of its former uses for fuel, etc., much old beech coppice has grown to maturity.

Among the other trees which make up the woodland mosaic, the hornbeam is notable, much of it planted in the 18th century. It is a beautiful tree, with a distinctive fluted trunk which divides into a number of ascending branches, giving a symmetrical outline. In spring the female flowers hang down like pale green silken tassels. A native tree, it is mainly represented in the Blean by old coppice among standard oaks. These oak/hornbeam woods represent one of only a few outstanding localities in the U.K. and have led to their being nominated as Special Areas of Conservation. Hornbeam is an exceptionally hard wood with only a limited number of specialised uses but it is good as fuel and provided firewood and charcoal in earlier times. It grows from seed, but is not a pioneer tree and is rarely found in new woodland, unless planted, which is unusual nowadays. While hornbeam mainly occurs in the Blean on northern slopes, it is also found in great density on the southern slopes overlooking the A2 road together with chestnut.

Two species of birch are present, springing up wherever there is coppicing and apparently increasing in numbers. The black birch has brownish-red bark, which remains smooth even in older trees, leaves with small teeth, and hairy twigs. The silver birch has a conspicuous white bark, with black fissures in age, double toothed leaves, and pendulous twigs with warts. Hybrids between the two species occur. The twigs of both appear purple from a distance, which gives a wonderful liveliness to the winter woods. Both male and female catkins are borne on the same tree. Quantities of pollen are produced in spring by the male catkins. which is blown by the wind to fertilise the female catkins. The resultant very light and small winged fruits are released in autumn and are disseminated by the wind over considerable distances.

Hazel is widespread, and there can be few more heartening sights than its pale yellow catkins swinging from bare branches in February. Male and female catkins are borne on the same tree, the female catkins being small and brown but made noticeable by the bright red of their styles. Self-pollination is largely prevented by their ripening after the male catkins on the same tree. The pollen is dispersed far and wide by the wind. In order to produce fruit the hazel needs light and has suffered from the decline in coppicing. It is weakly competitive and easily shaded out by hornbeam and chestnut. Much of the hazel in Church Wood and elsewhere produces few nuts and these are often taken by squirrels before they are fully ripe. The nuts are also an important element in the diet of dormice. The conservation bodies are at pains to improve the growing conditions of hazel and the production of nuts should therefore increase. The hazel's pliable but strong shoots, produced after coppicing, were used for a variety of purposes. The Blean has moderate areas of hazel coppice, often in low-lying, wet places, although it is not specially tolerant of wet soils. Such areas may have been planted with hazel because of the relative ease with which it could have been extracted from these difficult sites.

Ash is a calcicole and therefore not common on the acid soils of the Blean although there are some well-grown trees. A native tree, it reproduces by seed contained in the distinctive ash keys. It is late to come into leaf and early to shed its leaves in the autumn. Some trees have good yellow autumn colour.

Evergreens
Holly occurs widely but sparsely in the woods of the Blean, its bright green glossy leaves and solid shape among the bare trees particularly welcome in winter. Female trees produce crops of berries and it seeds quite freely. Holly has prickly leaves on the lower part of the tree while those on the higher part, out of reach of browsing animals, are largely without spines.

Other evergreens include Douglas fir and Scots and Corsican pine, of which there are plantations in Church Wood and elsewhere, although a number were lost in the Great Storm of October 1987, uprooted or their trunks snapped. In the nineteenth century the Ecclesiastical Commissioners planted pine as boundary markers along the New Road through the woods to Denstroude and on the road from Thornden Wood to West Blean Wood, some of which survive as sturdy and attractive specimens. Those on the plateau near Denstroude can be seen from across the valley and include the Bishop Pine, a native of California. Its curious clustered cones remain intact for many years. How appropriate that a tree so named should be planted in a wood owned by successive Archbishops of Canterbury for over a millenium.

Yew occurs occasionally, sometimes bird-sown from

nearby churchyards and gardens, surviving well on the miry clay despite its supposed need for sharp drainage.

Indicator species

A number of species regarded as indicative of ancient woodland occur in many of the woods of the Blean and point to their continuity as woodland over a very long period. They have had many centuries in which to adapt to the way the woods were managed, and in particular to the periods of light and shade provided by coppicing. They tend to seed poorly and do not readily spread into newer woodland, so that more recent woodland tends to be composed of trees better adapted to colonising such sites, or which survive from previous use of the land. Taken with characteristic associated plant communities and evidence of past management going back over many years, indicator species when present in good numbers as in the Blean are a useful clue as to whether woodland is ancient. (See this Chapter - Flora)

Service tree, an important ancient woodland indicator, is scattered through many of the woods of the Blean. Inconspicuous during most of the year, in autumn its maple-shaped leaves assume rich colour, crimson, orange and russet. It has prominent pale green buds on bare twigs in winter. Large clusters of creamy flowers, somewhat hawthorn scented, are followed by big brownish fruit, quickly found by blackbirds and the thrush family. Seedlings seldom establish but it spreads by suckering. Most of the trees in the Blean are rather lax, unlike the large robust trees found in Ham Street Woods. A peculiarity is that very rare hybrid forms exist in the Blean where it has crossed with whitebeam. In some, service predominates, in others whitebeam. Beside one of the rides in Church Wood there is a curious and rather beautiful tree which appears to be a hybrid between a rowan and a whitebeam.

A notable ancient woodland indicator is the woodland thorn. A lanky bush or small tree, its fruit has two pips and the shiny leaves have more rounded lobes than common hawthorn, with which it hybridises. It is found scattered in some of the woods in the Blean.

Small-leaved lime occurs in just two places, in small groups consisting of only a few rather attenuated trees. Church Wood is one such location. It is very unlikely to have been planted and is probably a residue of the lime woods which were present in prehistory. It coppices. It is an important indicator species and found in very few places in Kent.[2]

Small-leaved lime - Tilia cordata

Aspen, which springs up ever more thickly after coppicing, and with bigger leaves, is noticeable in March when catkins are borne on the bare branches. Separate male and female catkins are borne on separate trees, with the female tending to be the commoner tree in the Blean. The leaves, which tremble constantly on their flattened stems, turn pale yellow in autumn. Aspen produces suckers from the roots which develop into trees, forming circular patches of trees called clones, all genetically identical to the parent tree. Cherry behaves in the same way, as does the service.

Maple is found scattered in some woods. A calcicole, it is rare to find it on acid soils. It is a native tree and coppices and seeds. Its foliage turns a beautiful clear yellow in autumn and remains on the tree for quite a long time.

Crab apple crops up in places. It is possible to miss or confuse it with hawthorn when dormant, but it is easy to spot when the small greenish-yellow fruits are scattered on the ground. These make a delicious jelly when combined with haws.

Alder buckthorn is found in some moist places. It has red fruits, turning black, and its glossy green leaves, a little like those of alder turn yellow in the autumn.

The most frequent ancient woodland indicator in these woods is the sessile oak, but this is not such a strong indicator as some others, e.g. service. The lovely wild cherry, alder, rowan, whitebeam and sallow also occur, adding to the variety and beauty of the woods.

Semi-natural Woodland in the Blean
Coppice with standards - consists of standard trees, mainly oak, between which grows an underwood of mixed tree and shrub species. In traditional woodmanship the standard trees

were retained for timber, felled as needed, and the whole of the underwood was coppiced, i.e. cut to ground level on a regular cycle for a wide variety of uses such as fuel, fencing, tools, etc. (See Chapter V). The Blean has areas where the underwood is composed of chestnut, much of it probably originally planted. It is more common in the south of the woods, while hornbeam and oak predominate in some northern parts such as parts of North Bishopsden Wood. The standards are mainly of sessile oak and there are smaller areas of ash and hazel with standards of pedunculate oak. Beech is also present as standards and underwood. Some areas of chestnut coppice have few or no standard trees, as in parts of Church Wood.

Standards (High Forest) - are areas where standard trees are allowed to grow to maturity. If they are closely spaced the trees grow straighter, and as the canopy develops little can grow beneath the heavy shade, particularly where the standards are beech.

Scrub - refers to young woodland, composed of the seedlings of tree species and shrubs, which in time will become woodland. Almost any vacant land in Britain if left to its own devices and free from grazing animals will turn into woodland. An example can be seen near the Short Tenement, where the woodland is spreading into the fields. This is also occurring on Wraik Hill.

Planted woodland - consists of modern conifer plantations in many of the woods, some of them large. In Clowes Wood these include Corsican pine, Scots pine, Western hemlock, Norway spruce and Japanese larch. After the Great Storm of 1987, Corsican pine and pedunculate oak were planted in this wood to fill gaps. Earlier, red oak and Norway maple were planted along the main rides, and these give good autumn colour.

Conclusion
Considerable parts of the Blean still survive as semi-natural broadleaved woodland and are likely to remain so, as the recent plantations of conifers are slowly being reduced in size by the conservation bodies which now own large tracts of the woodland. Many of these plantations have proved unsuccessful. The list of trees of the Blean which forms an appendix to this account is not exhaustive but serves to show what can be seen and enjoyed in the

Blean at all times of year. Even in winter there is plenty of colour in the subtle greens and greys of the tree bark, the russet of dead bracken and the occasional bright red bramble leaf, and there is always the sight of the sky through the canopy of the woods.

Mary Fox

References
1. Rackham,O.1990 Revised Edition. *Trees and Woodland in the British Landscape,* J.M. Dent & Sons Ltd. Page 125.
2. *Philip's Atlas of the Kent Flora.* 1982. Kent Field Club.

Fig. 7.1: Trees Found in the Blean

Trees of Semi-Natural Woodland

Common Name	Scientific Name
Alder	Alnus glutinosa *
Alder-Buckthorn	Frangula alnus **
Ash	Fraxinus excelsior*
Aspen	Populus tremula ***
Beech	Fagus sylvatica ****
Birch, Silver	Betula pendula ***
Birch, Black	Betula pubescens ****
Blackthorn	Prunus spinosa ***
Cherry (wild)	Prunus avium *
Chestnut, Sweet	Castanea sativa *****
Crab Apple	Malus sylvestris **
Dogwood	Cornus sanguinea**
Elder	Sambucus nigra **
Elm	Ulmus minor *
	Ulmus glabra*
	Ulmus procera *
Guelder Rose	Viburnum opulus *
Hawthorn, Common	Crataegus monogyna**
Hawthorn, Woodland	Crataegus laevigata***
Hazel	Corylus avellana ****
Holly	Ilex aquifolium ****
Hornbeam	Carpinus betulus ****
Lime, Small-leaved	Tilia cordata *
Maple, Field	Acer campestre *
Oak, Sessile	Quercus petraea *****
Oak, Pedunculate	Quercus robur ***
Poplar	Populus
Rowan	Sorbus aucuparia **
Sallow	Salix cinerea **
	Salix caprea **
Service Tree	Sorbus torminalis **
Service x Whitebeam	Sorbus vagensis *
Spindle	Euonymus europaeus*
Whitebeam	Sorbus aria *
Yew	Taxus baccata *

Trees of Plantations

Common Name	Scientific Name
Beech	Fagus sylvatica ****
Fir, Douglas	Pseudotsuga menziesii*
Fir, Silver	Abies, alba *
Larch, European	Larix decidua ***
Larch, Japanese	Larix lepolepsis ***
Norway Spruce	Picea abies ***

Pine. Bishop	Pinus muricata *
Pine, Scots	Pinus sylvestris ***
Pine, Corsican	Pinus nigra laricio****
Western Hemlock	Tsuga heterophylla***

Other Trees

Horse Chestnut	Aesculus hippocastanum *
Maple, Norway	Acer platanoides *
Oak, Red	Quercus borealis *
Sycamore	Acer pseudoplatanus **

***** Most common; **** Common;   *** Fairly common;   ** Uncommon

Vegetation - General Character

Some of the woods of the Blean in spring present an idyllic picture, with bluebell following wood anemone and primrose, violet and ladies smock edging paths, as the bare canopy gives way to the fresh green of emerging leaves. In general, however, the flora is rather restricted, sparse, and fairly uniform, much of it dominated by bramble, bracken and honeysuckle as well as ivy and woodsage. There are no nationally or regionally scarce plants but a good number of species indicative of ancient woodland.

As is usual in woodland on clay, much of the interest is provided by the margins, the clearings and the rides; and in the valleys, where the soil tends to be more friable. This is particularly so in Ellenden Wood, where ravines cut by streams support a rich woodland community.

In places where the oaks are even-aged and fairly closely spaced, with underwood of hazel, hawthorn, honeysuckle and bramble, the combined shade of the trees and underwood inhibits growth of ground flora.

In some areas of chestnut coppice nearing felling, the dense shade and thick leaf litter prevent the growth of most plants, even bramble, so prolific in other parts of the woods. Such places spring into life, however, after the coppice is cut, when the sunlight stimulates the germination of the buried seed of such plants as foxglove and wood-spurge and encourages other plants which do poorly in the years of shade, such as bluebell and wood anemone, to flower and spread. The densely planted conifer plantations have little ground vegetation.

Ancient Woodland Indicator Species - [Ancient Woodland Vascular Plants]

Species indicative of ancient woodland occur in many of the woods, reflecting their long history. These are plants which have become adapted to the periods of light and shade provided by coppicing over many centuries. They spread only slowly into newer woodland, or seed poorly, so that their presence in large numbers suggests old woodland. The occurrence of some ancient woodland vascular plants may have little or no significance but as the number of such species on a site increases, so the statistical probability of the wood being ancient increases.

A list of plants considered to be indicator species in the south-east of England and which occur in the Blean is in Fig. 7.2. Both Rose and Peterken, who have done much work in this field, warn of the pitfalls associated with using such lists uncritically, however, when seeking to determine whether a wood is ancient. They stress that they should be used as a tool, in combination with historical and other information, and not as an infallible guide. The proximity of ancient woods with rich flora may result in secondary woodland acquiring slow-colonising vascular plants. This is exemplified in the Blean by Crawford's Rough, secondary woodland bordered on three sides by ancient woodland, where ancient woodland indicators are present. The situation in which plants are found may also have a bearing, particularly where wild plants which are also used in gardens, such as Soloman's-seal, are concerned. Some ancient woodland may lack significant numbers of ancient woodland vascular plants for various reasons while some secondary woodland may have acquired them.[1 & 2] But as Rackham has shown some species have nearly always a strong affinity with ancient woodland e.g. woodland hawthorn.[3]

Flora - Species Present

Two striking plants characteristic of the Blean are the sulphur-yellow-flowered wood spurge, particularly beautiful when seen with bluebells, and pendulous sedge whose tall flower spikes arch over the large clumps of bright green strappy leaves. There are also a number of smaller sedges, together with such typical

Blean species as great woodrush and hairy woodrush.

Cow-wheat is present in many of the woods of the Blean. This annual semi-parasitic plant with its rather insignificant yellow flowers grows from buried seed and needs light to flourish. It thus benefits from the coppicing undertaken by conservation bodies and also by some private owners, as in Ellenden Wood. It is important as the food plant of the caterpillar of one of Britain's most endangered butterflies, the heath fritillary.

Church Wood and Hunstead Wood have lily-of-the-valley, a native plant sometimes found in old woodland. It has an elusive sweet scent, produces quantities of leaves in most years flowers, rather shyly. Small bright red berries follow the flowers.

Some woods are carpeted with wood anemone in early spring. The delicate white flowers are sometimes pink - or mauve-tinged according to the particular clone. The leaves are fresh green and dissected and the whole plant then dies down by early summer. It rarely sets seed and spreads through its root system extremely slowly. Its presence is an indication that the woodland is ancient.

Bluebell, not an indicator of ancient woodland in Kent, is absent or sparse in some of the Blean woods. One theory is that rooting swine might have been responsible. Pigs are clearers of land par excellence and there were extensive swine pastures in the Blean in Anglo-Saxon times as indicated by the number of woods with 'den' in their names - Den Lees, North Bishopsden, Bossenden, Ellenden. This theory is not entirely convincing, however, since pigs are unlikely to have completely denuded the woods of bluebell and it grows in the Weald where dens are equally prolific. The distribution of bluebell is generally very patchy and it is absent in many other apparently suitable ancient woods in eastern England. Bluebell does, however, grow in profusion in some places, among them East Blean Wood, an old coppice wood owned by the Kent Wildlife Trust and now a National Nature Reserve, and in Stock Wood, where the ground slopes steeply to a little stream. The scent is heady on warm days.

Lesser periwinkle occurs in a number of woods, with sky-blue flowers among the narrow evergreen leaves. Although it seems well adapted to its woodland situation it is generally regarded as a 'garden escape' and can be found near to the sites of what are believed to be old habitations. Its long trailing stems were used in the past in funeral and other wreaths.[4]

A variety of plants edge the wide rides through the woods. Where the sward is rabbit-nibbled, low growing plants such as yellow pimpernel, wild strawberry, tormentil and milkwort carpet the ground. Primrose, ladies smock, feathery grasses like bent, wavy hair grass and woodrush make a most attractive picture on the damp sides of the ditches beside them.

Violet and primrose edge many of the smaller paths but not usually in great numbers. Primrose thrives however in the woods near Harbledown, in parts of Church Wood and on the north facing slopes of Blean Wood, near Dargate. Here it comes into flower late but continues for a long period, flourishing on the wet sticky clay. Oxlip does not occur at all in Kent, unlike Essex where it is present in great profusion in certain ancient woods. Greater stitchwort is abundant in sunny places, often growing with bluebell, red campion, yellow archangel and wood-spurge. Wood sage crops up everywhere, wet and dry, often associated with bramble, heather and bracken.

The Blean woods are not noted for orchids, but the common spotted orchid occurs in several places, including Church Wood, where it is increasing very well despite suffering the depredations of rabbits in some years. Early purple orchid can also be found in Church Wood and in the adjoining Willows Wood. Clowes Wood has common spotted and marsh orchid. Greater butterfly orchid occurs in possibly only two locations in the Blean.

A plant of clearings and woodland rides, St. John's wort (*Hypericum pulchrum*) is frequent in dry spots. Ragwort, a grassland plant, occurs in similar sunny places, where it attracts butterflies to its bright yellow flowers over a long period. It is the food plant of the largely nocturnal cinnabar moth. A striking plant in the mass, it is poisonous to grazing animals and particularly so when cut and mixed in hay. Golden-rod often completes the trio of yellow-flowered plants.

The rosebay willow herb growing strongly in July and August in large drifts, particularly where there have been bonfires, makes a beautiful sight in a woodland setting. The flowers are followed by feathery seed-heads which are dispersed far and wide by the wind. The mysteriously named enchanter's nightshade grows in wet shady spots. It has small pale flowers, having none of the bravura of the rosebay but with its own quiet charm.

In boggy parts, such as the moat in North Bishopsden Wood, creeping jenny can be found. In other wet places, the divided petals of ragged robin distinguish it from the more frequent red campion. Soft rush occurs in large patches in parts of Ellenden Wood and other places which lie wet. The pith of this plant was valued in the past as it was used to make rushlights. Bugle is fairly widespread, as is figwort.

Dog's mercury is absent from many of the woods although it grows well in parts of Ellenden Wood. As far as I know, herb Paris does not occur in the woods of the Blean.

Wood sorrel, a delicate little plant with bright apple green trefoil leaves and pure white violet-veined flowers, is not common in the Blean but all the more welcome when one comes across it. Woodruff, another delightful small plant, crops up in places. A member of the bedstraw family, it has a high value as an ancient woodland indicator and smells of new-mown hay when dried. Lousewort, a semi-parasitic plant, can be found, notably in the RSPB reserve in Church Wood, where it is increasing.

Damp, shady places on banks and in crannies provide suitable conditions for ferns, including buckler, soft shield, hart's tongue, hard fern and polypody; their fresh graceful fronds a restful and beautiful addition to the woodland scene. Male fern, although more luxuriant in moist places, can withstand dry shade.

Grasses, which are described elsewhere, add much to the beauty of some parts of the woods, particularly associated with heather in the clearings and along some of the rides.

Undershrubs
Bramble, of which there are many species, grows prolifically in the Blean, in some places forming an impenetrable mass. Its flowers are valuable for insects and the fruits provide food for birds and small rodents. Many birds including nightingales nest among its tangled thorny stems.

Butcher's broom, an ancient woodland indicator species, grows in many of the woods of the Blean. It is a curious spiny evergreen shrub and surprisingly a monocotyledon. It is usually less than a metre high, and spreads very slowly, eventually forming large clumps 2-3 metres wide. Scarlet berries are carried on the leaf-like flattened stems. As its name suggests it was used in the past to scour butchers' chopping blocks. It is often included, rather incongruously, in florists' bouquets.

Heather (*Calluna vulgaris*) is common along sunny rides and in clearings. Heathlands are rare in north-east Kent and the conservation bodies which own many of the woods in the Blean are now trying to redress this imbalance by felling parts of the chestnut coppice and poisoning the stumps, to create areas free of trees and scrub. Heather has quickly re-colonised these areas, growing from buried seed which responds to the light.[5] The honey-scent of the flowers in bloom is a delight on sunny days. When lizards bask on the dead stools of the chestnut, their colouring so like that of the wood, they are difficult to see unless they move.

Broom and gorse occur along paths, in clearings and along the edges of coppiced areas, their bright yellow scented flowers always a pleasure. In some clearings gorse mingles with sedges and purple moor-grass. The gorse in the Blean is common gorse (*Ulex europaeus*) except that western gorse (*U. gallii*) is reported to have been found in Clowes Wood. This species is otherwise virtually absent from Kent. The main flowering period of common gorse is from January to June, although flowers can be found at most times of the year.

Spurge laurel, with shiny evergreen leaves and greenish-yellow flowers in the top leaf tuft, occurs in a few places where the soil is less acid but much less frequently than in the chalk woods to the south of Canterbury. It is a charming small shrub, a daphne, its fugitive scent in January delightful.

Guelder rose is noticeable in autumn, when its leaves turn scarlet. Its white flowers are followed by red berries.

Rhododendron ponticum can grow well under the shade of trees and flourishes in parts of Church Wood and elsewhere in the Blean especially where clay is absent. A non-native, it may have been planted as cover for game birds but can become dominant to the detriment of the area. In Homestall Wood there are some choice cultivars, now very large, which are said to have been planted for the enjoyment of an Archbishop of Canterbury who reputedly had plans to build a summer residence in the Blean. The building was never constructed but the rhododendrons bloom on. A well can be found just inside the wood near them.

Honeysuckle is a frequent plant in the Blean, its fresh green leaves appearing very early in the year - indeed it rarely seems to be out of leaf. The deliciously sweet scent of its flowers on a summer evening can be detected a long way from the plant. It was given short shrift by foresters in the past because its woody entwining stems damaged trees but it is now recognised as a valuable plant for wildlife - for dormice, which use its shredded bark in their nests, and for the White Admiral, a woodland butterfly whose larvae feed on honeysuckle.

Influential Factors
The flora and vegetation of woods are influenced by many factors. Some that affect the Blean are mentioned below.

Topography and Soils - The two main soil types in the Blean are London clay and gravel drift deposits. The clay which surfaces in valleys supports quite lush vegetation, in contrast to the plateau areas, where it and the more strongly acidic gravel soils also found there are poor in nutrients. Of less importance is brickearth in valleys and around Blean Church.

Browsing - The absence of deer allows the natural regeneration of trees and shrubs and the development of an understorey of vegetation. Woods with many deer usually lack much of an understorey and it is possible to see for quite long distances between the trunks of the trees under the browsing line. This is not the case in most of the Blean, except where densely shaded, as under the canopy of beech, chestnut or hornbeam, or in conifer plantations.

Shade - The dense or light shade of trees has an effect on the vegetation growing beneath. Predominantly oak woodland usually has a well-developed field and shrub layer, provided the oaks are not too many or too close, and there are trees of different ages. In most places in the Blean the leaf canopy is not sufficiently dense to prevent sight of the sky.

Coppicing - Plant communities to a great extent reflect

woodland management, particularly the occurrence and frequency of coppicing, with its alternating periods of light and shade. Some plants tend to be associated with different trees, bluebell and bramble with oak, for example. (Chapter VIII, giving descriptions of individual woods, shows the distribution and composition of some plant communities). It is difficult to predict which plants will predominate after coppicing. An example of such variation occurred recently in Ellenden Wood, where two almost adjacent areas of oak coppice were felled in successive years after an interval of 40 years. In the first an abundant crop of cow-wheat appeared in the following summer. In the second area, although cow-wheat also occurred, the most abundant plant was soft-rush. The land lies wetter there than the first area but the difference was nevertheless striking.

Continuity - Of the greatest significance is the continuity of much of the Blean as woodland over a very long period, as reflected by the large number of indicator species present, and the uses made of it by man from earliest times. Its stability and lack of fragmentation largely result from much of it having been owned by religious foundations for many centuries.

Conclusion

Centuries of management have left their mark on the woods of the Blean, and although not spectacular in botanical terms the flora and vegetation are of interest because they reflect the history of these ancient woods, with their coppicing, areas of wood pasture, boundary banks and ditches. The species which have become adapted to such habitats over very many years are those we see today, giving the woods their distinctive character.

Mary Fox

References
1. Rose, F. April 1999. *British Wildlife,* pages 241-251. Indicators of Ancient Woodland. The use of vascular plants in evaluating ancient woods for nature conservation.
2. Peterken, G. Feb 2000. *British Wildlife,* Pages 153-158. Identifying ancient woodland using vascular plant indicators.
3. Rackham, O. 1990 Revised Edition, *Trees and Woodland in the British Landscape.* J.M. Dent & Sons Ltd., Page 132.
4. Mabey, R. 1996. *Flora Britannica.* Sinclair-Stevenson, Page 300.
5. Rackham, O. 1986. *The Woods of South-East Essex.* Rochford District Council, pages 58, 59.

Fig. 7.2: Ancient Woodland Indicator Species in the South-East of England Found in the Blean.

Acer campestre	Field Maple
Adoxa moschatellina	Moschatel
Anemone nemorosa	Wood Anemone
Blechnum spicant	Hard Fern
Bromus ramosus	Hairy-brome
Carex laevigata	Smooth-stalked Sedge
Carex pallescens	Pale Sedge
Carex pendula	Pendulous Sedge
Carex remota	Remote Sedge
Carex sylvatica	Wood-sedge
Carpinus betulus	Hornbeam
Chrysoplenium oppositifolium	Opposite-leaved Golden Saxifrage
Conopodium majus	Pignut
Convallaria majalis	Lily-of-the-valley
Crataegus oxycanthoides laevigata	Woodland Hawthorn
Daphne laureola	Spurge-laurel
Dryopteris carthusiana	Narrow Buckler-fern
Epipactis helleborine	Broad-leaved Helleborine
Equisetum laevigata	Wood Horsetail
Euphorbia amygdaloides	Wood Spurge
Festuca gigantea	Giant Fescue
Frangula alnus	Alder Buckthorn
Galium odoratum	Woodruff
Holcus mollis	Creeping Soft-grass
Hypericum androsaemum	Tutsan
Hypericum pulchrum	Slender St. John's wort
Ilex aquifolium	Holly
Lamiastrum galeobdolon	Yellow Archangel
Lathyrus montanus	Bitter-vetch
Luzula pilosa	Hairy Wood-rush
Luzula sylvatica	Great Wood-rush
Lysimachia nemorum	Yellow Pimpernel
Malus sylvestris	Crab Apple
Melampyrum pratense	Common Cow-wheat
Melica uniflora	Wood Melick
Milium effusum	Wood Millet
Moehringia trinervia	Three-veined Sandwort
Orchis mascula	Early-purple Orchid
Oxalis acetosella	Wood-sorrel
Phyllitis scolopendrium	Harts-tongue
Platanthera chlorantha	Greater Butterfly orchid
Poa nemoralis	Wood Meadow-grass
Polygonatum multiflorum	Solomon's-seal
Polypodium vulgare agg	Polypody
Polystichum setiferum	Soft Shield-fern
Populus tremula	Aspen

Primula vulgaris	Primrose
Prunus avium	Wild Cherry
Quercus petraea	Sessile Oak
Ranunculus auricomus	Goldilocks
Ribes sylvestre	Red Currant
Rosa arvensis	Field-rose
Ruscus aculeatus	Butcher's-broom
Sanicula europaea	Sanicle
Scutellaria minor	Lesser Skullcap
Solidago virgaurea	Goldenrod
Sorbus torminalis	Wild Service-tree
Stachys officianalis	Betony
Tamus communis	Black Bryony
Tilia cordata	Small-leaved Lime
Ulmus glabra	Wych Elm
Viburnum opulus	Guelder- rose
Vicia sepium	Bush Vetch

Grasses, Sedges, Rushes, Woodrushes of the Blean

These three grass-like families colonise and occupy a large proportion of the earth's surface and dominate the ecological zones between the deserts and the rain forests. In woodlands they occur where the light intensity is not severely limited, in clearings and on the edges of rides and pathways.

About 400 species of grass, over 120 species of sedges, 30 rushes and over 10 woodrushes are listed in the United Kingdom (Hubbard[1] (1984) and Fitter, Fitter and Farrar[2] (1987) but far fewer can be easily found in the Blean. These are mainly species adapted to shade and acid or wet conditions. They add interest to the ground flora and are valuable in helping to stabilise soil on the sides of streams and of paths.

The most common species in the Blean are listed at the end of this section (Fig. 7.3). Those of greatest interest are referred to below with a comment on their preferred habitat and those of indicators of ancient woodlands are indicated thus*.

Soft grass and *Agrostis canina* are common and wood millet is frequent and all three occur most commonly in damp shaded areas. In drier areas and on path edges wavy hair grass is frequent and wood melick, one of the most attractive grasses, is quite common. Of the sedges the pendulous sedge with its graceful inflorescence is often seen on damp areas and on the edge of streams and a variety of smaller sedges including wood sedge and remote sedge can be found, some on the drier areas. The hairy woodrush occurs, sometimes in clumps up to a metre square, in damp shade, and the giant woodrush is also present. Hairy Woodrush which is common in the Blean, is illustrated.

William Holmes

References
1. Fitter R, Fitter A. and Farrer A., (1987) Collins Guide to Grasses, Sedges, Rushes and Ferns.
2. Hubbard C. E. (1984) Grasses, a Guide to their Structure, Identification, Uses and Distribution in the British Isles, 3rd edition, Penguin Books, Harmondsworth.

Fig. 7.3: Species Recorded in the Blean

Luzula pilosa - 'Hairy Woodrush'

Grasses
Cocksfoot	(*Dactylis glomerata*)
Tussock Grass	(*Deschampsia caespitosa*)
Common Bent	(*Agrostis canina*)
Wavy Hair Grass	(*Deschampsia flexuosa*)
Floating Sweet Grass	(*Glyceria fluitans*
Wood Melick	(*Melica uniflora*) *
Purple Molinia	(*Molinia caerulea*)
Wood Millet	(*Milium effusum*) *
Soft Grass	(*Holcus mollis*)*
Yorkshire Fog	(*Holcus lanatus*)
Sweet Vernal	(*Anthoxanthum odoratum*)

Sedges
Pendulous Sedge	(*Carex pendula*)*
Remote Sedge	(*Carex remota*)*
Wood Sedge	(*Carex sylvatica*)*

Rushes
Soft Rush	(*Juncus effusus*)

Wood Rushes
Hairy Woodrush	(*Luzula pilosa*)*
Giant Woodrush	(*Luzula sylvatica*)*

* = ancient woodland indicator species

Mosses & Liverworts (Bryophytes) of the Blean

The relatively dry climate of East Kent has meant that mosses and liverworts are not abundant. The acid nature of the clay on much of the Blean also restricts diversity although greater variety occurs where the upper deposits have a raised pH level or the underlying chalk is exposed. This account deals with the most common and noticeable plants, together with a mention of some more unusual finds.

In deciduous woodlands of the Blean the main places to find bryophytes would be on the bases and stumps of trees, embankments and the edges of paths and trackways, and they only occasionally cover level ground. The most common species are *Mnium hornum*, a fairly robust upright growing moss and *Hypnum cupressiforme*, feathery-shaped with hooked leaves. Two characteristically acid-loving mosses are sometimes seen; one is *Leucobryum glaucum* which forms neat, rounded whitish-green cushions. The other is *Campylopus introflexus*, an introduced species now common in Britain. The leaves have a white hair-point at the tip, which, when the plants dry out, tangle into a star-like cluster at the end of the shoot. On living tree bases can also be seen *Isothecium myosuroides*, another feather-moss in which the shoots are curved to give the sward a curly appearance. Epiphytic mosses, those growing only on trees at a height of more than about a metre, are generally scarce, probably due to the dryness and possibly air pollution. The most frequent is *Dicranoweisia cirrata*, forming small cushions in which the leaves curl tightly when dry.

Acid Habitats

Banks and path edges give areas where shelter and lack of leaf litter provide a better habitat for further mosses. Typical of acid soil banks is *Dicranella heteromalla*, a small narrow-leaved plant, giving the slopes a green velvety texture. Here also some liverworts can be found, usually the common species of *Lophocolea* and *Calypogeia*. Even these are never abundant in the Blean.

Heaths and acid grasslands provide areas of bare ground often dominated by mosses, the chief of these being *Hypnum jutlandicum*. This is more robust than its woodland relative. The feather-like shoots are often erect and are a pale green. Recently cleared ground is frequently colonised by *Campylopus introflexus*. Another moss of these habitats is *Polytrichum juniperinum*, one of the larger narrow-leaved species in which the massed upright shoots look like miniature pine forests.

Sweet Chestnut coppice produces its own range of bryophytes which vary with the stages of the coppicing cycle. When the wood is cut the resulting open ground allows a heath-like flora in which *H. jutlandicum* can dominate. As the new shoots grow and the light is reduced these mosses disappear and a certain amount of *M. hornum* takes over. Species growing on the coppice stools are those which tend to be permanent, usually *H. cupressiforme* and a largish curved-leaved cushion-moss, *Dicranum scoparium*. Characteristic species of rotted-wood such as *Tetraphis pellucida* are usually quite scarce.

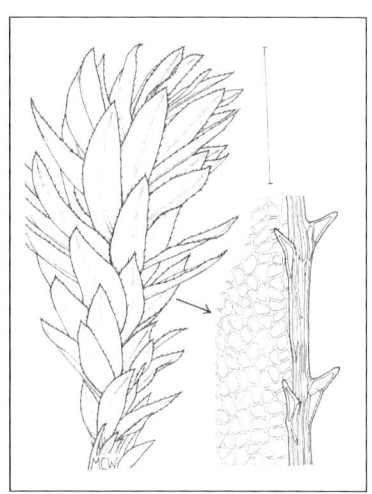

Mnium hornum

Coniferous plantations have interiors which are as devoid of bryophytes as of most other vegetation, but the edges, paths and deciduous parts of these woods can be productive. When clear felling has occurred the disturbance of the ground opens up a profitable niche for soil-colonising mosses which would not normally be found in the woods. Conspicuous on the exposed clay would be *Pleuridium acuminatum*, in which the yellowish capsules are retained down amongst the dark green velvety leaves. Also here might be *C. introflexus* and other species of the heathlands. These will disappear as the ground is shaded by new trees.

A Rare Find

Probably the most unusual find is *Ditrichum subulatum*, a rare moss usually found in the west of Britain, which was recorded in Honey wood in 1948. Species which are generally common but rare in the Blean, can turn up in the appropriate habitats. *Fontinalis antipyretica*, one of the few truly aquatic mosses, occurs in the stream running through Church Wood. Bog mosses can be found in water-retaining ditches: *Sphagnum fimbriatum* in Clowes Wood, *S. auriculatum* var. *auriculatum* in Clowes Wood and Church Wood and *Sphagnum palustre* x *subnitens* in moat in North Bishopsden Wood. An unusual form of a *Dicranella* species, possibly of hybrid origin, grows in an alkaline flush next to a shaded portion of forest track in Clowes Wood. The most remarkable bryophyte is the parasitic white liverwort, *Cryptothallus mirabilis,* in the bog at Hunstead Wood.

Hypnum jutlandium

The relative sparsity of bryophytes might be a discouragement to the naturalist who is looking for them, but experience shows that perseverance can be rewarded. Most of the species normally expected in lowland woods have been found, even if only in small isolated colonies. The question of climate change raises the possibility of additional bryophytes for places like the Blean. Even a temporary increase in rainfall noticeably enhances their abundance: a long term one should cause the scarcer types to become more common and allow the appearance of species further west and south. A more continental type of climate, on the other hand, might bring the introduction of plants from Europe. It is clear that there is still much to be done in terms of bryophyte studies in the Blean, both to complete the present picture and to follow future developments.

Malcolm Watling

Bibliography.
1. *British Mosses and Liverworts*, E. V. Watson, 3rd Edit. 1981, CUP [For beginners].
2. *The Moss Flora of Britain and Ireland*, A. J. E. Smith, 1978. CUP.

Lichens of the Blean

Lichens are epiphytes, consisting mainly of two mutually interdependent life forms, one algal the other fungal. This symbiotic relationship ensures a protective fungal matrix for the algal component while fungal growth and maintenance are sustained by the provision of nutrients by the algal cells.

Lichens can be grouped as crustose, foliose or fruticose. They are often highly decorative especially on walls and graveyard headstones and have been investigated in the past for their colouring and medicinal properties. More recently they have been used as indicators of air quality and environmental change as they are sensitive to sulphur dioxide and other pollutants.

The lichens found at a given site depend on air quality, light and moisture, the age and nature of the substrate and nutrient availability. Blean Woods are an example of broad-leaved woodland much of which has been regularly coppiced in the past. The late Dr Francis Rose, an acknowledged authority on the botany of south east England, recorded 56 lichen species in Blean of which *Thelotrema lepadinum*, an old forest species, was of particular interest. In a brief visit with Dr. L Garraway, an amateur enthusiast, we identified about a dozen species. Perhaps somewhat disappointingly, but not surprising in view of its position, downwind of London and the Medway towns, and between two busy roads, the lichen flora of Blean Woods is sparse being confined mainly to crustose and foliose species. Crustose lichens are readily visible on the trunks of oak, while foliose lichens, mainly *Parmelia* species, are confined to the uppermost surfaces of the branches. Other tree species appear not to support such a varied lichen flora, occasionally only one or two crustose species. Inevitably *Cladonia* species are present on dead and decaying wood.

The rather restricted range of lichens in Blean must be viewed within the context of air quality throughout south-east England and the composition and nature of the woodland.

Lyn Garraway & William Holmes

Bibliography
1. Broad K. (1989) *Lichens in Southern Woodlands*, Forestry Commission Handbook No. 4 London, H M S O.
2. Orange A. (1994) *Lichens on Trees*, British Plant Life, No. 3, Cardiff,

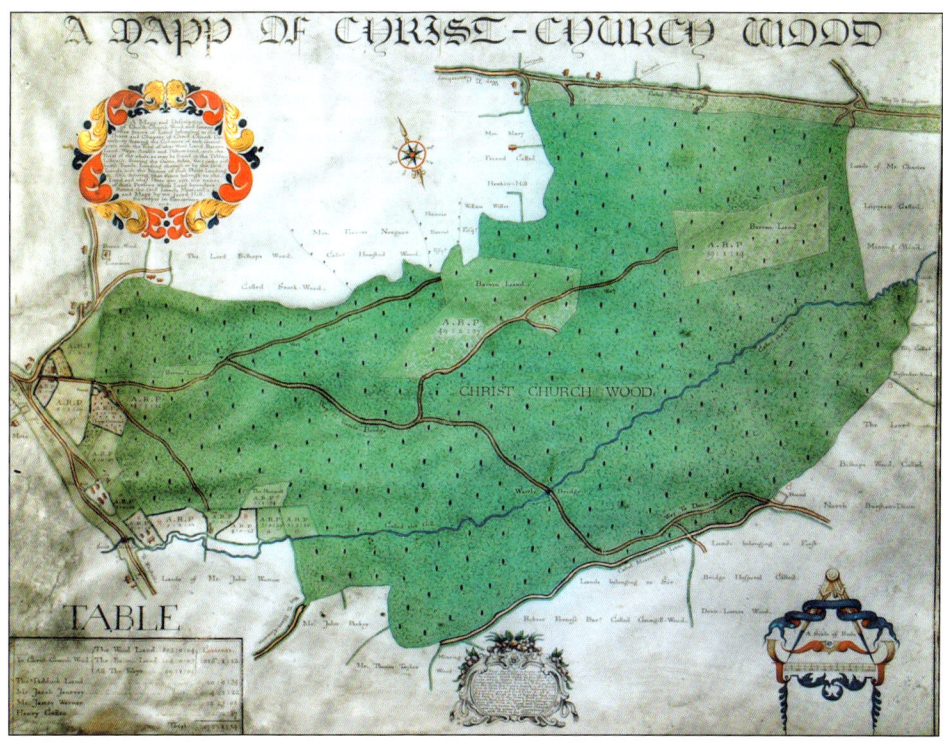

Above - A mediaeval map of Church Wood

Left - Stone Age artefacts found in the Blean and a first century Roman cremation pottery vessel

PLATES I & II

Above - 15th century roof timbers Faversham Abbey Great Barn - Oliver Rackham

Above - Pistius Truncatus RDB 1. This tiny spider measuring 4 to 5mm from head to tail is the rarest spider recorded in the Blean - Dr A Russell-Smith

Left - Heath fritillary - Professor S. Harrop

PLATES III, IV & V

Top left - Pyramidial Orchid (Anacamptis pyraridalis)   Top Right - Yellow Archangel (Lamiastrum galeobdolon   Bottom Left - Primroses (Primula vulgaris) Bottom right - Common Spotted Orchid (Dactylorhiza fuchsia)

PLATE VI, VII ,VIII & IX

Above - Fly agaric (Amanita muscaria)
Right - Stinkhorn (Phallus impudicus)
Below - Great Spotted Woodpecker (Denchocopops major)
Right - Female Whitethroat - Heather Nightingale

PLATES X, XI ,XII & XIII

Bluebells in Church Wood - Professor S. Harrop   PLATE XIV

Coppice Stools in Thornden Wood - Alexander Wheaten

PLATE XV

Above - This old marker tree in Bossendon Wood eventually died after being in total shade for so long.

Left – A veteran beech tree that stands on a bank on the edge of a woodland ride is a beech cant-mark A strip of woodland demarcated by two such markers on a bank showed an area of about an acre which was known as a cant. The wood in cants was auctioned in early autumn and cut from October to March by the buyers who sold them for a variety of uses such as fencing, stakes and bean poles.

PLATES XVI & XVII

A typical eroded way through the London Clay - Alexander Wheaten

PLATE XVIII

Above - What appears to be a bank indicating a boundary between one field and another is not. It was actually a boundary between what was once woodland, on the right and pasture on the left. The ditch on the pasture side would have been constructed to prevent grazing animals to get into the coppice (wood) and the hedge planted and laid on top to increase the difficulty of entry. Now after many years the hedge has "grown out" to give an impression of separate tree stems.

Above - Part of an old beech hedge that separated the edge of the wood from the pasture shown in the photograph above.

PLATES XIX & XX

Above - A beech pollard growing on a bank that marked the boundary between Bossenden Wood bank and North Bishopden wood.

Above - A woodbank c1250 on the old northern boundary of Thornden Wood - Alexander Wheaten

PLATES XXI & XXII

Right - A woodbank and ditch on an old boundary of Church Wood near Rough Common- Alexander Wheaten

Left - North Bishopden Wood showing the 19th Century road with one of the pines planted alongside it - Alexander Wheaten

PLATES XXIII & XXIV

Former disused road from Herne to Canterbury in the Blean shown on maps as "The Radfall" - Alexander Wheaten

PLATE XXV

Fungi of the Blean

There are many natural history interests of The Blean Woodlands, not least - the fungi.

Most people recognise the mainly autumn growths to be found beside paths and under trees as 'mushrooms' or more likely calling them 'toadstools' - without appreciating the vital role they play in the overall ecology of the woodland.

Fungi, to use the correct terminology, along with soil insects and bacteria, are an absolutely essential component in ensuring a woodland's sustainability. In the spring the development of leaves and flowers - a period when trees take up nutrients from the soil using photosynthesis to create tissue - is perhaps our most familiar aspect of the woodland. Through the summer the trees develop their full cover and fruits, then comes the autumn. That is the time when recycling occurs - leaves fall, boughs fall, even trees fall - and fungi are then a major factor in breaking down the vegetative growth into the essential humus and nutrients which the trees require again in the next spring. Woodlands are one of the very few truly naturally sustainable habitats as they are never artificially fertilised. Fungi play a vital role in their self regeneration.

Reproduction

Fungi reproduce by spores developed on the various forms of the cap - millions being produced and dispersed when the cap is allowed to open. Those spores develop into a thread like mycelium which lives in the soil, or within the tree and its root system - deriving nutrients from the wood or from the surrounding soil. Indeed some trees actually depend on the presence of a fungus to obtain essential chemical nutrients. A mutually beneficial system exists - symbiosis. The trees need the fungi, the fungi need the trees or other ground floor plants of the woodlands for their survival. Some fungi are harmful to trees - causing decay and eventually death of the tree - but these are the exception rather than the normal process.

Conditions in the woodland will also affect abundance and diversity of fungi - sandy heathland, heavy clay, dry autumns, north facing slopes and many more physical factors will greatly affect the production of the fruiting bodies in any year. We can never anticipate what the next fungus season will bring.

Identification

What can we hope to see on an autumn stroll through the woodland? Armed with our field guide, what can we hope to identify? Some books imply that the task is easy - including identification of those which are edible and good, with helpful symbols for edible or poisonous. In reality it is very much more difficult. Field guides may illustrate only a small proportion of the fungi which will be encountered, leaving many more which cannot even be considered in making our identification. It is very much a matter of experience and we should try to learn from those who already have the essential knowledge, rather than to experiment and possibly have an unpleasant experience. We can find as many as 140 or more species on a single study day in The Blean, and the total of fungi recorded there over the years amounts to around 500. It is therefore not surprising that for the inexperienced the task of identification is not easy.

It is the form and colours of the fungi, their essential natural beauty that we should appreciate, but for many there is always the question - is it edible? Only a small proportion are edible and good and only a very few are truly harmful. The vast majority have no special interest. We can find common species such as the yellow russula *Russula ochreoleuca,* the charcoal burner *Russula cyanoxantha* and the blackening russula *Russula nigricans* in most years. Occasionally we can find a parasitic fungus living on another fungus! *Asterophora lycoperdiodes* is a small white fungus found growing only on decaying specimens of the blackening russula! With beech trees we find the beechwood sickener, another russula - *Russula maireii* - which causes nausea if eaten. That is only a small selection of more than 150 russula species found in Britain!

Another widespread group is the Lactarius - the milk caps - which exude a milky fluid when damaged. Many of these species are associated with specific trees - such as the oak milk cap *Lactarius quietus*. Sometimes the milk is creamy white but in others the milk may be orange or purple. Others demonstrate their capacity to produce recognisable smells - these are often important aids to identification! The curry scented milk cap *Lactarius camphoratus* smells just as it sounds. Another milk cap, *Lactarius glyciosmus.* smells of cake baking - or coconut.

Edible Fungi

For those whose interest is edibility then The Blean holds examples of both ends of the spectrum. The Cep or Penny Bun *Boletus edulis* occurs regularly, as does the similar Bay bolete *Boletus badius*. In the same area the Death Cap *Amanita phalloides* also occurs. This is one of the few seriously dangerous species and its identification is vital to those collecting for the pot. Easily separated by the experienced but a challenge to the unwary! Other members of the Amanita group include the false death cap *Amanita citrina* - with its smell of raw potatoes - edible in theory - but beware of a false identification! The Blusher *Amanita rubescens* - recognisable by the tendency to flush red when bruised.

The Boletus group is recognisable because they develop pores on the underside of the cap instead of the more usual gills, on which the spores develop. The most common is the Brown Birch bolete - *Leccinum scabrum* found with birch trees. A more robust species with a bright orange cap, *Leccinum quercinum* is found with oak trees. A range of this group is often found associated with conifers - including the Slippery Jack *Suillus luteus*, a slimy capped species. Elsewhere, in association with larch trees, is found the Larch bolete *Suillus grevillei*. Similarly with pine is *Suillus bovinus* - and associated with this is sometimes found the very uncommon *Gomphidius roseus*, with its rosy coloured cap.

Historic Indicators

A good place to look for these is in the clearing near the car park! A good range of fungi occur here, but it is a good example of the need to exercise great care - or many species will simply be trodden underfoot, prevented from developing their caps and producing spores to renew the species for other years. Some fungi are also good indicators of the past history of the woodland. In a deciduous area, with oak, beech, chestnut, we find a small bright yellow club fungus growing from a stump. *Calocera viscosa* only grows on conifer stumps and shows that in the past conifers have grown here.

Other delights include the almost black trumpets of the Horn of Plenty *Craterellus cornucopioides*, At some path sides is found the Elfin saddle *Helvella crispa* - with a creamy white twisted cap, appearing to be turned inside out, with spores produced on the upper surface of the cap. Also by some paths is found Hare's Ear - *Otidia onotica* - an ochraceous yellow erect fungus five inches high, very reminiscent of those animal ears!

A strong smell of rotting meat can indicate the presence of the Stinkhorn *Phallus impudicus*. Easily identifiable by its overall appearance of a white netted cap on a thick stem - a fungus which uses a strong smell to attract flies and other insects, which consume the slimy spore bearing cap surface and fly off to deposit them elsewhere; an association of the fungi with the insect world.

Bracket Fungi
We must mention the bracket fungi, whose mycelium grows in the wood of the tree and produces fruiting bodies on the outside surface. The Birch polypore or Razor strop fungus *Piptoporus betulinus* - standing out rigidly from the birch stems. It is reputed to have been used to sharpen cut throat razors! Usually these brackets have a pore surface on the underside, hence the name polypores. On chestnut and yew we sometimes find the brightly coloured *Laetiporus sulphureus* - the Chicken of the Woods or Sulphur polypore, a reputedly edible species when young but very tough and woody when old. Another group are the bonnet caps, small species of Mycena and Marasmius. There are so many species they challenge even more experienced mycologists!

Puffballs are familiar to most people. Some grow on the woodland floor, others grow on wood. Their more uncommon relative, the earth star *Geastrum triplex* - like a small round puff-ball supported by 'legs' which raise it off the ground - produce their spores inside the rounded top of the fungus. They puff out spores through a vent in the top when rain drops fall. The Blean Woodlands is one of the best sites in Kent for its diversity and abundance of fungi. Though only a small selection of species have been described here, a separate species list follows. It will reward the casual interest of those who appreciate the colour and form of the fungi, and provide a challenge to those with a more serious wish to learn more about one of the most interesting disciplines of the natural history world.

Over collection of fungi is potentially harmful to the survival of some of the rarer species, and forays to gather specimens for identification should only be made with permission of the owners of the wood.

Enjoy the experience of the fungi, together with the many other natural history delights of the The Blean woodlands, but also recognise the important role these mushrooms and toadstools play in working to sustain the health and vigour of this woodland habitat.

**Fred Booth
in association with Michael Walters**

Fig. 7.4   Fungal Species List for Blean Wood
(From forays conducted by the British Mycological Society in 1981 & 1982)

MYXOMYCOTA

*Arcyria cinerea; A. denudata
A. incarnata;   A ovelata
A. pomiformis
Badhamia utricularis
Ceratiomyxa fruticosa
Collaria arcyrionema
Comatricha nigra
Enteridium intermedium
E. lycoperdon   T. persimilis
E. splendens   T. varia
Lycogala epidendrum*

*Physarum leucophaeum
P. leucopus; R. robustum
Pocheina rosea
Stemonitis flavogenita
S. fusca
S. virginiensis
Stemonitopsis typhina
Trichia decipiens*

EUMYCOTA
*Discomycetes
Arachnoscypha aranea
Ascocoryne sarcoides
Bisporella citrina
monogyna
Calycellina punctiformis
Chlorosplenium aeruginascens
Colpoma quercinum
Dasysscyphus apalus
D. carneolus var. longisporus
D. diminutus
D. dumorum
D. niveus
D. soppittii
Hyaloscypha flaveola
H. peudopuberula
Hymenoscyphus fructigenus
H. scutula
Microscypha grisella
Orbilia leucostigma
O. luteorubella
O. xanthostigma*

PLECTOMYCETES
*Erisyphe heraclei on Heracleum sphondylium
E. trifolii on Lathyrus pratensis
Microsphaera alphitoides on Quercus sp.
Podosphaera clandestina on Crataegus*

Sphaerotheca pannosa on Rosa Sp.

PYRENOMYCETES
*Bolinia lutea
Daldinia concentrica
Diatrype disciformis;   D. stigma
Diatrypella favacea
Hypoxylon fragiforme; H. multiforme
H. fuscum;   H. serpens
Melogramma spiniferum
Nectria cinnabarina; N. episphaeria
Ustulina deusta
Xylaria hypoxylon; X. polymorpha*

Phragmonaevia hysterioides
Polydesmia pruinosa
Propolis versicolor
Pseudopeziza trifolii
Rutstroemia americana
R. echinophila
R. sydowiana
Trochila ilicina

HETEROBASIDIOMYCETES
Melampsora capraearum on Salix caprea
Melampsora capraearum on Salix cinerea
Melampsora populnea on Populus tremula
Melampsoridium betulinum on Betula sp.
Phragmidium violaceum on Rubus sp.
Puccinia annularis on Teucrium scorodonia
P. coronata on Holcus lanatus
Tranzschelia discolor on Prunus sp.
Auricularia mesenterica

Dacrymyces stillatus
Exidia glandulosa

HOMOBASIDIOMYCETES - APHYLLOPHORALES

Coniophora puteana
Coriolus versicolor
Cristella farinacea; C.sulphurea
Cylindrobasidium evolvens
Fistulina hepatrica
Ganoderma adspersum
Hapalopilus nidulans
Hydnum repandum
Hymenochete rubiginosa
Hyphoderma radula
Incrustoporia semipileata
Lachnella villosa

Merulius tremellosus
Mycoacia uda
Peniophora lycii; P. quercina
Phellinus ferreus: P. ferruginosus
Phlebia merismoides
Piptoporus betulinus
Polyporus lentus
Ramaria stricta
Schozopora paradoxa
Stereum gausapatum; S. hirsutum
S. Rameale;   S. rugosum

Butterflies of the Blean

The Blean Woods were renowned as a paradise for lepidopterists in the 19th century collections. E. Newman and his colleagues, in particular W. O. Hammond, made many sightings and recordings of butterflies and moths in Kent and Blean was mentioned frequently. Indeed one of the justifications for scheduling part of the Blean as a National Nature Reserve was that this would make it possible to manage the area for the benefit of the rare heath fritillary butterfly.

The species of butterfly which occur in an area depend largely on the presence of the appropriate food plants for their larvae. As a result of changes in woodland management and the pressures of modern agriculture on the habitat, insect populations have declined in the Blean as elsewhere in the country. However sympathetic management of selected areas has been of considerable benefit to the heath fritillary. This management has taken the form of the provision of 'wide rides' and corridors trimmed on a two-year cycle, to encourage the growth of the comparatively rare cow-wheat. These rides also provide 'corridors', so that the butterfly, which is a weak flier and tends to stay fairly near the ground, may move more easily throughout the wood and migrate to newly coppiced areas.

Other butterflies seen include the speckled wood, the meadow brown and the gatekeeper, the larvae of which feed on grasses, the common blue, feeding on trefoils and other legumes and the brimstone, on alder buckthorn. The ringlet is abundant and the comma has also been seen. Peacocks, red admirals and small tortoiseshells probably fly in from areas outside the woods where their larvae feed on nettles.

A Brief Attraction

For a relatively brief period of about 8-10 weeks each year, butterflies become the most obvious and attractive element of the Blean's wildlife. Easily the commonest is a group of predominantly brown species, known collectively, for obvious reasons, as the Browns; a single exception is the marbled white, which is strikingly patterned in black and white. Most years the hedge brown (popularly known as the gatekeeper) is easily the commonest, but also vying for this accolade is the ringlet, a delightful butterfly with dark chocolate-brown on the upper wings, set off perfectly by the thinnest of white lines along the edges, whilst the paler underwing is punctuated by striking rows of cream-rimmed black eyespots. Normally scarcer than the gatekeeper, the ringlet can in occasional years be twice as common, seeming to benefit from the lusher vegetation prevalent in damper summers. The meadow brown is never as common as either of these other two browns, but all three prefer the sunniest areas, whereas the much scarcer speckled wood is found in shadier parts. The caterpillars of all the browns feed on a variety of grasses, which may explain their abundance. The relatively acid, nutrient-poor soils of the Blean do not support a great wealth of herbaceous plants, so inevitably the butterflies which are dependent on species other than grasses are bound to be less common.

Colourful Species

Most of the more colourful species belong to the family

Nymphalidae, and include familiar garden species such as peacock, comma and red admiral, but these are far less abundant than the Browns, though much more conspicuous. Interestingly, the small tortoiseshell has always been quite scarce, and in recent years has become rare. The caterpillars of all these species feed on nettles that thrive in areas of nutrient enrichment, and are noticeably more abundant in areas of the woods used by dogs.

Another colourful group, the Fritillaries, are also Nymphalids. Only one species, the heath fritillary, is now recorded annually in the Blean, but it is the species for which the area is most famous. Occurring at only a handful of sites in the West Country, and a few woods in Essex where it was reintroduced in the 1980s and 1990s, its main British stronghold is the Blean, and it is no coincidence that its larval food plant, cow-wheat, is one of the few flowers to be found abundantly in parts of the Blean during summer. Adults are on the wing mainly in June and July, but with some present in May and August, whilst in recent years there has been a small second generation at East Blean Woods in September. These later individuals are presumably doomed, as by that time the cow-wheat is dying back, and there is nothing for their caterpillars to feed on before hibernation. The eggs hatch two to three weeks after being laid on or near cow-wheat, and the caterpillars immediately start to feed up, over wintering in curled-up oak leaves on the woodland floor, then resuming feeding in spring once the cow-wheat, an annual plant, has germinated. In a particularly good year, the full-grown caterpillars can be seen in their hundreds or thousands, crawling over areas of cow-wheat, or wandering across the ground in search of uneaten food plant. Pupation occurs in May or June, the striking orange-and-black chequered adults emerging some two to three weeks later. The best populations are currently in East Blean Wood, but colonies are also found in Thornden, West Blean and the Blean Woods National Nature Reserve.

In the 1980s the pearl-bordered fritillary was a regular, albeit uncommon, species to be found in various parts of the Blean. A brighter orange than the heath fritillary, and appearing earlier in the spring, its larvae feed exclusively on violet leaves, particularly those growing up in freshly-coppiced parts of the woods. After a good spell in the late 1980s, numbers suddenly plummeted in the 1990s, with the last known record around 1997.

This mirrors the national decline (the species is now nearing extinction in Kent), but the reason for the decline is harder to find, given that coppicing has been maintained within a number of the Blean woodlands.

White Species

Five species of white butterfly occur annually - large, small and green-veined whites, plus orange tip and brimstone. The first four lay their eggs on a range of plants in the cabbage family, but the orange tip tends to specialise on the lovely lilac-flowered lady's smock which occurs in damper areas such as ditch margins, and perhaps for this reason the orange tip is the rarest of the four. The brimstone is different, for not only is it yellow but its caterpillars feed on purging buckthorn (not normally found in the Blean) and alder buckthorn. The sulphur-yellow male and paler female are amongst our largest and longest-lived butterflies, as the adults, which emerge in July or August, hibernate and then breed the following spring and summer. A sixth species of white is also yellow! This is the clouded yellow, not a native of this country, but one which appears in variable numbers, depending on how many make the flight across the Channel. Most years none are seen, but in the occasional good season, which occurs every ten years or so, individuals of these bright butterflies may be encountered almost anywhere in the woods.

The other main group are the skippers, rather small, hyperactive, moth-like butterflies, whose caterpillars feed on grasses. All three of the species which occur at Blean are an orangey colour; the small and Essex skipper are indistinguishable except at very close range, but the large skipper is noticeably bigger and has a slightly different patterning. Formerly amongst the commoner of the Blean butterflies, small and Essex skippers have suffered a dramatic decline in recent years, and have now become scarce on the Blean NNR, perhaps associated with a general scrubbing up of the ride verges - these insects prefer herbaceous growth.

Butterfly Management

Management for butterflies, at its simplest, involves ensuring that there are always sunny areas containing the larval food plant and may be achieved by mowing or coppicing. However, over a period of years of regular management, the habitat structure tends to change subtly - species composition may change, bare patches disappear and so on. This is particularly critical for the heath fritillary; managing permanent open space for cow-wheat results in the plant's decline, and moreover the caterpillars do better where the cow-wheat grows on bare soil and not surrounded by other vegetation which depresses the temperature. For the heath fritillary, the best long-term solution is to ensure an area of coppice supporting cow-wheat is cut each year. Provision of open tracts (rides) then assist the butterflies in moving to new habitats as the old ones become unsuitable.

Some species have maintained fairly stable populations over the years, but most have experienced marked fluctuations related to short-term weather patterns, or longer-term upward or downward trends which may be associated with climate or deteriorating habitat. Most dramatic and numerous, unfortunately, have been the declines; in the past ten years wall brown, small heath, pearl-bordered fritillary and brimstone have become extinct on the Blean Woods NNR, and some other declines have already been described. Only one species colonised the reserve, the brown argus, but that proved short-lived, the colonies apparently becoming extinct after three years. The most marked increase has been that of the ringlet; weekly counts along a two-mile transect on the NNR in 1982 produced an annual total of just 150, whereas in 2002 the figure was as high as 1559. An interesting effect of global warming has been the steady advance of the season; first ringlets are now seen about ten days earlier than they were in the 1980s. Even more dramatic is the life history of the red admiral, now first seen in February or March, whereas twenty years ago it would not be recorded until June. In the past, winters were too cold for this continental species to survive, so its presence in Britain depended on annual influxes from abroad, which did not occur until early summer. Nowadays, red admirals can survive the milder winters, re-emerging in the first mild days of spring to mate and lay eggs.

Occasional years stand out in my mind as exceptional for one reason or another. The purple hairstreak is unusual in that it normally spends its entire life around the tops of oak trees, where it lays its eggs, and is not generally seen by ground-based humans; but on one memorable afternoon in 1983 what appeared to be the entire population of purple hairstreaks descended to ground level and were to be seen swarming everywhere. What caused this phenomenon, which I have not experienced since, is totally unknown. More recently, in 1996, there was a much larger than usual influx of painted ladies which laid their eggs on thistles; for a brief period in July the newly-emerged adults were almost the commonest butterfly in the woods.

The Future

What does the future hold for our butterflies? Climate warming has already resulted in many species appearing earlier, as described above, and may lead to some normally single-brooded species having a second brood. So far, however, there has been little sign of continental species colonising, although red admiral could, arguably come into that category, and it may soon be joined by the painted lady. Cow-wheat becomes stressed by prolonged drought, so we may find heath fritillary populations declining in hotter summers. In the 1940's, white admiral and silver-washed fritillary were both resident in parts of the Blean; the former has now become re-established at East Blean and puts in an occasional appearance at the Blean NNR, whilst the strikingly large silver-washed fritillary has, tantalisingly, dashed down the rides from time to time, but has so far failed to re-establish a population. Perhaps its time will come shortly.

Gerald Flack and Michael Walter

Fig. 7. 5: Species List for Blean Butterflies

Hedge brown *(Pyronia tithonus)* - Abundant, commonest species

Small heath *(Coenonympha pamphilus)* - Frequent in 1980s, becoming rare in 1990s, and now extinct on the reserve.

Speckled wood *(Pararge aegeria)*- Scarce, but commoner in some parts of the Blean than others

Wall brown *(Lasiommata megera)* - Common in 1982-3, then becoming rare, and now possibly extinct in the Blean.

Marbled white *(Melanargia galathea)* - One or more seen most years

Meadow brown *(Maniola jurtina)* - Common

Ringlet *(Aphantopus hyperantus)* -Common in 1980s, abundant (second commonest) in 1990's

Pearl-bordered fritillary *(Boloria euphrosyne)* - Frequent in 1980's, rare in 1990's, becoming extinct 1998

Small pearl-bordered fritillary (*Boloria selene*) - Recorded occasionally in Church Wood in 1895

High brown fritillary *(Argynnis adippe)#* - One recorded in Church Wood in 1893

Silver-washed fritillary *(Argynnis paphia)* - Recorded in 1947. One seen in July 1997.

Heath fritillary *(Mellicta athalia)* - Increasing in 1980's, frequent in 1986-7, sudden decline to scarcity, minor recovery in 1990s. Successful introduction in west end of wood in 1998.

Niobe fritillary *(Fabriciana niobe)** - One in Church Wood in June 1895

Camberwell beauty *(Nymphalis antiopa)* -Two records Aug-Sept 1995, one March 1997

Red admiral *(Vanessa atalanta)* - Fairly scarce. Painted lady (Cyanthia cardui) -Very rare most years, massive influx 1996

Small tortoiseshell *(Aglais urticae)* - Fluctuates, scarce-occasional

Large tortoiseshell (*Nymphalis polychloros*) - Recorded in 1947, but may not refer to reserve

Comma *(Polygonia c-album)* - Fluctuates, occasional-rare

Purple emperor *(Apatura iris)* - One in Bossenden Wood in 1912

White admiral *(Ladoga camilla)* - One+ in 1985-6 and 1992, also recorded in 1947. In 2000 appeared to be colonising other parts of the Blean.

Duke of Burgundy fritillary *(Hamearis lucina)* - Bossenden Wood in 1908, also seen there in 1947.

Brown argus *(Aricia agestis)* - First recorded in 1997, small increase in 1998-9 then disappearing again.

Common blue *(Polyommatus icarus)* - Occasional
Holly blue *(Celastrina argiolus)* - Absent-rare most years, occasionally more frequent e.g. in 1990.

Small copper *(Lycaena phlaeas)* - Absent/very rare

Green hairstreak *(Callophrys rubi)* - One+ recorded in some years

Purple hairstreak *(Quercusia quercus)* - Frequent

Large white *(Pieris brassicae)* - Occasional/frequent

Small white *(Pieris rapae)* - Scarce/occasional

Green-veined white *(Pieris napi)* - Occasional/frequent

Orange tip *(Anthocharis cardamines)* - Rare

Clouded yellow *(Colias croceus)* - Very rare – seen 1983, 1990, 1991, 1996

Brimstone *(Gonepteryx rhamni)* - Occasional/frequent

Grizzled skipper *(Pyrgus malvae)* - One in May 1990

Small skipper *(Thymelicus sylvestris)* - Frequent/common

Essex skipper *(Thymelicus lineola)* - Occasional/frequent

Painted lady *(Cyanthia cardui)* -Very rare most years, massive influx 1996

Peacock *(Inachis io)* - Occasional/frequent

Moths of the Blean

Compared with our butterflies, the number of moth species in the British Isles is very large, numbering in the thousands. Moths can be divided into two groups, the macro-Lepidoptera, which have both English and scientific Latin names, and the micro-Lepidoptera which, with few exceptions, are known only by their scientific names.

Altogether about 500 species of moth have been recorded in and around the Blean. Most of my recording has been done in parts of the Blean Woods National Nature Reserve - Church Wood, Crawford's Rough, and occasionally in Bossenden Wood - where 294 macro-moth species have been recorded, but I have also recorded in West Blean and Clowes Woods. Not surprisingly, there is a great variety of species in the Blean and, although some are local, with distinct habitat preferences, others are common and well-distributed.

Noctuids

Moths are divided into families, the largest being the *Noctuidae*, or Noctuids, also known locally as owlets, millers and buzzards, with over 400 species. They are mostly medium-sized and dull coloured, and nearly all are nocturnal and attracted to light, especially ultra-violet light. For this reason, mercury vapour (MV) lamps, which emit strongly in the ultra-violet region, are much more attractive to insects than ordinary lightbulbs. Noctuid moth larvae mostly feed at night, hiding by day on the ground, spun between leaves, or in a tree crevice, and nearly all of them pupate in or near the ground. Typical common Noctuids in the Blean are the ingrailed clay, angle shades and flame, whose larvae feed on many plants including dock and bramble. The larvae of dark arches, smoky wainscot, flounced rustic, the clay and straw underwing all feed on various grasses. The early grey is one of the first moths to appear in spring and its larvae, like those of the copper underwing, feed on honeysuckle. Several other moths in the Blean are associated with only one food plant, including the lychnis which feeds on red campion, the bordered sallow which feeds on rest-harrow, and the centre-barred sallow which feeds on ash. Many Noctuids depend on oak trees for their survival, such as the chestnut, which appears commonly in the autumn and again after hibernation in the spring. Other oak-feeders include common quaker, clouded drab, small quaker and grey shoulder knot. The adults of all these species, along with red chestnut, twin-spotted quaker, Hebrew character and the pine beauty, are readily attracted at dusk to sallow blossom in March and April. An interesting group of Noctuids which fly from August through to November are readily attracted to over-ripe blackberries and ivy blossom. Examples include chestnut, pink-barred sallow, yellow-line quaker and the satellite, whose larvae, like those of the dunbar, have a voracious appetite for the caterpillars of other Lepidoptera.

Geometers

The second largest group of macro-moths is the *Geometridae*, or Geometers, represented by more than 300 species in Britain. The adults mostly have broad forewings and hindwings and could be described as butterfly-like. The vast majority fly at night and are attracted to light. Many species fly slowly at dusk, the small white wave being an example. Others may be easily disturbed during the day, such as the treble bar, which is associated with St John's wort, and the common white wave, which flies up at the least disturbance, whilst brown silver-lines can easily be flushed when walking through or near bracken. Geometer caterpillars are extremely variable, and are widely known as loopers or inchworms on account of their progressing by alternately arching and straightening their bodies. Birch feeders include the peppered moth, large emerald and birch mocha; the orange underwing, as an adult, can be seen flying around the tops of birch trees in March sunshine, and occasionally visits sallow blossom. Oak feeders include blotched emerald, brindled pug (which can be common), and oak beauty which, as an adult rests by day low down on tree trunks, where it is perfectly camouflaged (the female is not attracted to light and is rarely seen). Two species feeding on broom are the streak and broom tip, whilst wild rose feeders include the streamer and shoulder stripe. Moth larvae feeding on rosebay willowherb include the small phoenix, a pretty moth with an intricate wing pattern, and the scarce white-banded carpet. The first British specimen of the latter moth was recorded in north-west Kent in 1924 and again in 1950 at Ham Street; since then it has spread north and eastwards and was first recorded at Church Wood in May 1999. Other common Geometers to be found in the Blean include green carpet, July highflyer, light emerald, winter moth (which can be abundant) and little emerald.

The winter moth is a member of an interesting group of Geometers in which the females are wingless or have such stunted wings as to be useless for flight. Most occur during winter and early spring, and winglessness may have evolved to make them less liable to be blown away in gales, and also makes them less conspicuous to predators such as birds. The scare umber, mottled umber and northern winter moth all occur in parts of the Blean in October and November. In February and March the spring usher, March moth, pale brindled beauty, small brindled beauty and the very common dotted border emerge, and may be seen, by torchlight, crawling up tree trunks or sitting on twigs.

Arctiidae

The tiger moths and footmen make up the next group, known as the *Arctiidae*. The footmen (*Lithosiinae*) are a group of small- to medium-sized species with elongated forewings which fold down tightly around the body when the moth is resting, suggestive perhaps of a footman in livery. Scarce footman, four-dotted and rosy footman are all fairly widespread in the Blean, and their larvae feed mostly on various species of lichen. Tiger moths are a group of medium to large, mostly brilliantly coloured moths with very hairy caterpillars, popularly known as "woolly bears", which feed on a variety of herbaceous plants, and pupate in silken cocoons on or near the ground. Typical examples in the Blean include the muslin moth, cinnabar and ruby tiger. Curiously, the best-known of this group, the garden tiger, has not been recorded in the area. The bright colours of the adult moths are a warning to predators that they are toxic.

Drepanidae

The *Drepanidae* or hooktips are an interesting group of moths with a distinctive wing shape. Several species occur in the area, the commonest being the pebble hooktip. The scalloped hooktip is fairly common and the oak and barred hooktip, although mainly nocturnal, may be seen flying in afternoon around oak and beech trees.

Sphingidae

The *Sphingidae* or hawkmoths are some of the largest and

best-known moths in Britain. The larvae can be very large and are usually adorned with brightly coloured stripes or eye-like spots, plus a horn at the tail end. The poplar hawk and elephant hawk are common in Church Wood; the lime hawk has only been recorded sparingly, and the hummingbird hawk moth, a migrant from southern Europe, is sighted occasionally. The privet hawk, the largest hawkmoth in Britain, does not seem to occur in the Blean, but is fairly common in nearby Larkey Valley Wood, south-west of Canterbury.

Lesser families

Several other lesser families are represented in the Blean by many species. The swifts (*Hepialidae*) are a primitive family with elongated wings and short antennae. They usually fly from a short time before dusk until dark, and are also attracted to light. Apart from the common swift and the more local map-winged swift, the most familiar species here is the gold swift. In the June gloaming the males can be seen hovering back and forth over the bracken, presumably looking for the less active females.

The prominents (*Notodontidae*) are rarely seen during the day, but the males are readily attracted to MV light traps. Many of the adults, including buff-tip and pale prominent resemble a small twig when at rest, to avoid detection by birds. The pebble prominent, sallow kitten and swallow prominent are all fairly widespread in the Blean. Less common is the lobster moth, and the puss moth may be found only where poplar or aspen grow.

The tussocks (*Lymantriidae*) are represented by a few species in the woods, by far the commonest being the pale tussock, which is readily attracted to light. The brown tail and yellow tail occur less commonly in more open areas and hedgerows at the woodland edge. The larvae feed on hawthorn, bramble, blackthorn and oak. Some of the larvae of this family, which are all very hairy, may cause a severe skin rash if handled. These irritating hairs are passed on to the hairy pupae, which are spun up in silk cocoons usually amongst the food plant.

The *Thyatiridae* are commonly known as the lutestrings, almost certainly because of the group of thin wavy lines on the fore-wings. There are nine species in this group and all but the frosted green have been recorded to my knowledge in the Blean. Buff arches, common lutestring and peach blossom are all widely distributed. The beautiful satin lutestring, although local in other areas, is fairly common here. The rare figure of eighty has only been recorded once and the poplar lutestring, whose larvae feed on aspen, is also quite local.

Three species of the family *Lasiocampidae*, or eggars, are present. The fox moth and oak eggar males may be seen flying very fast in a zigzag fashion during the day in search of females, which only fly at night and are attracted to light. The adult males have very sensitive feathery antennae and can detect a female downwind from a great distance. The December moth one of the last to emerge, occurring from late autumn to the New Year.

Last but not least, the family *Limacodidae* is represented by one species, the festoon. Locally distributed, the strange-looking larvae feed on oak and beech. The adults occasionally fly in sunshine around the tops of oak trees but more frequently at night, when mostly the males are attracted to light.

Diurnal Moths

Relatively few moths are diurnal, flying mainly in sunshine. Of the geometers, the most frequently seen is the speckled yellow, which is common and widely distributed throughout the Blean in May and June. The cinnabar is seen in good numbers in some years, as in 1997. Their orange and black striped caterpillars may be seen feeding on ragwort in July and August, and the vermilion and grey adults are distasteful to birds. The mother shipton, whose wing markings were said to resemble a Yorkshire witch, is another dayflyer. The female muslin moth, a member of the tiger moths, flies fitfully in warm, sunny weather, and there are several other moths which may fly up readily from the undergrowth during warm weather, such as the silver Y, which sometimes migrates in large numbers from the continent. Another day flyer is the orange-coloured male vapourer moth, which can be seen dashing about in parts of the Blean in late summer and autumn. The males search for the wingless females, which emit a volatile scent and never leave the cocoon from which they hatched. After mating the female begins laying up to 300 eggs. The caterpillars feed on hawthorn, broom, hazel and many other plants.

One rare moth, whose status is uncertain, is the beautiful snout. First recorded in the Blean in 1989, I have seen only one specimen, a female, in Church Wood in July 1998. Whether this was an immigrant or a member of an established colony is unknown. The normal food plant, bilberry, does not occur here, but the moth may have adapted to heather as an alternative. Other migrants, including pearly underwing, dark swordgrass and turnip moth have all been recorded in the Blean. The dotted rustic, another possible migrant, became quite common in Kent in the 1980s and was first recorded in the Blean in the summer of 2001. Another very rare species, which has declined nationally, is the common fanfoot. Fortunately, it turned up at light in numbers in June 2001 in West Blean Wood, and may await discovery in other areas soon.

A vast number of species of micro-Lepidoptera occur in the British Isles, and the Blean is no exception. They are divided into many groups, including the pyralids, tortrix moths and the plume moths. Some of the more obvious species include the green oak tortrix, which can be common, the bramble shoot moth, the black-and-white *Anania funebris* or eight-spot, which also flies in sunshine, the brown china-mark, easily disturbed from undergrowth around ponds, and the leafminers, tiny moths whose larvae feed within the leaf tissue of many trees and shrubs, leaving characteristic patterns (unique to each species) where the larvae have burrowed.

Predators
One of the predators of moths and their larvae is the ubiquitous wood ant (*Formica rufa*). Common in the Blean, their familiar nests may each hold up to 300,000 workers, which spend much time supplying the enormous amount of food needed by the larvae inside the nest. The nests are never far from trees, where the ants hunt for insects, especially moth caterpillars. The ants kill their prey by spraying them with formic acid which paralyses the victim. The lifespan of a worker is from one to two years, but queens can live as long as fifteen years. Undoubtedly wood ants have an impact on many insects, including moths.

Ian Clark

Wood Ants of the Blean

Wood ants (*Formica rufa*) are a common feature of the Blean woods. They are the largest of the ants commonly found in Britain, up to ¼in in length. In spring and summer, trails of ants can be seen as they travel from their nests to forage, or to the oak trees where they harvest honey dew from the aphids. Their dome shaped nests (up to 2m in diameter and up to 1m high) commonly occur on the edges of rides but can also be seen within the woods

Apart from their intrinsic interest these ants are regarded by some as valuable predators on woodland pests, such as the larvae of winter moths and other Lepidoptera, indeed attempts have been made to introduce them where they do not occur naturally, although they may also be harmful to other beneficial species.

Coppicing of trees is considered to be generally beneficial to woodland wild life but it can cause some disruption of the nests of ants. The possible effect of coppicing on the ant population is therefore of interest. Welch (1978)[1] studied an area in the Blean which had been coppiced, for a subsequent period of 10 years and his paper also includes a comprehensive review of earlier work. More recently Dr. K. Adams, a former member of the Blean group, conducted detailed studies on the ant. These are reported in an M.Sc. thesis of the University of Kent (Adams 1991)[2] and summarised in Adams (1993)[3].

The present work was carried out by members of the group during 1993-98 with the prime object of studying the influence of coppicing on the proliferation and survival of ant nests

Location

In February 1993 two contiguous areas (A and B) each of just under an acre, one of which had been coppiced in the previous winter were examined and 10 nests were found in each. In 1994 two further contiguous areas, C (coppiced) of over an acre with 1 nest and D (not coppiced) of just under an acre with 11 nests were included. In 1995 a further area, E (0.25 ha.) was coppiced. This included half of B, with 3 nests, and a similar adjoining area also with 3 nests. The sequence of areas and their approximate locations are shown in Fig 7.6

Normal development

Observations were made regularly throughout 1993-1996 followed by intermittent observations in later years The normal seasonal pattern of development was that little activity could be seen in winter, but on warm days in February the ants clustered (like caviar) in sunny spots on or near the nest and also began to explore their territory. Foraging activity increased during March - April and nests were built up with pine needles, leaf petioles or pieces of grass, depending on local resources. New nests, within a few metres of the original, might appear in April-May with busy ants carrying building materials and eggs from the old to the new nest. A few winged ants might be seen. By July some of the old nests had been abandoned, many of the new nests had also disappeared but some would survive. From August onwards consolidation of surviving old and new nests and 'thatching' of the nest against the winter took place.

Fig.7.6: Areas recorded in each year

Coppiced	Area in ha	Not coppiced		Area in ha
1993 A - - -	0.5	B1 and B2	-	0.5
1994 A C - -	0.65	B1 and B2	D	0.9
1995 - C B1 E	0.65	B2	D	0.65
1996 C B1 E	0.65	B2	D	0.65

There were few predators on the ants in Blean. The commonest damage was from woodpeckers which dig into the nests, especially in winter and spring, in search of ants and eggs. Badgers have become increasingly harmful in recent years.

Observations

The size and activity of the nests was recorded at two week intervals in April - June and at monthly intervals later. Records included the activity of each nest on a scale of 1 to 5, whether additional 'satellite nests' had developed, their position relative to the original nest and, at the end of the season, the diameter and height of each nest. A final count of nests was made in winter 1998-99.

Results

Detailed results are provided in the annual reports for 1993-1996 and only a summary is included here.

The data in Fig. 7.7 show that numbers of nests increased for one or two years after coppicing but remained fairly static till 1996 and on non coppiced areas. However Adams (personal communication) found that one nest which was shaded artificially declined rapidly and Maylam (personal communication) believes that in the long run ants eventually abandon deep shade. Dr. Adams observed that in May and June the ants derived nourishment from the extra-floral nectaries in the unfurling frond of bracken [Adams 1991].

Fig: 7.7: Changes in Number of Nests Over the Seasons

Observation Date		NUMBERS OF NESTS							
		Coppiced site					Site not coppiced		
		A	B1	C	E	Total	B2	D	Total
1993	Spring	9	-	-	-	9	9	-	9
	Autumn	15	-	-	-	15	9	-	9
1994	Spring	10	1	-	-	11	10	11	21
	Autumn	8 + 7*	1 + 7*	-	-	23	9	8 + 2*	19
1995	Spring	8	3	4	3	18	5	10	15
	Autumn	7	3	4	4	18	5	12	17
1996	Spring	-	5	8	6	19	3	11	14
	Autumn	-	3	5	8	16	4	11	15
1999	Spring	-		5	5	10	4	5	9

New nests in 1994 are shown thus- *

Fig. 7.8 Volumes of nests (cubic metres)
from Volume (cubic metres) +diameter ^{2} (metres x 0.3927

	A	B1	C	E	B2	D
1994	-	-	0.14	-	0.145	0.43
1995	0.19	0.15	0.19	0.38	0.51	0.57
1996	-	0.07	0.22	0.07	0.45	0.34

Although individual nests varied in volume (Fig. 7.8) those in the non-coppiced area were generally much larger averaging 0.48 m^3. compared with 0.18 m^3 on the areas which had been coppiced. It is possible that shade favoured nests in the hot summers of 1995 and 1996.

Nests per unit area

The data in the previous tables show that nests per hectare ranged from 18 in 1993 to 24 in 1996. Peak values of 35 and 26 were recorded in coppiced and not coppiced areas in 1994 and 1995 respectively. These figures are not dissimilar to those quoted by Welch (1978) and give no strong evidence of a decline in numbers over the period of the study. The 1999 data are equivocal and because of the increasing density of the undergrowth it was not possible to be certain that all nests had been seen in 1999.

Discussion

This study was conducted over a period of 4 years including two which were unusually hot. In each spring, ant activity increased in these areas which had been coppiced and several new nests developed. Some nests were temporary but several did remain till the end of the season. It is probable that the increase in light intensity encouraged the proliferation of young plant material such as the re-growth of chestnut and oak stools and also of ground cover plants, which provided attractive food for aphids, although these were seldom noticed during inspections. Further observations became impossible because of bramble growth in the shaded uncoppiced areas.

Conclusion

Ant nests in areas which have been coppiced tended to exhibit increased colonisation in the subsequent summer but it is doubtful whether the total population of ants in the area increased. Proliferation of nests also occurred within the uncoppiced woodland and indeed the greatest increase in numbers from one nest occurred there. Especially in the hot summers of 1995 and 1996 the size of the nests in the uncoppiced areas in late summer was substantially greater than in the coppiced areas.

The study has given further information on the normal activity of the wood ant and on its response to the practice of coppicing. Although there was an increase in numbers of nests in the year after coppicing the present data give no evidence that if the practice is adopted on a regular basis it has any long term effect on the ant population.

William Holmes and Irene Marchant

References

1. Welch R C (1978) Changes in the distribution of the nests of Formica rufa at Blean Woods National Nature Reserve, Kent, during the decade following coppicing. Insectes Sociaux, Paris 1978, Tome 25, No 2 pp.173-186t
2. Adams K (1991) M. Sc. Thesis, University of Kent
3. Adams K 1993) Notes on the ecology of the wood ant, Formica rufa (Hymenoptera: Formicidae) in Blean woods National Nature Reserve, Kent, during 1989 and 1990. Transactions of the Kent Field Club,13 (1),29-49.

Spiders of the Blean

The Blean provides an interesting mixture of habitats for invertebrates. Ancient woodlands (coppiced or otherwise) and their associated rides together with small areas of heathland and patches of sphagnum supply a mosaic of types of ground cover, light conditions and moisture regimes that favour different spider assemblages and contribute to an exceptionally high spider species diversity in the area as a whole.

Although serious work on spiders in the Blean complex only started 35 years ago, it was soon evident that the spider fauna included some exceptionally interesting species. A programme of pitfall trapping in an area of abandoned chestnut-beech coppice in Great Den Lees in 1967 (part of the Blean Woods NNR) produced several rarities. These included large numbers of the amaurobiid *Coelotes terrestris* (Notable B) and two linyphiids *Centromerus cavernarum* (RDB 2), a species known from a few other beech woodland sites in southern Britain and *Walckenaeria mitrata* (RDB 1). The latter was then new to the British fauna and, sadly, was only recorded once again at the same site in 1968 despite intensive searches. (RDB refers to the Red Data Book lists of rare species 1 is extremely rare and 2 vulnerable).

It was not until the author moved to Kent in the early 1990's that further detailed work on spiders in the Blean was started. Thus by 1990, only 73 spider species had been recorded from the Blean Woods complex as a whole whereas today the figure stands at 216 species. This total represents just over one third of all spiders recorded from Britain and makes the Blean one of the most important areas for spiders in the whole country. Amongst the species recorded, 129 (60% of all species) are characteristically associated with woodland habitats while 97 (45% of all species) are more typical of heathland. Interestingly, although the two habitat types tend to intergrade in the Blean, (particularly along the edges of woodland rides), only 32 species (15% of the total) are commonly found in both types of habitat.

The studies in Great Den Lees between 1967 and 1972 suggest that the ground-active component of the woodland element is dominated by the linyphiids *Microneta viaria*, *Centromerus sylvaticus*, *Macrargus rufus* and *Lepthyphantes zimmermanni*, all common inhabitants of woodland litter throughout Britain. The other common inhabitants of the litter are the small hahniids, *Hahnia helveola* and *H. montana*. On the surface of the litter, the wolf spider *Pardosa saltans* is common in spring and early summer whilst the large amaurobiid, *Coelotes terrestris* (Notable B) has a peak of adult activity in autumn. Although listed as nationally notable, this species is widespread and often abundant in woodlands in Kent. Apart from the two linyphiids mentioned above, four other ground-active woodland species are worthy of comment. The gnaphosid *Haplodrassus silvestris* (Notable B) is widespread in recently coppiced woodland throughout the Blean and is largely confined in Britain to an area south-east of the line between the Wash and the Severn estuary. The wolf spider, *Xerolycosa nemoralis* (Notable B) is a species commonly seen in recently coppiced areas of the Blean and is reasonably abundant here. It is largely confined to the south-east corner or Britain. The linyphiid *Trichoncus affinis* (RDB 2) is normally found on maritime shingle in Britain and its discovery in litter of recently coppiced chestnut in Church Wood in 1995 came as a complete surprise. However it is known from this type of habitat in France and subsequent work in the Blean Woods NNR indicates that it is not uncommon in the litter around the bases of recently coppiced chestnut, the only red data listed species from the area that can be found reasonably regularly. Finally, the small liocranid *Agraecina striata* (Notable B) is, like *Trichoncus affinis*, found both in coastal shingle and in ancient woodland. A single specimen was collected in pitfall traps by Michael Walter in an area of coppiced hornbeam with oak standards in North Bishopsden Wood in June 2002.

The heathland component of the Blean spider fauna has been less extensively studied than that of the woodlands. However, pitfall trapping in early summer in an area of grass heath near the south end of Church Wood showed that the dominant ground-active species include the wolf spiders *Pardosa pullata*, *Alopecosa pulverulenta* and *Trochosa terricola*. Other commonly occurring species include *Zelotes apricorum*, *Zora spinimana*, *Evarcha falcata*, *Pardosa nigriceps* and the linyphiids *Walckenaeria atrotibialis*, *Peponocranium ludicrum* and *Lepthyphantes tenuis*. All of these are reasonably common spiders and not exclusively associated with heathlands.

The rarer ground-active spiders associated with heathland or patches of heather in the Blean include the small ant-mimicking liocranid *Phrurolithus minimus* (notable A) which has been found both in the National Nature Reserve and East Blean Woods. It is largely restricted to the south-east in Britain and is known from dry chalk grassland as well as clearings and rides in ancient woodlands. The linyphiid *Gonatium paradoxum* (RDB 2) has only been found in Mincing Wood, deep in the roots of patches of heather and wood sedge along the edge of rides. It is a species that elsewhere in Britain is restricted to small areas in Sussex, Surrey and Kent and found on heathland and chalk grassland.

Uncommon species associated with the canopy of heather in the Blean include the small black theridiid *Dipoena tristis* (notable A) which feeds exclusively on ants. It has been found in Blean Woods NNR and East Blean Woods LNR and is recorded from about ten localities in southern England, from Devon in the west to Kent in the east. It is most frequently collected elsewhere on gorse bushes but is found also in the field layer of heathland and grassland. Other species from heather in the Blean include *Tetragnatha pinicola*, *Zilla diodia* and *Hyposinga sanguinea* (all notable B). The first two of these are in fact not particularly uncommon in southern and south-eastern England respectively. The small orb-web weaver *Hyposinga sanguinea* is, however, very local and largely confined to the south-east of England. As well as heathland, it occurs occasionally on chalk grassland.

The remaining rarer spiders from the Blean are all associated with the foliage of trees. Four of these belong to the crab spider-like genus *Philodromus*. They include *Philodromus albidus*, *P. collinus* and *P. praedatus* (all notable B) which have been beaten from the foliage of oaks and, in the case of the first two, swept from heather in the NNR. All three species are largely confined to an area south-east of a line between the Wash and the Severn estuary in Britain. The fourth species, *Philodromus longipalpis*, has only recently been discovered in Britain and has no formal designation as yet. It is, however, very uncommon with records from some fifteen sites in southern Britain. In the Blean it was swept from the central heathland area in Church Wood in 2001. Another unusual species is the bright green orb-web weaver *Araniella inconspicua* (Notable B) which has been beaten from an oak in East Blean Woods LNR. This also is a species that is restricted to south-east England.

Spiders Collected in the Blean Woods Area
The rarest spider recorded from the Blean is undoubtedly the crab spider *Pistius truncatus* (RDB 1). *Pistius truncatus* was first recorded in Britain from near Brockenhurst in the New Forest

in the 1870s. although the exact locality is not known. It was not seen again in Britain until a single female was taken in a woodpile by Mr. Eric Bradford on the edge of a small detached wood at the western end of East Blean Woods on 19th May 1985. Two immature specimens were collected by myself and Rod Allison by beating branches of a small oak in East Blean Woods on 24th July 1993, and reared to maturity by the late Frances Murphy. Since then, many attempts have been made by the author to collect this species in the same area and elsewhere in the Blean Woods, but without success. Finally I collected another female, again by beating a small oak, very close to where it was found in 1993, on the 29th July 2001. It would seem therefore that there is probably an established population in East Blean Woods, albeit probably at extremely low densities.

Some of the rarer ground-active spiders from the Blean are particularly associated with open ground in the early stages of the coppice cycle and continued coppicing is thus essential to their survival. Likewise, for species such as *Dipoena tristis, Zilla diodia, Hyposinga sanguinea* and *Gonatium paradoxum*, management of areas within the woods to ensure survival of patches of heathland would also be essential. None of the species characteristic of tree foliage are known to be specifically associated with ancient woodland. Some, such as the *Philodromus* species, may originally have been characteristic of woodland clearings and have colonised trees outside woodland as the total area has shrunk over the past two millennia. If this is the case, periodic coppicing would also benefit them by increasing the relative area of woodland edge habitats. One species. *Pistius truncatus*, deserves special mention given as it is currently only recorded from the Blean in Britain. If the observation from continental countries that it is normally associated with 'scrub' oaks holds true in the Blean, it would be important to ensure the continued coppicing of a reasonable proportion of oaks, as opposed to *'promoting'* them to high forest trees.

A. Russell-Smith

Fig. 7.9: Spiders from the Blean

SPIDERS COLLECTED FROM THE BLEAN WOODS AREA

Family	*Species*	*East Blean LNR*	*Blean Woods NNR*	*National Status*
Dysderidae	*Dysdera erythrina*	*v/94*	*vi/67*	*common*
Dysderidae	*Dysdera crocata*	*iv/95*		*common*
Dysderidae	*Harpactea homberg*	*iv/94*	*vi/68*	*common*
Mimetidae	*Ero cambridgei*	*ix/02*		*common*
Mimetidae	*Ero furcata*	*viii/92*	*ix/97*	*common*
Theridiidae	*Episinus angulatus*	*v/94*	*iv/95*	*common*
Theridiidae	*Dipoena tristis*	*vi/00*	*vi/95*	*Na*
Theridiidae	*Anelosimus vittatus*	*vii/93*	*x/97*	*common*
Theridiidae	*Achaearanea lunata*	*vii/93*		*local*
Theridiidae	*Theridion sisyphium*	*vi/92*	*vi/95*	*very common*
Theridiidae	*T. varians*	*vi/92*	*vi/95*	*common*
Theridiidae	*T. melanurum*	*vi/95*		*common*
Theridiidae	*T. mystaceum*	*vii/97*		*common*
Theridiidae	*Simitidion simile*	*v/97*		*local*
Theridiidae	*Neottiura bimaculatum*	*vi/92*	*vi/95*	*common*
Theridiidae	*Paidiscura pallens*	*viii/92*	*iv/95*	*common*
Theridiidae	*Enoplognatha ovata*	*vi/92*	*vi/98*	*very common*
Theridiidae	*Enoplognatha latimana*	*viii/01*		*common*
Theridiidae	*Enoplognatha thoracica*	*v/02*		*very common*
Theridiidae	*Robertus lividus*	*v/94*	*i/67*	*very common*
Theridiidae	*R. arundeneti*	*vi/00*	*vi/00*	*uncommon*
Theridiidae	*Pholcomma gibbum*	*v/94*	*v/95*	*common*
Linyphiidae	*Ceratinella brevipes*		*vi/67*	*common*
Linyphiidae	*Ceratinella brevis*	*viii/01*		*common*
Linyphiidae	*Walckenaeria acuminata*	*x/95*	*ii/67*	*very common*
Linyphiidae	*W. mitrata*	*iv/67*	*RDB1*	
Linyphiidae	*W. antica*	*v/94*	*ix/01*	*common*
Linyphiidae	*W. cucullata*	*x/95*		*common*
Linyphiidae	*W. atrotibialis*	*v/94*		*uncommon*
Linyphiidae	*W. incisa*	*v/67*		*Nb*
Linyphiidae	*W. dysderoides*	*v/67*		*uncommon*
Linyphiidae	*W. nudipalpis*	*viii/70*		*common*
Linyphiidae	*W. obtusa*	*xii/71*		*uncommon*
Linyphiidae	*W. monoceros*	*viii/99*		*uncommon*
Linyphiidae	*W. furcillata*		*vi/67*	*uncommon*
Linyphiidae	*W. unicornis*		*iii/76*	*common*
Linyphiidae	*W. cuspidata*		*iv/95*	*common*
Linyphiidae	*Dicymbium nigrum*		*vi/67*	*common*
Linyphiidae	*Entelecara erythropus*		*vi/01*	*common*
Linyphiidae	*Gnathonarium dentatum*		*viii/92*	*common*
Linyphiidae	*Gongylidium rufipes*	*vi/00*	*vi/98*	*common*
Linyphiidae	*Dismodicus bifrons*			
Dysderidae	*Dysdera erythrina*	*v/94*	*vi/67*	*common*
Dysderidae	*Dysdera crocata*	*iv/95*		*common*
Dysderidae	*Harpactea homberg*	*iv/94*	*vi/68*	*common*

Family	Species	East Blean LNR	Blean Woods NNR	National Status
Mimetidae	*Ero cambridgei*	*ix/02*		*common*
Mimetidae	*Ero furcata*	*viii/92*	*ix/97*	*common*
Theridiidae	*Episinus angulatus*	*v/94*	*v/95*	*common*
Theridiidae	*Dipoena tristis*	*vi/00*	*vi/95*	*Na*
Theridiidae	*Anelosimus vittatus*	*vii/93*	*x/97*	*common*
Theridiidae	*Achaearanea lunata*	*vii/93*		*local*
Theridiidae	*Theridion sisyphium*	*vi/92*	*vi/95*	*very common*
Theridiidae	*T. varians*	*vi/92*	*vi/95*	*common*
Theridiidae	*T. melanurum*	*vi/95*		*common*
Theridiidae	*T. mystaceum*	*vii/97*		*common*
Theridiidae	*Simitidion simile*	*v/97*		*local*
Theridiidae	*Neottiura bimaculatum*	*vi/92*	*vi/95*	*common*
Theridiidae	*Paidiscura pallens*	*viii/92*	*iv/95*	*common*
Theridiidae	*Enoplognatha ovata*	*vi/92*	*vi/98*	*very common*
Theridiidae	*Enoplognatha latimana*	*viii/01*		*common*
Theridiidae	*Enoplognatha thoracica*	*v/02*		*very common*
Theridiidae	*Robertus lividus*	*v/94*	*i/67*	*very common*
Theridiidae	*R. arundeneti*	*vi/00*	*vi/00*	*uncommon*
Theridiidae	*Pholcomma gibbum*	*v/94*	*v/95*	*common*
Linyphiidae	*Ceratinella brevipes*	*vi/67*	*common*	
Linyphiidae	*Ceratinella brevis*	*viii/01*		*common*
Linyphiidae	*Walckenaeria acuminata*	*x/95*	*ii/67*	*very common*
Linyphiidae	*W. mitrata*	*iv/67*		*RDB1*
Linyphiidae	*W. antica*	*v/94*	*ix/01*	*common*
Linyphiidae	*W. cucullata*	*x/95*		*common*
Linyphiidae	*W. atrotibialis*	*v/94*		*uncommon*
Linyphiidae	*W. incisa*	*v/67*		*Nb*
Linyphiidae	*W. dysderoides*	*v/67*		*uncommon*
Linyphiidae	*W. nudipalpis*	*viii/70*		*common*
Linyphiidae	*W. obtuse*	*xii/71*		*uncommon*
Linyphiidae	*W. monoceros*	*viii/99*		*uncommon*
Linyphiidae	*W. furcillata*	*vi/67*		*uncommon*
Linyphiidae	*W. unicornis*	*iii/76*		*common*
Linyphiidae	*W. cuspidata*	*iv/95*		*common*
Linyphiidae	*Dicymbium nigrum*	*vi/67*		*common*
Linyphiidae	*Entelecara erythropus*	*vi/01*		*common*
Linyphiidae	*Gnathonarium dentatum*	*viii/92*		*common*
Linyphiidae	*Gongylidium rufipes*	*vi/00*	*vi/98*	*common*
Linyphiidae	*Dismodicus bifrons*			
Hypomma comutum				
Dismomodicus bifrons		*vii/97v/03*	*vii/97*	*very common*
Linyphiidae	*Metopobactrus prominulus*		*vi/95*	*local*
Linyphiidae	*Gonatium rubens*	*viii/92*	*iv/95*	*very common*
Linyphiidae	*Gonatium rubellum*		*ix/97*	*common*
Linyphiidae	*Gonatium paradoxum*		*ix/02*	*RDB2*
Linyphiidae	*Maso sundevalli*	*viii/92*	*iv/67*	*common*
Linyphiidae	*Peponocranium ludicrum*		*vii/97*	*common*
Linyphiidae	*Pocadicnemus pumila*			

Family	Species	East Blean LNR	Blean Woods NNR	National Status
	Pocadicnemus juncea			
	Hypselistes jacksoni	vi/97	v/02vi/03	very common
Linyphiidae	*Oedothorax gibbosus*		iv/95	common
Linyphiidae	*O. fuscus*	vi/92	vi/99	very common
Linyphiidae	*O. retusus*	vi/92	vi/98	very common
Linyphiidae	*O. apicatus*	vi/99		common
Linyphiidae	*Cnephalocotes obscurus*	vii/00		common
Linyphiidae	*Trichoncus affinis*	iv/95		RDB2
Linyphiidae	*Tiso vagans*		v/02	common
Linyphiidae	*Troxochrus scabriculus*		iv/95	local
Linyphiidae	*Tapinocyba insecta*		vi/95	local
Linyphiidae	*Microtetonyx subitanea*		v/99	uncommon
Linyphiidae	*Thyreosthenius biovatus*	v/94	v/03	local
Linyphiidae	*Monocephalus fuscipes*		vi/95	very common
Linyphiidae	*Gongylidiellum vivum*		vii/97	common
Linyphiidae	*G. latebricola*		iv/95	uncommon
Linyphiidae	*Micrargus herbigradus*		iv/67	common
Linyphiidae	*Erigonella hiemalis*	v/95	v/95	common
Linyphiidae	*Diplocephalus picinus*	v/94	vi/67	common
Linyphiidae	*D. latifrons*	v/94		common
Linyphiidae	*Panamops sulcifrons*	v/94		local
Linyphiidae	*Milleriana inerrans*	vi/95		local
Linyphiidae	*Erigone atra*	vi/92	iv/95	very common
Linyphiidae	*E. dentipalpis*	vii/93	vi/95	very common
Linyphiidae	*Jacksonella falconeri*		iv/67	uncommon
Linyphiidae	*Ostearius melanopygius*			
	P. pygmaeum	vi/00	vii/03	viii/99 common
Linyphiidae	*Porrhoma microphthalmum*	vi/99	vii/67	common
Linyphiidae	*Meioneta rurestris*			
	Meioneta saxatilis	vi/94	x/97v i/03	common
Linyphiidae	*Microneta viaria*			
	Maro minutus	v/94	iv/67	vi/03 common
Linyphiidae	*Centromerus sylvaticus*	v/94	i/67	common
Linyphiidae	*C. prudens*		i/67	local
Linyphiidae	*C. dilutus*		x/67	common
Linyphiidae	*C. cavernarum*	iv/67		RDB3
Linyphiidae	*Centromerita concinna*	x/97		common
Linyphiidae	*Sintula corniger*	v/94	x/97	local
Linyphiidae	*Saaristoa abnormis*		vi/67	common
Linyphiidae	*S. firma*		xii/01	uncommon
Linyphiidae	*Macrargus rufus*	v/94	i/67	common
Linyphiidae	*Bathyphantes gracilis*	vi/92	v/67	very common
Linyphiidae	*Bathyphantes parvulus*	vi/00		common
Linyphiidae	*Diplostyla concolor*		v/67	very common
Linyphiidae	*Drapetisca socialis*		viii/70	common
Linyphiidae	*Tapinopa longidens*		ix/68	common
Linyphiidae	*Floronia bucculenta*		ix/97	local
Linyphiidae	*Taranucnus setosus*		i/67	very local
Linyphiidae	*Labulla thoracica*		x/97	common

Family	Species	East Blean LNR	Blean Woods NNR	National Status
Linyphiidae	*Stemonyphantes lineatus*		/99	common
Linyphiidae	*Lepthyphantes obscurus*		/00	common
Linyphiidae	*Lepthyphantes tenuis*	vi/92	ii/67	very common
Linyphiidae	*L. zimmermani*	vi/94	ii/67	very common
Linyphiidae	*L. mengei*	viii/67		very common
Linyphiidae	*L. flavipes*	v/94	x/95	common
Linyphiidae	*L. tenebricola*	vi/67		local
Linyphiidae	*L. ericeus*	viii/92		very common
Linyphiidae	*L. pallidus*	viii/67		common
Linyphiidae	*Helophora insignis*		vii/67	common
Linyphiidae	*Linyphia triangularis*	viii/92	ix/94	very common
Linyphiidae	*L. hortensis*	vi/92	iv/95	common
Linyphiidae	*Nereine montana*		v/68	common
Linyphiidae	*N. clathrata*	v/94	iv/67	very common
Linyphiidae	*N. peltata*	v/94	iv/95	very common
Linyphiidae	*Microlinyphia pusilla*	iv/95		common
Tetragnathidae	*Tetragnatha extensa*	vi/95		very common
Tetragnathidae	*T. pinicola*	v/94	vi/95	Nb
Tetragnathidae	*T. montana*	vii/93	vi/99	very common
Tetragnathidae	*T. nigrita*	vi.98		uncommon
Tetragnathidae	*Pachygnatha clercki*	ix/00		very common
Tetragnathidae	*Pachygnatha degeer*	ix/9 4	v/67	very common
Tetragnathidae	*Metellina segmentata*	vi/92	vi/71	very common
Tetragnathidae	*Metellina menge*	iv/94	ix/94	very common
Tetragnathidae	*Meta menardi*		/99	local
Araneidae	*Gibbaranea gibbosa*		v/02	common
Araneidae	*Araneus diadematus*	viii/92	ix/94	very common
Araneidae	*A. sturmi*	vi/95		uncommon
Araneidae	*A. triguttatus*	vi/94	vi/01	local
Araneidae	*Nuctenea umbratica*		/99	common
Araneidae	*Agelanatea redii*			
Neoscona adianta		vi/00	iv/9 vii/03	uncommon
Araneidae	*A. cucurbitina*	vi/94	vi/95	common
Araneidae	*Araniella opistographa*	vi/92	x/97	common
Araneidae	*A. inconspicua*	v/94		Nb
Araneidae	*Zilla diodia*	vi/92	iv/95	Nb
Araneidae	*Hyposinga pygmaea*	vi/98		local
Araneidae	*H. sanguinea*	v/94	vii/97	Nb
Araneidae	*Zygiella x-notata*	viii/67		common
Araneidae	*Zygiella atrica*	viii/93		common
Araneidae	*Mangora acalypga*		vi/02	local
Araneidae	*Cyclosa conica*	v/94	x/97	local
Lycosidae	*Pardosa palustris*		/00	common
Lycosidae	*Pardosa pullata*	v/94	iv/95	very common
Lycosidae	*P. prativaga*	vii/68		common
Lycosidae	*P. amentata*	v/94	vi/68	very common
Lycosidae	*P. nigriceps*	vi/67		common
Lycosidae	*P. saltans*	vi/92	v/67	common
Lycosidae	*P. hortensis*	vi/92	iv/95	very local

Family	Species	East Blean LNR	Blean Woods NNR	National Status
Lycosidae	*Xerolycosa nemoralis*	vi/94	iv/95	Nb
Lycosidae	*Alopecosa pulverulenta*	vi/98		very common
Lycosidae	*A. cuneata*	vi/99		uncommon
Lycosidae	*Trochosa terricola*	ix/97		very common
Lycosidae	*Trochosa ruricola*	iv/02		very common
Lycosidae	*Pirata latitans*	vi/03		common
Pisauridae				
Pisaura mirabilis	vii/93	-	iv/95	very common
Agelenidae	*Tegenaria sylvestris*		iii/02	local
Hahniidae	*Hahnia montana*	vii/93	i/71	common
Hahniidae	*H. nava*	vi/71		local
Hahniidae	*H. helveola*	v/94	i/67	common
Hahniidae	*H. pusilla*	ix/97		uncommon
Dictynidae	*Dictyna arundinacea*	vi/92	iv/95	common
Dictynidae	*D. latens*	vi/92	vi/95	local
Dictynidae	*Lathys humilis*	viii/93		local
Dictynidae	*Cicurina circur*	i/67		very local
Amaurobiidae	*Coelotes terrestris*	ii/67		Nb
Anyphaenidae	*Anyphaena accentuata*	ix/94		common
Liocranidae	*Agroeca brunnea*	v/94	ix/97	common
Liocranidae	*Agroeca proxima*	ix/02		common
Liocranidae	*Agraecina striata*	/02		Nb
Liocranidae	*Scotina coelans*	ix/02		local
Liocranidae	*Phrurolithus festivus*	v/94		local
Liocranidae	*P. minimus*	v/94	vi/00	Na
Clubionidae	*Clubiona corticalis*	vii/97		common
Clubionidae	*C. reclusa*	vi/95		very common
Clubionidae	*C. terrestris*	viii/92	ix/67	common
Clubionidae	*C. compta*	v/94	x/71	common
Clubionidae	*C. brevipes*	vi/94	ix/94	common
Clubionidae	*Clubiona diversa*	/00		local
Clubionidae	*Clubiona subtilis*			
Clubionidae	*Cheiracanthium erraticum*		vi/95	common
Clubionidae	*Cheiracanthium virescens*	vi/01	vi/01	local
Gnaphosidae	*Drassodes cupreus*		iv/95	local
Gnaphosidae	*Drassodes pubescens*	v/94	iv/95	local
Gnaphosidae	*Haplodrassus silvestris*	v/94	iv/95	Nb
Gnaphosidae	*Zelotes apricorum*	v/94	vi/00	common
Gnaphosidae	*Zelotes latreillei*		/00	common
Gnaphosidae	*Drassyllus pusillus*		/00	local
Gnaphosidae	*Micaria pulicaria*	v/94	vii/97	common
Zoridae	*Zora spinimana*	vi/92	v/67	common
Sparassidae	*Micrommata virescens*	vii/93	vi/68	very local
Philodromidae	*Philodromus dispar*	vi/92	/68	common
Philodromidae	*P. aureolus*	vi/00	vi/95	common
Philodromidae	*P. praedatus*	vi/92	vi/00	Nb
Philodromidae	*P. cespitum*	vi/95		rare
Philodromidae	*P. collinus*	vii/97		Nb
Philodromidae	*P. albidus*	v/94	v/97	Nb

Family	Species	East Blean LNR	Blean Woods NNR	National Status
Philodromidae	Tibellus oblongus	viii/92	vi/95	common
Thomisidae	Misumena vatia	vi/92	vi/98	common
Thomisidae	Pistius truncatus	vii/93		RDB1
Thomisidae	Xysticus cristatus	vi/92	iv/95	very common
Thomisidae	X. audax	viii/92		common
Thomisidae	Xysticus lanio	v/94	vii/97	local
Thomisidae	Xysticus kochi	/00		local
Thomisidae	Ozyptila simplex			
	Ozyptila trux vi/00	vi/0	vi/03	local common
Thomisidae	O. atomaria	ix/01		common
Salticidae	Salticus scenicus	vi/95		common
Salticidae	Salticus cingulatus		vii/97	common
Salticidae	Heliophanus cupreus	viii/92	vi/68	common
Salticidae				
H. Salticidae flavipes				
Bianor aurocinctus		vii/97	iv/03	common
Salticidae	Ballus chalybeius	vi/92	ix/94	local
Salticidae	Neon reticulates	v/95	vi/67	common
Salticidae	Euophrys frontalis	v/94	vi/99	common
Salticidae	Evarcha falcata	v/94	iv/95	common

Totals   216   101   205

Birds of the Blean Woods

The Blean is a wonderful area for birds and one of the most important ornithological sites in East Kent which range from the Medway estuary and the Swale to the water meadows and reed beds of the Stour valley, the chalk downlands and the south Kent coast. The proximity of the English Channel and the European continent are two of the reasons for the rich and varied population. Climate is also important since the South East is warmer and drier than most other areas of the British Isles. Severe weather in Europe forces birds to seek the usually better conditions of the South East of England. In the Blean woods the great storm of 1987 brought down stands of mature conifers and many individual oak and other trees. This opened up areas of the woods to glades and heath and these clearings in fact were of benefit to many birds including the nightjar. Management of the woods is also important; improvement and widening of rides, creation of open areas by regular coppicing of chestnut and other species, and maintenance of stands of mature deciduous trees, all contribute to the diverse habitat in the Blean which favours a variety of birds.

Habitat: Extensive young coppice/conifer plantations **Species:** Nightjar, tree pipit, whitethroat

Habitat: Deciduous high forest **Species:** All the expected birds of southern woodland: (tits, woodpeckers, nuthatch, treecreeper, thrushes, robin, tawny owl, wood pigeon, woodcock In addition, wood warbler, hawfinch, redstart and golden oriole, which are all scarce as breeding species in SE England, regularly bred in small numbers until the late 1990s, but are now generally absent.

Habitat: Woodland edge **Species:** Little owl, kestrel

Habitat: Conifer high forest **Species:** Goldcrest, coal tit, crossbill

Habitat: Dense coppice **Species:** Warblers, nightingale

Habitat: Open areas – glades, heath and scrub **Species:** Common whitethroat, lesser whitethroat, tree pipit, yellowhammer, linnet, redpoll

Habitat: Streams, ponds, wet areas **Species:** Moorhen, mallard, teal*, heron*, reed bunting, kingfisher, pied wagtail, grey wagtail*, sedge warbler

(Apart from asterisked species, all have bred in The Blean within the last 15 years

---

Fig. 7.10: Main Habitats in the Blean and their Associated Birds

Botanical surveys of the woods made by members of the group have recorded the range of woodland types which occur, mostly within the W8 and W10 groups, according to the classification of the National Vegetation Survey (Rodwell 1991).

Changes in the population follow the seasons. Autumn sees the migrants returning to their winter quarters and they and the resident birds take advantage of the seeds and berries in the arable and grassland areas and in the hedgerows and woods, and also the well stocked bird tables in nearby gardens. Winter visitors, such as fieldfares and redwings, then pass through though some may stay to feed in the woods, hedgerows and nearby apple orchards.

Siskins, redpolls and bramblings are mainly recorded on passage but a number of redpolls may spend the winter feeding in the birch trees and the ground beneath. Mixed flocks of tits can be heard and sometimes seen moving through the tree canopy. In a harsh winter snipe may be seen near the frozen ditches. When spring returns the welcome song of the chiffchaff is its harbinger and soon thereafter the summer visitors begin to arrive.

Blean Woods RSPB Reserve is one of the sites where the song of nightingales can be heard in April and May. Other migrant songbirds such as tree pipits, willow warblers, whitethroat and turtle dove are also to be heard and a quiet summer evening is the time to see and hear the woodcock "roding" and male nightjars wing-clapping.

Birds are identified by song and sighting. A good book, a good ear, and binoculars are needed.

A comprehensive list of birds that have bred or attempted to breed in the Blean between 1978 and 2003 (prepared by Michael Walter, the site manager of the RSPB Blean Woods Reserve) is in Fig 7.11.

Heather Nightingale and Michael Walter

Fig. 7.11: Birds that Have Bred or Attempted to Breed in The Blean between 1978 and 2003

Mallard* (*Anas platyrhynchos*) - Annual, a few pairs at ponds.

Sparrowhawk (*Accipiter nisus*) - Now well-established breeding and wintering.

Kestrel (*Falco tinnunculus* - Occasional at woodland edge.

Hobby (*Falco subbuteo*) - A few pairs now breed annually, reflecting the marked increase in Kent in the past few years.

Red-legged partridge (*Alectoris rufa*) - Not normally associated with woodland, a few birds are known to have been released by a shooting tenant on the RSPB reserve in the late 1990s, and in 2000 at least one pair was present throughout the spring, though without proof of breeding.

Pheasant (*Phasianus colchicus*) - Numbers augmented by some breeding for sport.

Moorhen* (*Gallinula chloropus*) - At several small ponds.

Woodcock (*Scolopax rusticola*) - Fairly widespread, at low density.

Stock dove (*Columba oenas*) - Scarce in mature woodland, possibly scarcer in recent years.

Wood pigeon (*Columba palumbus*) - Widespread.

Collared dove (*Streptopelia decaocto*) - Occasional in conifers near woodland edge.

Turtle dove (*Streptopelia turtur*) - Declining in the 1980's, stabilising in the 1990s, but with a sudden further marked decline since 1998; now a very scarce summer visitor in older coppice or mature woodland with understorey.

Cuckoo - (*Cuculus canorus*) - Thinly spread and declining since 1996, with very few now encountered within the woodland; more likely to be heard in surrounding open countryside.

Little owl (*Athene noctua*) - A few pairs at edge of woodland.

Tawny owl (*Strix aluco*) - Thinly spread in mature woodland.

Long-eared owl (*Asio otus*) - Occasional in small blocks of mature conifer.

Nightjar (*Caprimulgus europaeus*) - Up to c15 pairs, depending on area of suitable habitat available.

Kingfisher* (*Alcedo athis*) - Nests along small streams in some years.

Green woodpecker (*Picus viridis*) -Widely, but thinly, spread throughout mature woodland.

Great spotted woodpecker (*Dendrocopos major*) - Commonest of the woodpeckers, in all mature woodland, including conifer.

Lesser spotted woodpecker - (*Dendrocopos minor*) - Only about a third as common as the great spotted woodpecker, not normally in conifer, absent from extensive areas of apparently suitable habitat.

Sand martin* (*Riparia riparia*) - At least two colonies have been established in old sand quarries.

Sedge warbler* (*Acrocephalus schoenobaenus*) - Occasional around ponds within woodland.

Lesser whitethroat (*Sylvia curruca*) - Very scarce in scrub or woodland edge.

Whitethroat (*Sylvia communis*) - Scattered distribution in denser patches of young scrub with grassy clearings. Numbers crashed in the early 1980s, and have only made a partial recovery since.

Garden warbler (*Sylvia borin*) - Fairly widespread in young coppice.

Blackcap (*Sylvia atricapilla*) - Fairly widespread, with a marked increase in the 1990's, mainly in understorey associated with open mature oakwood.

Wood warbler (*Phylloscopus sibilatrix*) - Sporadic breeder in mature birch coppice, oakwood and beechwood; no breeding records for the past five years.

Chiffchaff (*Phylloscopus collybita*) - Increased in 1980's and early 1990s, but with a definite decline in the late 1990's, but with a massive comeback in 2002, in mature oakwood with an understorey.

Willow warbler (*Phylloscopus trochilus*) - Declining until the mid 1990's, when there was a fairly marked revival in young coppice and open rides.

Goldcrest (*Regulus regulus*) - Fairly common in conifer plantations from thicket stage onwards; much scarcer in mature oakwood, favouring areas where ivy and/or holly is present.

Spotted flycatcher (*Muscicarpa striata*) - Rather thinly spread in some of the mature woodland with marked decline since 1997, and now very scarce; site faithful, many apparently suitable areas no longer occupied.

Long-tailed tit (*Aegithalos caudatus*) - Reasonably widespread, especially where there are open areas of woodland with dense scrub eg gorse for nest-site.

Marsh tit (*Parus palustris*) - Always fairly thinly spread through mature woodland, becoming extremely scarce in the late 1990s. Mirrors a trend in large parts of Kent, the reason is unknown.

Willow tit (*Parus montanus*) - Always scarce, has declined alarmingly in past 15 years in Blean and the wider countryside, and may now be extinct within the woodland; favours conifers, and scrubby coppice, especially near water.

Coal tit (*Parus ater*) - Can reach quite high densities in maturing conifers; present at much lower density in mature oakwood.

Blue tit (*Parus caeruleus*) - Reasonably common in mature oakwood, less so in conifer and older coppice.

Great tit (*Parus major*) - Scarcer than blue tit, more likely to be present in older coppice.

Nuthatch (*Sitta europaea*) - Widespread at low density in mature oakwood. Sustained decline since 1995. On the RSPB reserve only one territory was located in 2001, compared to an average of 20 in 1991-1995. Partial recovery in 2002-3.

Tree creeper (*Certhia familiaris*) - Rather scarce in mature woodland, numbers fluctuating wildly from one year to the next, but usually leaving large expanses of woodland untenanted, with some suggestion of a downward drift since the mid-1990's.

Golden oriole (*Oriolus oriolus*) - A few bred annually in the late 1970's and early 1980's; now much more sporadic - and no longer even recorded annually.

Jay (*Garrulus glandarius*) - Common.

Magpie (*Pica pica*) - Increased dramatically in 1980's, now stabilised, with birds nesting around the edges of the woods.

Jackdaw (*Corvus monedula*) - Scattered through the mature woodland, usually in small colonies.

Rook (*Corvus frugilegus*) - Not strictly a bird of the main Blean woodland blocks, but nesting in some copses that occur within the area occupied by The Blean.

Crow (*Corvus corone*) - Scarce, but probably increasing, nests sometimes well within the wood.

Starling (*Sturnus vulgaris*) - Formerly fairly common, nesting in loose colonies, but with a marked decline in the 1990s, and now very scarce breeder. Post-breeding flocks which fed on caterpillars in the oak canopy in the 1980's are no longer seen.

House sparrow (*Passer domesticus*) - A few nest in disused sand martin holes and outbuildings. Like starling, used to be found just inside the oakwoods feeding on caterpillars in late spring; this behaviour is no longer recorded.

Tree sparrow (*Passer montanus*) Used to nest, now almost certainly extinct.

Chaffinch (*Fringilla coelebs*) - Fairly scarce in mature woodland.

Greenfinch (*Carduelis chloris*) - Very scarce.

Goldfinch (*Carduelis carduelis*) - Occasional at edge of woods.

Siskin (*Carduelis spinus*) - Occasional mid-summer records of adults, and once of juveniles, in Canterbury area, indicates possibility of a pair breeding in conifer woodland in The Blean. Variable numbers recorded on spring and autumn passage.

Linnet (*Acanthis cannabina*) - Very scarce in young scrub and young conifer plantations.

Redpoll (*Acanthis flammea*) - Formerly abundant in some winters, with flocks of hundreds, and a few staying to nest. No longer breeds, and very scarce in winter.

Crossbill (*Loxia curvirostra*) - Has bred in past; affected by the loss of so many mature pines in the 1987 storm, but small post-breeding flocks still seen in some years, and known to have bred in 2000.

Bullfinch (*Pyrrhula pyrrhula*) - Widespread but scarce in a wide range of habitats. Limited monitoring suggests marked decline since 1996.

Hawfinch (*Coccothraustes coccothraustes*) - Very scarce and declining, mirroring a regional trend. Last peak, in the late 1980's, coincided with a major winter influx from the continent, so it is possible that numbers in Kent depend on occasional topping up from abroad. Associated with mature oak, beech and hornbeam.

Yellowhammer (*Emberiza citrinella*) - Formerly fairly frequent in scrub and young coppice, now quite rare and known to be declining in the wider countryside. A winter roost of 25 in gorse in a woodland clearing in 1999 constituted a significant flock for Kent.

Reed bunting (*Emberiza schoeniclus*) - Has bred in wet areas of scrub in the past.

Mammals of the Blean

The grey squirrel is the most frequently seen mammal of the Blean woods. It is numerous and widespread and its dreys, rather untidy nests of twigs and leaves high up in the trees, are readily seen in winter. The squirrel is a pest because it causes considerable damage to young trees by nibbling their bark

Foxes are common and widespread and their characteristic smell may be detected almost anywhere in the woods especially in the breeding season, early in the year and in humid conditions.

There are a number of badger setts in the woods. One of these is unusually extensive. It covers a large area and is situated in the midst of woodland instead of the more normal position near the wood edge adjacent to open fields. In the grass rides the turf is kept short by rabbit grazing but the rabbit population is not large. East Blean Wood is unusual in also having a population of hares. Moles are widespread and create their mounds, or 'hills', in some open areas, along woodland edges and sometimes within the wood even on heavy clay soil.

The Blean, unlike many other parts of Kent, was free from deer but in recent years they have been reported on the outskirts of the woods both near Tyler Hill and near Dunkirk. It is thought that both fallow and muntjac deer have been sighted. This is likely to be followed by further colonisation with serious implications for the future structure of the wood.

Fig. 7.12: Mammals - Blean Woods including the National Nature Reserve

Hedgehog	Single record in Blean Woods NNR in 20 years
Mole	Frequent In some years in 1980's up to 30 dead individuals found
Common shrew	Fairly common
Pygmy shrew	Much scarcer than common shrew
Water shrew	One found dead in Blean Woods NNR in 1980's
Common pipistrelle (45KHz)	Fairly scarce
Soprano pipistrelle (55KHz)	Fairly scarce
Noctule	Rare - occasionally seen
Rabbit	Common on periphery in some years; much scarcer in middle of wood. Myxomatosis evident most years
Hare	One in wood near Bossenden Farm in April 2002, but evidence of a population in East Blean Wood
Grey squirrel	Common in oakwood, apparently becoming more abundant in 1990's
Brown rat	Associated with pheasant release pens. Also seen near NNR car park in 2002
Bank vole	Fairly common
Water vole	Occasionally seen in pond or along main stream
Wood mouse	Much less common than bank vole
Yellow-necked mouse	Occasionally found nesting in dormouse boxes.
Dormouse	Very occasionally disturbed in nest boxes or during winter management. Several pairs breed in boxes each year
Fox	Occasional - apparently scarcer in 1990s in NNR, but some evidence of more in other woods
Weasel	Very occasionally seen, usually crossing rides
Stoat	Much scarcer than weasel - few records
Badger	Three established setts in the Blean Woods NNR. Occasional scat in various parts of the reserve may relate to animals from off-reserve setts.

21 species recorded

Notes: A proper bat survey would probably reveal the presence of further species, including long-eared and whiskered.
No deer have been recorded on the reserve, but muntjac and fallow deer have been reported more frequently since the 1990s in and around the Blean, so it is probably only a matter of time before one or both species becomes established within the Blean

The dormouse, a rarity in many parts of England, still inhabits the Blean and, its nests are occasionally found in hedge and bramble thickets. Also to be found are the wood mouse, the yellow-necked mouse, the pigmy shrew, the bank vole and several species of bat.

Irene Marchant and Michael Walter

THE WOODS FROM WEST TO EAST

Chapter VIII

The Blean Woods - A Selection

During its activities the group visited over 20 woods within the Blean, a small proportion of over 80 woods, but by far the most important and accounting for most of the total area. For the purposes of this book the Blean Woods are those listed below. Members of the group and Oliver Rackham visited the principal woods of the Blean and these are described.

Group A - Woods west of Church Wood

This group includes North Bishopden and Bossenden Woods which now form part of a National Nature Reserve together with Church Wood and some others.
1. Ellenden Wood, near Seasalter.
2. Blean Wood, near Dargate.
3. Bossenden Wood in Dunkirk.

Group B - Woods south of Watling Street (A2)

These woods are on the southern edge of the London Clay on which most of them are situated.
4. South Bishopden.
5. Fishpond Wood in Dunkirk.
6. Denstead Wood near Chartham Hatch.

Group C - Woods west of Blean village

These woods lie between Watling St (A2) and the Canterbury - Whitstable road, (A290). Church Wood is the largest area of woodland here and most is within the National Nature Reserve.
7. Shimhill Wood, near Rough Common.
8. Church Wood, near Blean village.
9. Radfall Road (west), near Blean village

Group D - The Former 'Blean Woods National Nature Reserve'

These woods stretch for about one mile along the northern boundary of Church Wood. They were acquired by the Nature Conservancy and the former Nature Conservancy Council

between 1953 and 1985.
10. Crawford's Rough, near the main road, A 290
11. Town Wood now part of Mincing Wood
12. Mincing Wood, near the Royal Oak, Blean.
13. Grimshill Wood, near Denstroude valley.
14. Great Den Lees next to North Bishopden Wood
15. Little Den Lees, near Denstroude Valley

Group E -Woods east, north and south of Blean Village
16. Marley Wood, north of the village.
17. Park Wood, part of the University campus.
18. Brotherhood Wood, part of the University campus.
19. The Radfall.
20. East Blean Wood, next to the road to Herne (A 291)
21. Great Hall Wood, to the east of Tyler Hill
22. Herne Park Elmwood.

Other Woods of the Blean are:
(a) next to Watling Street and Church Wood: (i) Poundfall (ii) Hospital (iii) Brotherhood (iv) Willows (v) Homestall

(b) near Tyler Hill and Great Hall Wood: (i) Honey (ii) Paddock (iii) Timber (iv) Daws (v) Little Hall (vi) Barton

(c) next to Clowes Wood: (i) Lypeatt (ii) Woodside (iii) Mintey's (iv) Cane (v) Hempshall (vi) Butler's Court

(d) next to West Blean Wood: (i) Cripps (ii) Round (iii) Banker's (iv) Hoath (v) Farthings (vi) Belce.

This chapter contains descriptions of differing length, prepared by different individuals or small groups of the twenty two woods in Group A to E above. The first of these, Ellenden Wood is the subject of a detailed report by Dr Oliver Rackham. Four woods Church, Clowes Thornden and Blean themselves occupy over 3,000 acres. The descriptions are arranged geographically beginning with those woods in the north west corner of the woodland area.

1. Ellenden Wood (including Coombe Wood and Tong Wood)

Ellenden Wood, now 224 acres, lies on the outer fringes of the Blean plateau and is divided by an internal valley. On the north-west, uniquely among the Blean woods, it descends down a narrow ravine to within half-a-mile of the coastal marshes. On the Ordnance Survey of 1801, and until recently, it formed part of a huge extent of woodland covering the whole western part of the Blean. It was separated from North Bishopsden Wood by a big clearing made between 1873 and 1896 Between c.1955 and c.1975 its south-western part was grubbed out cutting the wood

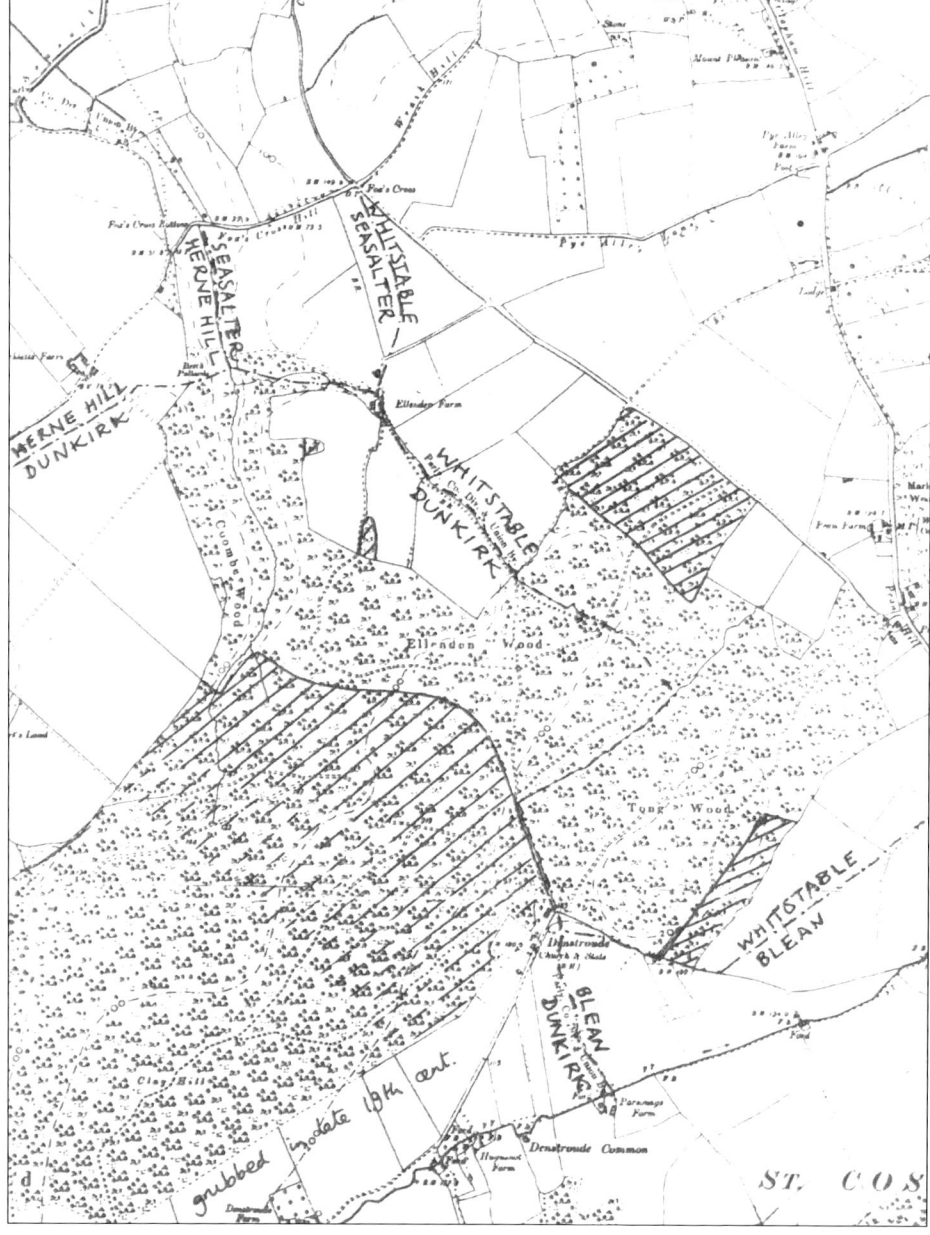

Fig.8.1: Ellenden Wood from the Ordanance Survey of 1896 showing ancient parish boundaries and areas of woodland since grubbed (hatched)

off from Old Blean Wood to the west.

Ellenden Wood properly refers to the middle part of the wood, between the two streams. The part south-east of the eastern stream is historically called Tong Wood; the part west of the northern stream is called Coombe Wood. Tong Wood and part of Ellenden proper are in the ancient parish of Whitstable. Tong apparently means 'tongue', Tong Wood forming a tongue of land at the southern end of Whitstable parish. The rest of the wood belongs to the extra-parochial territory of Dunkirk with small parts in Herne Hill and Seasalter.

History and Archaeology
Ellenden Wood seems to have been in an area of fragmented private ownership lying between the royal (later monkish) woods to the south-west and the great ecclesiastical woods to the east. The wood is named after Ellenden Farm (located at the triple junction of Dunkirk, Seasalter and Whitstable). This was a small independent manor. The place-name Elynden, going back at least to the mid-thirteenth century, apparently means 'the denn (outlying settlement) of elder'[1] which would be reasonable today.

Faversham Abbey had many woods in the north-west Blean, some of them given by King Stephen at the Abbey's foundation in 1147. At an unknown date the Abbey was given an estate including 64 acres of wood 'in Whitstable and Seasalter', which would fit the east side of the western ravine in the present wood.[2] If the Faversham Abbey barns are a guide to the timber output of these woods, their 15th century output included a large number of oaks smaller than most of those in the wood today, but it was almost impossible to procure 32 middle-sized oaks for the posts of the barns, which could easily be got from Ellenden Wood now.

Ellenden Manor, after centuries of private ownership, was bequeathed to Faversham Abbey in 1504. At the dissolution the estate was stolen by Henry VIII and sold to Thomas Arden of Faversham, later famously murdered. The property included 5 acres of '*tonge woode*', plus 3 acres of '*hedgerowes*' treated as woodland. Of these 18 acres two acres were 'waste' (having no trees on them) and the remainder was coppice-wood of from 0 to 16 years growth since last felling. Timber trees were only in the hedgerows. The produce included 20 wagon-loads of firewood per year.[3] The woods evidently formed part of what is now the eastern part of Ellenden Wood.

Arden acquired by lease the major part of the Abbey Woods - 1100 acres of coppice.[4] He also purchased another ex-Faversham property, *'Lambertisland'* (of which *'Lamberhurst'* is a modern corruption). This was both a farm and a tile-factory with eleven kilns. The estate included nine acres of coppice-wood and six acres of hedgerows, but more wood for the tile-burning came from other Faversham Abbey woods then in the king's hands.[5]

As well as tile-making, there was another big fuel-using industry: salt-boiling on the Seasalter levels, attested by documents back to Anglo-Saxon times. By the 15th century the woods were fully used, to judge by the remarkably small and crooked oaks that went into the great barn which still stands at Littlebourne.

Ownership continued to be sub-divided. A Jesus Hospital document of 1598 refers to:
> *'9 acres at Tonge Hill invironed with the woodland*
> *of Wm Rowth and Mychell Berisford Esq and*
> *wayes through the woods of the said Wm Rowth*
> *To the highway leading from Whitstable to*
> *Canterbury'*.[6]

This evidently refers to the public rights-of-way which still exist as an unusual feature of Tong Wood.

Ellenden Farm later acquired more woodland. When the estate was sub-divided in 1735-6 it included 70 acres of wood, which were tithe-free (indicating that they had once been abbey land) and were worth nearly as much as the 120 acres of tithe-free farmland.[7]

Like many other Blean Woods, Ellenden has lost most of its original perimeter and with it any massive boundary banks that Faversham Abbey or the kings their predecessors may have made. The remaining pre-1801 stretches of boundary often only have a ditch, which suggests unrecorded encroachments on the wood in the 18th century or earlier.

Miles of lesser, internal, woodbanks snake through the woods. They are truncated by the present boundary, showing that the woodbanks came earlier They confirm that this part of the woods was divided among smaller private owners. Cant-marks and small pollard trees show that some of the boundaries were still functional within the lifetime of living trees. Somewhere among these internal subdivisions - if we could identify them - lie the Ellenden and Lambertisland shares in the wood.

Since at least the 16th century the wood has been traversed by public rights-of-way. This unusual feature suggests a period as a common wood. The tracks are not usually demarcated from the surrounding wood; they are at least as old as the woodbanks, some of which terminate or change direction on meeting a track. One of the tracks, now long disused, is represented by a pair of woodbanks in the south of Tong Wood.

Soils

The soils of Ellenden Wood are particularly complex. The underlying London Clay is masked, as in other woods, by surface deposits of gravel and loess. On the plateau root-plates of windblown trees reveal a clayey silt containing small, rounded or shattered flints. These soils, which are probably typical of Blean plateau woods, are acid (pH ranging from 3.5 - 4.4) and low in nitrogen and phosphorus.[8]

The ravine ought to cut down into the London Clay, but here too it is covered, probably by the silty 'Head Brickearth' which the Geological Survey maps in other, larger valleys outside woodland. However the underlying clay itself varies and is evidently permeable. On the steep side of the ravine are springs and ancient landslips, with their characteristic crescentic shapes. Ledges of hard iron concretion create small waterfalls in the stream. The vegetation indicates less acid soils, uncharacteristic of London Clay.

Vegetation

Ellenden is probably the most complex wood on the Blean. It is an ancient, relatively natural, coppice-wood which has escaped modern forestry and was not much affected by the chestnut fashion. The combination of woodland types gives this wood its reputation for a rich flora in flowering plants and fungi.

The main body of the wood is composed of oak (mainly sessile), beech, chestnut, hornbeam and aspen. They form an irregular mosaic of patches of different trees, mostly not following management boundaries. Oak coppice and beech coppice are well represented. The ground vegetation is dominated by bramble, bracken, honeysuckle, the grass *Deschampsia flexuosa* and (in recently felled areas) heather.

The north-west ravine is very different: its trees are ash, maple, hazel, hornbeam, and elm (*Ulmus minor* - East Anglian Elm). There is a wide range of shrubs like spindle and dogwood. Service is more abundant than in most of the Blean woods. The ground vegetation is usually dominated by bluebell, dog's mercury, wood anemone or the grass *Poa trivialis*. Ash-maple-hazel wood and elmwood imply somewhat calcareous, less infertile soils. They are probably unique to the Blean, linking the plateau woods to a type of woodland more commonly found on chalky boulder-clay or even chalky soils.

Ancient stools of oak, hornbeam, ash and maple, over 6ft across, are to be found throughout the wood. They are the result of centuries of felling and regrowth, and confirm that nearly the whole wood is of at least 16th century antiquity. Beech reaches 7ft in diameter and chestnut 7½ft, which indicates that chestnut, though probably not a Roman introduction, has been in Ellenden longer than in most other woods.

Recent History and Present State

The wood is admirably managed and regularly coppiced by the present owner and his excellent contractors. It has the great advantage of having no deer.

In the late 1990's there was a proposal to site a large *'bioreactor'*, that is a dump for burying rubbish on the land previously grubbed out to the west of the remaining wood. This was rejected after a very extensive Public Enquiry. Part of the evidence against the proposal was concerned with threats to the integrity of Ellenden Wood. Although the wood would not have been directly encroached upon, it would have been uncomfortably near the dump, and liable to have nitrate, phosphate and calcium (if nothing worse) added from dust, bird droppings and effluent leaching into the ravine. Excess nutrients would be disastrous to this ecosystem based on plants that are adapted to making do with low fertility; bluebells, for example would be replaced by nettles.

Oliver Rackham

References

1 J.K. Wallenberg, *The Place-Names of Kent*, Appelberg, Uppsala 1934.
2 E. Hasted, *The History and Topographical Survey of the County of Kent*, Simmons & Kirkby, Canterbury (1790) 3 551.
3 P. Hyde, *The Role of Thomas Arden in Faversham: the man behind the myth*, Faversham Soc. (1996) p.184ff. translating PRO: E318/2/34.
4 Hyde, p.210f, translating PRO:E326/12266.
5 Hyde, p.192ff, translating PRO:E318/2/37; E. Jacob, *The History of the Town and Port of Faversham*, White, London (1774), p.184ff.
6 Kindly transcribed by Alexander Wheaten from Bunce, MS Register of Charities, p.1074ff (Canterbury Cathedral Archives).
7 Hasted (1778-90) 3 151.
8 Information kindly supplied by Dr. M. Nicholls.

2. Blean Wood

On the western edge of the Radfall Road is Blean Wood, where other botanical surveys were made (with permission of Mr. & Mrs. Dawes of the nearby Mount Ephraim). This wood lies on the western extremity of the London Clay belt, which stretches west from East Blean Wood. Since woods occupy nearly all the distance between them, the Blean woods stretch about eight miles from east to west. There is some further woodland on those less acid soils further west than Blean Wood, but this is not generally regarded as part of the Blean. A stream in a ravine crosses the wood in the direction of Dargate. The name Dargate suggests that that is where the woods already ended in medieval times.

Blean Wood was thus once part of a very large block of woodland to its south joining North Bishopden and to its east Clay Hill, but each of these have suffered large woodland clearance. At the time of the Domesday Book it was the property of William the Conqueror.[1] It was given by his grandson, King Stephen, as one of the original endowments of Faversham Abbey, which he founded. The abbey was dissolved in the sixteenth century[2] and after the dissolution the woodland was managed by a succession of lay owners. In this respect these woods differ from those at the eastern end of the Blean

Botanical surveys confirm that Blean Wood is one of many ancient woods forming the Blean. A representative area examined in detail in 1998 was about half an acre. Nine species of tree were recorded as well as eleven of ground vegetation. Butcher's Broom which occurs in a number of places in this wood is an ancient woodland indicator, as are Sessile Oak and Crab Apple.

Another survey made further to the west showed fewer species but also recorded, as before, old oak coppice, a comparatively rare occurrence in South East England but frequent in the Blean.

A road follows the eastern boundary of this wood and there is access to a public footpath at Dargate.

Alexander Wheaten

References
1. Morgan P. (Ed) *Domesday Book - Kent* (1983)
2. Phillimore 1.4. (1996) Faversham Society App. 13.

3. Bossenden Wood

Bossenden Wood is on the north side of Watling Street, some four miles west of Canterbury. On three sides it surrounds Bossenden Farm and it is itself surrounded on three sides by Bishopsden Wood to the north, South Bishopsden Wood and others to the south and Church Wood and Manson Wood to the east. Like the other Blean woods Bossenden lies on London Clay but it is close to the less acid soils of Dunkirk to the west. The Fishbourne stream which rises nearby to the south of Watling forms part of the boundary with Manson Wood to the south and then enters Church Wood and flows through it for about two miles. The southern boundary is Watling St. and the northern boundary with North Bishopsden Wood is indicated by a rather indistinct ancient woodbank. Another woodbank crosses the wood from north to south towards Church Wood. It would have crossed the area now occupied by Bossenden farm. Its meaning as a boundary was lost long ago. Presumably it was constructed when the land belonged to the medieval abbey at Faversham, which owned over one thousand acres of woodland west of Church Wood at the Dissolution. Unlike Church Wood and North and South Bishopsden Woods, the woods no longer had ecclesiastical owners after the Reformation. Bossenden wood is unique in Blean being the site of an incident that attracted national attention, the so called Battle of Bossenden Wood in 1838, when because of a protest, troops had to be sent to restore law and order

At that and earlier times the remoteness of these woods had provided shelter to those pursuing unlawful activities such as at Wat Tyler's rebellion of 1382.[1] References to the management of this wood in the 16th century are in reports following the dissolution of Faversham Abbey.[2] Indicators of ancient woodland such as wild service, woodland thorn and sessile oak, occur in the wood. The dominant timber trees are oak, some exceeding 60ft, and beech, while there are smaller growths of beech, birch, chestnut, hazel, holly and hornbeam, many coppiced; oak saplings also occur. The tree canopy averaged 75%. Ground cover ranged from 15 – 100% and was similar to that in other areas of the Blean. and included butchers broom, St. John's wort and woodrush. In view of the importance of this wood to the Blean complex much of it was acquired by the RSPB as part of a larger reserve. It was designated as an SSSI [Site of Special Scientific Interest] and has recently been included in a larger National Nature Reserve. The RSPB, through its warden Mr Michael Walter, maintains tracks and footpaths for public access. The severe storm of 16 October 1987 uprooted a number of timber trees, mainly beech, and most of these have been allowed to survive.

Heather Nightingale

References
1. Canterbury Cathedral *Charta Antiqu*, B 334.2. Hyde P.(1996)
2. *The role of Thomas Arden of Faversham*, Faversham Society App. 13.

4. South Bishopsden Wood

This wood, documented since before the 14th century, is so named because it was owned by the Archbishops of Canterbury until the 19th century.

The wood overlies the boundary between the London clay and the Oldhaven and Woolwich beds, however it should be noted that to the north-east most of the London Clay is overlain by more silty deposits although in the centre is a small patch of sand and gravel much of it dug away forming ponds. In other areas the

London Clay is at the surface and the soil is very poor. This area is of roughly level ground above 100 metres in height. In the south-western half the Oldhaven and Woolwich Beds are covered to a large degree by Head Brickearth, but on occasions drainage has eroded some quite deep ravines cutting down into the Oldhaven Beds. These streams, mainly of temporary duration flow into a larger stream, known to some as Fishponds Stream, which forms the southern boundary of the wood and which flows in a north-easterly direction then turning to enter the Great Stour, south of Canterbury.

For the most part South Bishopsden Wood is surrounded by other woods; indeed it was so entirely prior to about 150 years ago when an area was grubbed out to form what is now Forester's Lodge Farm. However the boundary between the farm and the wood has an old ditch and bank, which shows signs today of having been re-cut in places in the not too distant past. Today the boundary with Fishponds wood is ill-defined but an old wood bank separates off Brotherhood Wood. A feature of South Bishopsden Wood is an old trackway, which follows the northern boundary of Church Wood then the southern part of North Bishopsden before crossing Watling Street to enter and pass through South Bishopsden Wood in a SW/NE direction. Rights of Way also pass through the wood.

Documentation since medieval times lodged at Lambeth Palace refers to the management of the wood on behalf of the Archbishops. According to a report by a surveyor of timber in 1816 the wood was used as a source of oak and beech some of which was timber and other as coppice every twenty years or so. Today sessile oak standards are found throughout the wood with birch and beech coppice, the latter becoming more prevalent in the southern part of wood where the soil is of better quality. Coppicing however seems to have ceased, the last cut being at least ten years ago. The result of this is that there is complete canopy and ground flora is found mainly near the paths, although there is an area to the north-west where it seems tree growth since the last coppicing has been poor due to the nature of the soil and woodland grasses, heathers, broom, gorse and other woodland clearing species are to be found. Holly, bramble and honeysuckle are frequent along the trackways, but ancient woodland indicators are rather sparse; very little butcher's broom is present and some wild service. Wood ant colonies are found but could not be described as frequent. The Blean Research Group have carried out two botanical surveys in the wood. The first, in 1998 found oak standards predominating with chestnut and a small amount of holly forming a fairly dense canopy and consequently little below with bramble and honeysuckle predominating although butcher's broom was located. The second study, further eastwards but still near the southern boundary found a dense chestnut canopy with no oak (atypical for this wood) and again a similarly poor ground flora except that bluebells were well established here.

There is very little evidence of recent woodland management, indeed one site is progressing towards oak high forest. The wood has now become part of a nature reserve having been bought by the Kent Wildlife Trust. It will be interesting to see what is actually done with it.

Robert Foster

5. Fishpond Wood

Fishpond Wood is one of the woods of The Blean which lies just to the south of Watling Street. Access to the wood may be gained by a footpath which leaves the west bound carriageway of the modern A2 a few yards west of The Gate services at Dunkirk. The fuel station and associated motel occupy high land and Fishpond Wood slopes down to low lying agricultural land in the east. On the western flank lies South Bishopsden. Fishpond wood itself is on London clay and the farm land to the east is on brickearth. In times past Fishpond Wood extended as far as Denstead Lane and it totally covered what is now farmland; the change in land use being relatively recent. The proximity of this agricultural land to the east and orchards to the south east make Fishpond Wood ideal for the rearing of pheasant and other game. The wood is still managed for the benefit of these birds. They are often clumsy in flight and some never reach the cooking pot but instead are squashed by heavy traffic on the dual carriageway from Canterbury to Faversham. Hovering kestrels are alert to this fact!

Several streams and ponds are located in Fishpond Wood. Most of the water passes in a south-easterly direction through the wood and there are several connected ponds just outside its southern corner. These ponds are screened from general view by a line of conifers, under which a culvert passes carrying the waters of the Cranburne. This little river rises in Court Wood to the west of South Bishopsden. Its name comes from the Old English 'cran' (crane) and 'burna' (stream). The crane was abundant in marshy places and was a status symbol. (It stopped breeding in England around 1600.) It is possible that the original system of ponds was more extensive. Mudge's map of Kent (1801) labels Denstead Wood incorrectly as Fishpond Wood. However the site of the pond is very close to Denstead (which lies to the south) and this error may simply serve to confirm its location. Old maps also refer to Fishpond Cott[age]s and in the field above the ponds much debris from demolished buildings may be found. Brick, tile, pipe and pottery appear on the surface but the interpretation is difficult for some of the material has been dumped here from other locations. Certainly there was an important house here which was once home to Samuel Parker, rector of Chartham from 1667 until his death some 20 years later. During this time he was also chaplain to the archbishop of Canterbury and master of Eastbridge Hospital. Writing at the end of the 18th century Hasted records that the property had gone to ruin.

Entering Fishpond Wood by the path described above, one soon crosses a wood bank running east-west. This is the old boundary which separated the wood from the strip of cleared land at the side of Watling Street; in more recent times it seems that the wood invaded the 'tranche'. A little further on another wood bank is apparent on the west side of the path. This marks the boundary between neighbouring South Bishopsden and Brotherhood Woods. At this point the path divides with a south-easterly branch descending along the approximate boundary of Fishpond Wood and South Bishopsden whilst a southerly one enters South Bishopsden. The woods hereabout are much given over to coppiced beech and coppiced hazel. Charcoal derived from these species was used in Faversham for the manufacture of good quality gunpowder. Ideally charcoal from alder or alder buckthorn would have been first choice but the product from beech and hazel was a substitute. Indeed it is interesting to note that alder coppice is found alongside hazel on the lower ground in the east of Fishpond Wood. As these woods are amongst the most westerly of those in the Blean, close to Faversham, it seems reasonable to presume that this town received the bulk of the charcoal.

South Bishopsden bore the brunt of the 1987 storm and

many trees fell so consequently the wood was opened out. Fishpond Wood was protected and there was virtually no damage. The canopy is for the most part closed and little light penetrates. However, the edges of paths are frequented by primrose, wood spurge, wood sage and St. John's wort. The ground cover is dominated by ivy and bramble although woodrush and a number of sedges are also found. Hard fern thrives on the edges of the water courses. Apart from the beech and hazel coppice we also find chestnut with oak standards. The north-eastern slopes of the wood are interesting. Here oak and hornbeam coppice abound. On the boundary of Fishpond Wood and the farmland, ash and birch struggle to gain a foothold and where light permits aspen has appeared. Just on the eastern fringes butcher's broom forms a number of colonies; here also woodland hawthorn may be found. Within the wood holly is ubiquitous.

A public footpath follows the wood's eastern boundary from Watling Street and another its western boundary with South Bishopsden thus enclosing about seventy acres. Within this area of woodland is found a greater variety of tree species than in many other parts of the Blean.

6. Denstead Wood

Leeds Priory lies some 15 miles to the west of Denstead and in former times it is believed the wood was the property of that foundation. Now it is privately owned and managed primarily for game.

The wood is best approached from The Gate service station on the west bound carriageway of the A2 at Dunkirk. From here a footpath heads in a southwesterly direction through South Bishopsden. After about a mile the path takes a turn to the south and begins descending towards a stream in the bottom of the valley. This valley is steep along much of its length but here the slope is gentle. Almost certainly this was the point where drovers used to cross with their animals. Often there is no water in this stream but after prolonged heavy rain the flow can be rapid. Nearby a number of worked flints of the late stone age have been found.

On the other side of this valley lies Denstead. These north facing slopes are on London clay and they are packed with dense pine and poor birch. There is little light and the understorey is restricted to ferns, mosses, bracken, bramble and holly. The odd oak and occasional coppiced hazel betray the earlier style of management. After climbing to the plateau the walker is greeted by a fine beech pollard. Here one must turn left for to the right lies Court Wood. A wide track crosses the high land of Denstead and the Stour valley beyond but this is forbidden territory. Notices declaring 'Private Woodland - Keep Out!' shout their presence. Chestnut coppice with oak standards dominate the scene on the plateau, together with monotonous ranks of birch. Up here there is more light and consequently gorse, broom, aspen and rowan are found on the edges of the ride. Much of Denstead is wet and a willow grows next to the ditch at the side of the track. There is every sign of oak regeneration taking place: an unusual feature. Here and there are small pockets of oak, beech and hazel coppice.

On the high ground there is evidence of wind throw for some oak standards have fallen, especially in the west. Inspection of their root systems suggests that the immediate underlying geology is one of clay with flints. Their place in the canopy is now occupied by coppice chestnut whose stools push mighty tillers ever onward and upward. Chestnut is a deep rooting species and maybe they will not succumb in the same way as the standards. However, the height and width of the coppice poles indicate a sign of neglect. Fortunately there were signs that some coppicing was taking place for as the main track descends towards Primrose Hill at the eastern end some chestnut had been recently cut. Near the bottom is Denstead's one true glory; a mighty spreading beech. This has long been a focal point and today an archery club has its headquarters nearby. Beyond the beech it is best to turn left along a narrow path, cutting straight across the road at the bottom and hence into orchards. The open space permits a view of the eastern flank of Fishpond Wood and the route back to The Gate is evident.

The parts of Denstead that one is permitted to explore are not of any great interest. However a late September day revealed an enormous number of fungi. Much of the wood is dank and dark with a great density of vegetation, which may be the reason why fungi flourish here.

7. Shim Hill Wood

Shim Hill Wood, a small wood of 15 acres, lies on the southern edge of the Blean to the north of the valley through which runs the A2. It is one of a number of woods bordering Isobella Mead Farm. The most northerly part of this low lying agricultural land is surrounded on three sides by a number of ancient woods. The largest is Shim Hill which lies on relatively steep slopes to the north and west. From a geological point of view the area is complex. Just north of Shim Hill we find London clay overlaid with terrace gravels. The land here is dotted with pits from which gravel has been extracted for past maintenance of the old road (nowadays a bridleway) from Rough Common to Harbledown. As one descends Shim Hill in a southerly direction other levels become apparent. In the space of a couple of hundred yards a transition is effected through Oldhaven and Woolwich beds so that at the bottom even Thanet Sand is exposed.

The tithe map of 1837 describes Shim Hill as the property of The Lord Archbishop Himself and for centuries it had been in church ownership. In 1435 Simon Morle was appointed keeper of Stock Wood and the adjoining Shim Hill Wood. Some ancient documents appear to refer to Shim Hill Wood as South Stock Wood. Until quite recently Isobella Mead Farm belonged to the hospital of St Nicholas in Harbledown. This institution was founded for lepers by Lanfranc in 1084/5. Hugh de Orivalle, first Bishop of London, was appointed by William the Conqueror and consecrated by Lanfranc in 1075. Hugh de Orivalle died of leprosy in 1085 and it is possible that this circumstance may have influenced the decision to proceed with the hospital. It was laid down that the lepers should be cared for by a chaplain and by 'skilful, patient and kindly watchers', although it seems that there might have been additional reasons for relocating beggars with a variety of unsightly skin conditions away from the streets of Canterbury. We know that timber was taken from the woods surrounding Isobella Mead Farm by these unfortunate folk for the construction of their bothies. (By the turn of the 15th century the institution of St. Nicholas had been converted into almshouses, unchanged up to present time.)

Today for the greater part Shim Hill is managed as chestnut coppice with oak standards, especially in the east. Much of the western section has been largely invaded by sycamore and to a lesser extent by elder. Hazel coppice is found in the middle of the wood and rowan has established itself to a considerable degree on the more open areas of the slopes. Near the ancient wood-bank which marks the south-west boundary, coppiced hornbeam, beech, oak and hazel stand alongside one another. Hornbeam frequents the south facing slopes which overlook the A2 from Dunkirk to Harbledown. The rain water drains slowly and the species seems to thrive in these conditions.

From February lesser celandine, wood anemone and primrose may be seen. Later yellow archangel and bluebell form a striking contrast. A number of speedwells are found in this area including brooklime which is found in the damper, shadier regions at the bottom of the hill. Willow herbs grow on the lower slopes and yellow pimpernel also enjoys the moist conditions. Arum maculatum is found in dank places under trees. Self-heal and wood sage prefer the open slopes and greater stitchwort, foxglove, cow-wheat, bugle, wood spurge and red campion line the footpaths. Dog's mercury carpets much of the ground in the shade near the south-west boundary. Butcher's broom is also dotted in clumps along the woodbank here. Grasses are an important feature of Shim Hill; these include greater and hairy woodrush, wood millet, wood mellick and sweet vernal.

The boundaries of Shim Hill Wood are to a considerable extent well defined. Running along the northern edge there is a feature which looks like a massive earthwork. This is on a far grander scale than the normal woodbanks and the structure suggests a possible military purpose. It should not be forgotten that Bigbury with its Roman earthworks is just to the south across the valley. However, despite its rectilinear nature, it is possible that this is a natural phenomenon which man has adopted for his own purposes. With the potential for geolgical instability, there may have been some slippage here. The south-west limit is marked by a typical ditch and bank system. The ditch descends here in a south- easterly direction. Water would have run down here and then through a gully which forms the boundary of Shim Hill with Town Wood. It then passes through the more level ground between Town Wood and Three Acre Wood before reaching Isobella Mead Farm. These are times of lesser rainfall and the ditch has been partially filled, so water no longer flows along this course. However, a drain has been cut across Isobella Mead Farm from west to east so that formerly the water fed into the stream which flows south along the edge of Stock Wood. This drain effectively cuts off the most northern tongue of the farmland. In the tithe map of 1837 this area was described as Isobella Wood. Since that time it has become an orchard which has only been grubbed out in recent years. In older maps this part has been labelled as meadow and wood pasture. The variety of land use has almost certainly been dependent on the relative wetness of the ground over the centuries. The historical boundary of the Blean is clear, for where Shim Hill Wood, Stock Wood and the "old" Isobella Wood meet there is a stretch of the ancient woodbank. Once a hornbeam hedge stood here but it has been neglected for many a long year. This same woodbank still skirts the eastern side of Three Acre Wood, all suggesting that Isobella Wood encroached. The best preserved woodbank of Shim Hill borders Three Acre Wood.

The descending slopes give Shim Hill its particular character. On the lower reaches there are a number of standards that have grown to great heights in order to compete with trees rooted above them. Green and great spotted woodpeckers drum their messages from these giants. Hills enclose this area on three sides so that the signature of these birds echoes to great effect.

The intriguing geology of this part of the Blean is confirmed if one leaves the wood at the western corner. The bridleway drops down to Harbledown and once it may have been a drove road connecting with Bigbury road on the other side of the A2. This track has sunk more than twenty feet below the surrounding land, doubtless fashioned by the passage of animals and water over several centuries. London Clay would not permit such erosion but here the sand beds are exposed.

8. Church Wood

Church Wood is the largest of the woods to the west of the village of Blean covering some 1,400 acres. Most of the wood is on a plateau. It is longer than it is broad and the valley of a stream stretches eastwards from one end to the other.

It is an ancient wood, traceable in Domesday Book and with a documented history from the reign of King Henry I. It was given by Richard I in 1189 to the Cathedral Priory and was known for 500 years as Short Wood, only acquiring the name of Church

Wood in the nineteenth century. Much of it is now owned by the RSPB and the Woodland Trust. A large portion of the wood was designated a Site of Special Scientific Interest in 1951, and as such was one of the earliest SSSI's in the country. In 2000 the designation was extended to include all parts of the wood managed for nature conservation and since 2001 the reserve has formed part of the Blean Woods National Nature Reserve. The remainder of the wood, some 700 acres, is privately owned and commercially but sensitively managed, with conservation an important factor.

There are two main soil types: London Clay and gravel drift deposits. The gravel drift deposits of the plateau areas are acidic and poor in nutrients, while richer soil in the valleys supports more lush vegetation. The Fishbourne Stream, which has many windings on part of its course, runs from west to east for over a mile through the wood until it emerges into open country at its eastern edge. Early thirteenth century charters indicate that small water mills existed on it in earlier times but the wood of which these were built has long since rotted and it is only possible to surmise their position. The stream is always reduced to a trickle in dry summers but can rush in spate after heavy prolonged rain, occasionally overflowing its banks.

Medieval woodbanks follow ancient property boundaries, the most notable that forming the northern boundary of the wood, the substantial bank and ditch beside the Radfall Road.

Giant coppice stools of oak, hornbeam and beech are reminders of centuries of coppicing and regrowth. As in the rest of the Blean, oak is the most frequent native timber tree throughout the wood. Most is sessile but there is some pedunculate oak mainly in the valleys, together with hybrids between the two species. It is known that there was planting of oak in the wood in the nineteenth century. There are no oaks of great size, most being 100-150 years old, many rather craggy in appearance with twisted boughs. There is also chestnut, beech, hornbeam, hazel, holly and woodland thorn, and much birch. Less frequently occurring species include ash, aspen, crab apple, elm, alder, whitebeam, rowan, alder-buckthorn, wild cherry, sallow and sycamore. Honeysuckle is abundant everywhere except among the conifers.

Among notable ancient woodland indicators are small-leaved lime, of which there are a few rather spindly trees in one place on the plateau in the RSPB Reserve. Some other small-leaved lime has been planted fairly recently in the privately owned part of the wood. Service tree is scattered through the wood with some good specimens on the line of an old hedge on a boundary near the Short Tenement. Butcher's broom is found on banks and in most parts of the wood except close to the stream. Some spurge laurel occurs on the southern edge of the wood under oak, beech and hornbeam.

There are large areas of chestnut coppice, which were established over the past 200 years, although chestnut has been in this country from Roman times and some may have existed in the wood from that time. In the 1960's many oak standards were removed to increase coppice vigour. In most years crops of chestnuts of reasonable size are produced, most of which go uncollected except by birds and small mammals (they are particularly liked by yellow-necked mice). Chestnut coppice is a poor habitat in most respects. Along the Fishbourne valley the chestnut coppice gives way to hazel and hornbeam underwood.

The Blean in general, including Church Wood, was relatively fortunate in losing less of its native woodland to conifers than many other large woods, but conifer plantations were established in the wood as early as the 1930's and 1940's, although most date to the 1960's. The conservation bodies have already reduced the areas of conifer plantation and of chestnut coppice and are committed to continuing the process, returning some areas to oak high forest, others to natural regeneration of native species, with where necessary planting/sowing of indigenous species, preferably from the wood; other areas have been converted to heathland, a habitat rare in Kent. An area of chestnut coppice removed by the RSPB a few years ago has been particularly successful in converting to heath. Heather and gorse rapidly colonised it, and nightjars and tree pipits have bred there. The common lizard can be found sunning itself on chestnut stumps.

Glades and wide rides have been created to benefit the rare heath fritillary and other butterflies which need sunny corridors along which to fly. Nightjars, too, need open space in which to hawk for moths and other insects. Rotational coppicing is carried out to encourage the growth of flowering plants, in particular cow-wheat, on which the larvae of the heath fritillary feed.

Church Wood has a large colony of lily-of-the-valley, regarded as an uncommon native of old woodland, although it also occurs in moorland.[1] Cow-wheat grows in profusion in sunny places. Spring flowers are only locally abundant but some places are carpeted with wood anemone and bluebell. Primrose, violet and lady's smock are increasing along many rides now that the verges are mown periodically. Low-growing plants such as tormentil, yellow pimpernel and wild strawberry also grow along rides, while in the areas owned by the conservation bodies dead timber is left standing, providing a valuable habitat for insects and fungi, and piles of brushwood offer nesting sites for birds and decaying wood for insects. Over 500 species of fungi have been identified.

On the edge of the wood at its north eastern edge there is a rifle range built in the First World War, its walls only noticeable in winter or when the area has been newly coppiced. They have endured, unlike a farm known to have existed in another part of the wood in the nineteenth century, which has disappeared without trace, swallowed up by the woodland.

Church Wood is a beautiful and interesting place at all times of year. In late winter the drumming of great and lesser spotted woodpeckers resonates in the high forest and jackdaws call companionably to one another. In spring there is the influx of migrant birds including the nightingale, the woods of the Blean being one of its best breeding areas. Summer has the pleasure of butterflies and the sight of dragon and damsel flies darting along the rides, and at night the strange churring of nightjars, the calls of tawny owls and the greenish light of glow-worms along the edges of rides. In autumn there are the rich yellows and russets of the oak, beech and hornbeam and the occasional flare of service tree. With so much to offer it is not surprising that the wood, always valued, is increasingly appreciated.

The RSPB has a car park at Rough Common and there is convenient access to this wood from Blean village and the A2 as well as from woods on its northern and western sides.

Mary Fox

References
1. Rose, F, April 1999. *British Wildlife Indicators of Ancient Woodland.* The use of vascular plants in evaluating ancient woods for nature conservation. p.242.

9. Radfall Road

The road along the western boundary of Thornden Wood towards Swalecliffe is called the Radfall Road. Originally, when it was a track or droveway it crossed Clowes Wood and led to Amery Court, Chapel Lane, Blean and eventually via South Bishopsden Wood to the Stour valley. Part of this, which divided Church Wood from Grimshill Wood, is now wooded over. It was called Mearencold (Lane) in the 18th century but by the 19th century, when it ceased to be a lane or road it came also to be known as the Radfall Road. It is not clear whether those who gave it that name realised that it was a continuation of another Radfall Road next to Clowes Wood a mile away. Radfall Road as we are now describing it follows the crest of the plateau and is bounded with massive wood banks on each side which can be dated to the 13th century and stretch for about a mile.

This western Radfall Road is clearly marked on the early maps and was most likely used by commoners to drive pigs and cattle to pastures in the woods and to bring out timber, faggots, and heath or ling. At one time the road formed the parish boundary between St. Cosmus and St.Damian and the old Ville of Dunkirk. The road passes from Blean Common by Mincing and Grimshill Woods, Great Den Lees and North Bishopden Wood on the north side and Crawford's Rough and Church Wood on the south side of the road.

The wood banks are of historical, archaeological and botanical interest. At the western end of the road a pound (to hold stray cattle) is shown on the 1872 map and from this area several roads diverge to various destination

A large part of the woodland to the east of the road belonged to the Abbey at Faversham. After the dissolution of the monasteries in 1538 the links of the woods with Faversham were diminished and improvements to the ancient Roman Road of Watling Street may have made the Radfall Road less important. By the 19th century it was in such poor repair that new tracks were made on either side of the road. The south side is now the public footpath CB 7.

The original Radfall Road is 2–3 ft. below the surrounding

Land. The ditches on both sides vary from only a slight depression to nearly 2ft. in depth. The banks would have been much higher when built, but over the centuries they have weathered down and have filled the ditches. Trees planted as hedges on the tops of the banks can still be seen and in some places evidence of early hedge laying is apparent.

When this old road became woodland the trees which appeared were principally oak, including sessile and hybrid examples, with beech and birch next in frequency and a few chestnut, holly and hazel. Tree cover varied from 75 to 100 % but ground cover was in many places sparse; the most frequent were bramble and honeysuckle.

Margaret Matherne and Alexander Wheaten

10. Crawford's Rough

Crawford's Rough is next to the north east corner of Church Wood on the plateau on which the woods of the Blean Woods National Nature Reserve are situated. The soils contain amounts of plateau gravel over London Clay. There are traces of some old ditches, some of which appear to be vestiges of a very old field system.

This is a small wood shaped like a funnel, the open end of which leads to a cross-roads to the east, where an ancient track and road crossed. Oak is not as prominent in it as in surrounding woods and there is not a great deal of beech. More prominent in some parts are chestnut, birch, hazel and aspen. In medieval times it seems that Blean Common extended over where the wood now is, as suggested by its shape and situation. Then as now to its north was Mincing Wood and the former Town Wood and to the west, Church Wood.

This is secondary woodland, which probably dates from the 17th and 18th centuries and ancient woodland indicators do not occur to any great extent. The wood has a number of stools of coppiced chestnut, planted over 200 years ago. Most of the coppice in this wood is chestnut and much of it is dense.

In some places there is heath, in others there is a greater variety of ground flora than in the immediately adjoining corner of Church Wood, which is high forest. Among these are some ancient woodland indicators, found when botanical surveys were made in 1990 and 1995, such as woodrush, woodspurge, St.John's wort and cow-wheat. Their presence may be explicable since there is ancient wood on three sides of the wood. There are more grasses here than in the Blean generally, which may indicate that once there was pasture here. The environment appears to suit wood ants which have built prominent active nests. Most of the oaks here are standards some 80 to 100 years old but some have been coppiced. Some of the standard oaks appear to have been planted as was the chestnut.

The wood became part of the National Nature Reserve in 1953. Access is by public footpaths from the main Canterbury to Whitstable road and also from the adjoining woods, Mincing Wood and Church Wood.

Alexander Wheaten and William Holmes

11. Town Wood

Town wood is so called because it was once owned by the City of Canterbury. It is on the eastern side of the National Nature Reserve. As shown in a map of 1772 it was roughly triangular in shape. In 1840 its size was given as 12 acres. It is wholly surrounded by other woods, Crawford's Rough to the south and Mincing Wood on its other sides. Three footpaths follow most of its three sides at a short distance from them. Several oak pollards are on the western boundary, a prominent medieval ditch and bank mark the southern boundary and there are traces of other old woodbanks along its other two boundaries. Some of the ditches lie on the very old grid mentioned in Chapter IV. Town is a small wood but at least six soil types occur and there are some six main tree species. Oak and hazel are the most frequent followed by birch, hornbeam, beech and chestnut. Ancient wood indicators include sessile oak and woodland thorn and among the ground flora, butcher's broom and woodrush. Although ancient, the wood may be secondary woodland. Much has recently been coppiced and about half is now in coppice. The tree canopy varied from 20% and 80% cover, while the ground flora cover varied from 10% to 100%. A number of tree seedlings were present. Ivy was unusually frequent. There are some tall thin oaks in this wood as well as a small number of oak coppice stools. In between there are active nests of wood ants, some of which are quite large.

The wood is mentioned in 13th century charters, when it was acquired by the Poor Priests' Hospital, which still stands in Stour Street, Canterbury, although it was dissolved in the 16th century and the hospital's endowments then passed to the Overseers of the Poor by the wish of Queen Elizabeth I.. Documentation relating to the wood includes a lease granted by the City in 1654 and references in Somner's *Antiquities of Canterbury* written in the 17th century. Since 1958 this wood has been managed as part of the National Nature Reserve and for some years as part of Mincing Wood. Botanical surveys were made by the group in 1994 and 1995. The height of the northern wood-bank is up to 3ft and of the southern up to 6ft.

Alexander Wheaten

12. Mincing Wood

Mincing Wood takes its name from the fact that nuns once had rights there[1], probably the nuns of Minster in Thanet, since by a charter of 724 they were given a pig pasture in the Blean. The wood is situated in the north-east corner of the largest block of woodland in the Blean, where there are some dozen woods, the largest of which is some 900 acres in extent. Immediately to the west is Grimshill Wood and to the south is Crawford's Rough both of which, with Mincing Wood and Great and Little Den Lees together formed the Blean Woods National Nature Reserve. These woods are all on acid plateau gravel soil over London Clay, the acidity in Mincing Wood varying from pH 3.8 to 4.6 according to a report commissioned by the Nature Conservancy, with the most acid soils on the plateau gravel.

Unlike other nature reserves nearby, the Blean Woods

National Nature Reserve were never planted with conifers during the last fifty years. In Mincing Wood some woodland is managed as high forest, some as coppice, as coppice-with-standards and, in places, as heath. Six sites along the southern boundary of Mincing Wood were surveyed. A summary of the frequency of trees follows and the range of frequencies found.

Oak	30 - 95%	Chestnut	abs - 2%
Birch	abs - 10%	Beech	2 - 50%
Hazel	abs - 10%	Holly	abs - 7%
Hornbeam	abs - 90%	Woodland thorn	abs - 7%
Wild Service	abs - 20%		

The northern part of the wood slopes towards the coastal plain but its southern part is on a broad plateau that stretches east and west for miles. The western boundary is marked by a prominent ancient ditch and bank and other ditches appear to be traces of the old field system. The documentary evidence that the wood is ancient is corroborated by the presence of trees such as service tree and sessile oak and by plants such as woodrush, wood spurge, and wood melick which were found in botanical surveys by the Blean Group. Parts of this wood have been coppiced to encourage another ancient woodland indicator, cow-wheat. Among other plants bramble, honeysuckle and ivy were frequent. The ground cover was not dense and it did include saplings of a number of trees including service.

This wood can be entered from the Royal Oak on the main Canterbury-Whitstable road (A 290) and this track continues for some distance in a westerly direction and emerges from Great Den Lees Wood into the Denstroude. Alternative footpaths which also provide access to Mincing Wood run from Crawford's Rough, Church Wood and North Bishopsden Wood.

Alexander Wheaten

Reference
1. Somner W (1703) 37B C S no. 141.

13. Grimshill Wood

This is the central and largest wood of the original Blean Woods National Nature Reserve. Like the rest of the reserve it lies on a plateau whose northern side slopes towards the Denstroude valley and its more fertile fields. Two small streams, dry for much of the year, run into the valley.

Fig. 8.2 : Mincing Wood and Six Other Woods. From a Map of 1840

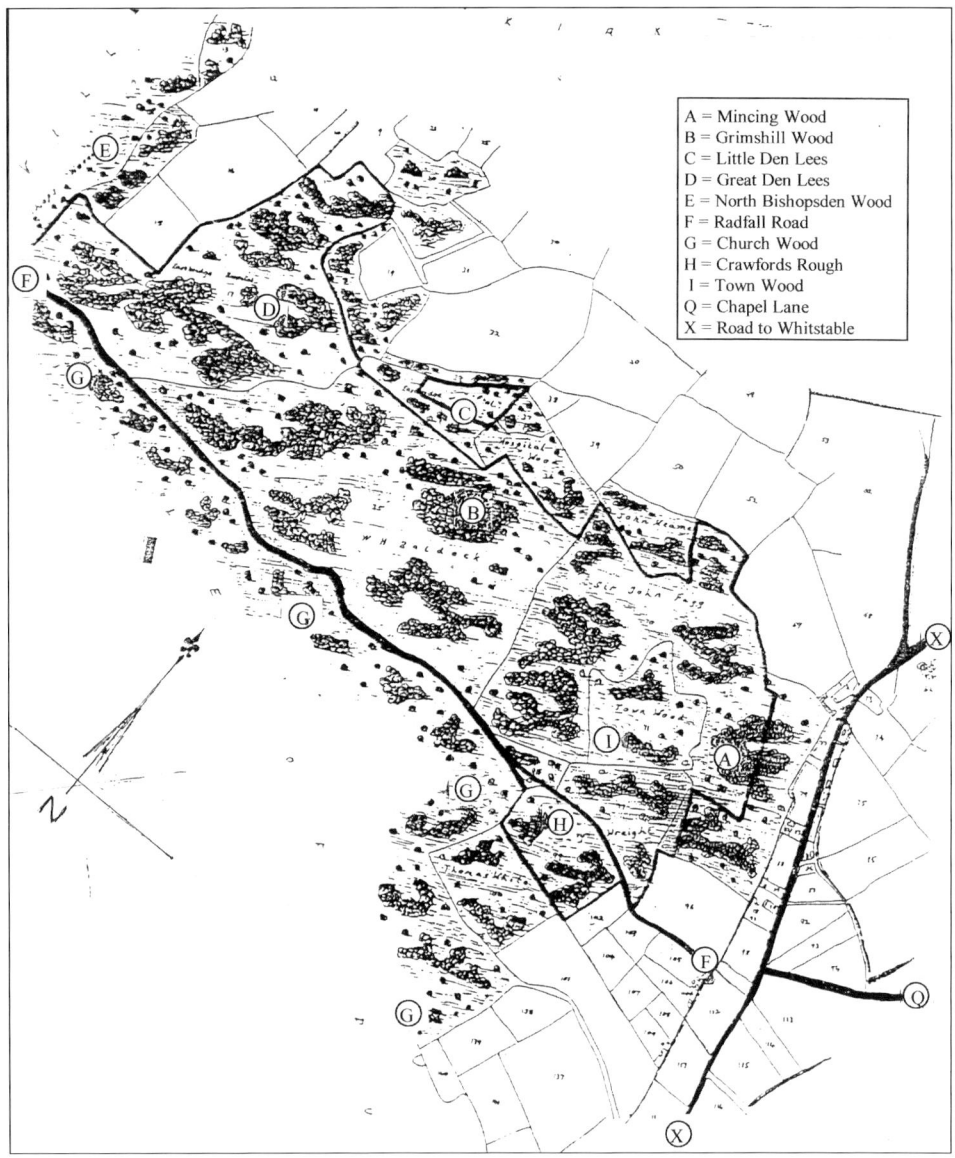

The wood of 83 acres contains planted hornbeam and chestnut, among timber trees of oak, mostly sessile. Some large old coppice stools of beech and some wild service trees are near the eastern boundary. The wood is surrounded by other ancient woods most of them in nature reserves. On the western boundary with Great Den Lees are the remains of a large medieval wood-bank, a larger wood-bank borders with Mincing Wood and on the southern boundary is the Radfall Road with large wood-banks and ditches on both sides. Little Den Lees is to the north.

Whether all this wood was dense in medieval times is not certain although the large surrounding wood-banks on its boundaries indicate that young underwood was protected from passing animals. A reference to *'Grymesfeilde in Blean'* in 1535 almost certainly refers to this wood, when some of it was owned by St. Jacob's Hospital in Canterbury, according to the *Valor Ecclesiasticus*. The view that the wood is ancient is supported by the presence of old coppice stools and of woodland hawthorn, wild service, yellow archangel and wood millet. It appears that coppicing mainly of oak but also of hornbeam and chestnut has been practised over centuries. The ground vegetation recorded included mainly bramble, honeysuckle and ivy with bracken, woodrush and archangel in some parts.

Since the wood became part of a National Nature Reserve in 1962 wide rides have been created. These provide pathways for the Heath Fritillary butterfly and encourage Cow-wheat its major food plant.

Alexander Wheaten

14. Great Den Lees & 15. Little Den Lees

Great Den Lees is the most westerly of the woods acquired by the Nature Conservancy Council to form part of their Blean Woods National Nature Reserve. Its name may in part be an abbreviation of that of the adjoining hamlet of Denstroude to the north and the addition of 'Lees' could signify that it was once pasture. It lies on the plateau where its neighbours are situated. A little stream flows northwards towards the valley occupied by the hamlet. Sessile oak and hornbeam are particularly prominent as is coppiced chestnut on its southern plateau. Other trees noted were beech and woodland hawthorn.

Except on its western side the wood's 57 acres are surrounded by woodland, most of which is managed as nature reserves. A path along its northern boundary follows an old woodbank. Other ancient woodbanks are on its eastern and southern boundaries; these appear to be of the same age as that on the south side of the Radfall Road nearby, that is to say of the 13th century.

This wood and its neighbours to the east were in the medieval manor of Blean given to Eastbridge Hospital, Canterbury in the 14th century[1] References to ownership of it are to be found in 16th century documents, where it is called *'Denne Lees'* (variously spelt).[2] The hospital did not cease to be the owner until in 1983 it sold it to the Nature Conservancy Council over four hundred years later.

There are several ancient woodland indicators here, such as service, yellow archangel and wood anemone. There is an abundance of bluebell near its northern boundary and foxglove near its western side. In places the ground vegetation is much richer than elsewhere and wood millet was noted as prominent; this ancient woodland indicator perhaps points to this wood having once been pasture, although for its medieval owner it was mainly important as its principal source of fuel.

A little to the east is Little Den Lees, which was bought from Eastbridge Hospital at the same time as Great Den Lees. It is small and lies to the north of the path leading to Denstroude. Here the understorey is somewhat dense. As in surrounding woods there is much bramble.

Alexander Wheaten

Bibliography
1. Rev.D.I.Hill, *The Ancient Hospitals and Almshouse of Canterbury*, published for the Canterbury Archaeological Society in 1969, when he was Master of Eastbridge Hospital.
2. *The Survey of the houses upon the mannors of Hothe and Blean and the lands belonging to the same mannors.* Lambeth Palace Library MS CM X111/9

16. Marley Wood

Marley Wood is a small wood which lies on the east side of the road from Canterbury to Whitstable at Pean Hill about two miles south of Whitstable. There is some evidence that the wood previously extended further towards Whitstable but it is now bounded on that side by housing. The road forms the western boundary, arable land running towards Hempshall Wood is on the east and the south is bounded by the curtilage of Blarney Court previously known as Fort Marion. The soil is of blue grey London clay and the surface slopes gently from east to west. There are no ditches or streams within the wood, nor any wood banks, but slight evidence of a ditch on the northern boundary. The wood is accessed by a track which runs east - west from the main road. The northern area is the more interesting botanically. No wood ants were seen.

There are about 1,000 mature oak trees, fairly densely planted (about 70 % cover) particularly in the northern half while hornbeam, hazel, field maple, beech, wild cherry, holly and a few wild service also occur. There is some coppice and a few oak stumps. Undergrowth includes bracken, broom, wood sage, wood anemone, bluebell, grasses and moss. The general vegetation indicates that the wood is ancient and this is supported by the presence of service trees and some of the other vegetation noted above. The wood is subject to a Tree Preservation Order. It was the subject of a planning enquiry in 1997 when an application to erect a dwelling was rejected.

Gerry Flack

17. Park Wood

Park Wood is one of several small woods on the 300 acre campus acquired by the University of Kent at its foundation in 1965. It is on the higher ground on the north western part of the site. It was probably named in the 17th century when together with Hothe Court it was owned by Eastbridge Hospital and leased to John Boys, a member of a prominent local family.[1]

The wood is described in the 16th century *'Survey of the houses and lands upon the manors of Hothe and Blean'*.[2] After describing *'One large hall and other buildings'* where Hothe Court now stands it speaks of: *'Two woods next the house, the one called the Upper wood, 17 acres by estimation and the Nether wood of 8 acres or thereabouts'* . The wood today is much reduced in size partly because some of it was used to provide housing accommodation for students at the university..

As part of the manor of Blean and Hothe Court, this wood had remained in the same ownership from medieval times, since Eastbridge Hospital became lords of the manor in the 14th century.

A nature trail has been created that passes through the wood. A booklet published by the University describes the wood as containing, *'Oak woodland, chestnut coppice, and to a lesser degree hornbeam coppice'*. Also noted were *'two-styled hawthorns'* and low bramble. This type of woodland was considered a type of *'classic oak woodland'*. These hawthorns, also known as woodland or midland thorn are, like sessile oak which is also present, regarded as indicators of ancient woodland. Their presence is not surprising since the wood has almost certainly been there since prehistoric times.

On the eastern boundary of this wood is an interesting feature of archaeological interest, noted by Oliver Rackham on one of his many visits to the University. This appears to be an ancient woodbank similar to a number in the Blean woods and probably of medieval origin. Another woodbank parallel to it is the boundary with the adjoining Brotherhood Wood. In between would have been a trackway leading from Blean Church to the city of Canterbury. However, not a great deal of these woodbanks survives and what there is remains not easy to find, perhaps one of the reasons they are still there. A road from Giles Lane near the centre of the campus to Hothe Court passes through this wood.

Alexander Wheaten

References
1. Canterbury Cathedral, *Charta Antiqua* , B 332
2. Lambeth Palace, M S, C M, xiii/ 9

18. Brotherhood Wood

The Brotherhood Wood also on the University campus derives its name from the previous owner, a medieval charitable foundation in Canterbury, the Hospital of St John the Baptist, in Northgate, founded about 1085.[1] A number of such foundations owned woodland in the Blean to provide fuel for their hearths and possibly to sell. These woods sometimes came to be known either as a Brotherhood Wood as here or as Hospital

Wood as elsewhere in the Blean. This small wood is triangular and like Park Wood now much reduced in size. On its southern side are some university buildings of the Estate Department, to the east is farm land and to the west is Park Wood. The wood slopes to the north to a stream, the Fishbourne, which flows to the east towards Thanet. This is another ancient wood and has much in common with Park Wood, as recorded in botanical surveys conducted there by the Blean Research Group. It is part of some 75 acres acquired from St John's Hospital which had belonged to the charity for at least six centuries.[2]

As were many other woods in the Blean it was managed as coppice with standards. The oak standards seldom reached more than 80 to 100 years of age, since ancient oaks are a rarity. In the 1991 Annual Report to the former University School of Continuing Education, the Blean Research Group noted that *'the ground cover varied; the area nearest the stream was found to have less vegetation than to the south on higher ground while the area near the University buildings was thick with brambles'*. Nevertheless the total number of plant species was greater than in many other parts of the Blean, although not dissimilar. Several ancient woodland indicator plants were found including yellow archangel, wood spurge, woodrush, wood anemone, and bluebell as well as wood millet although the presence also of cyclamen showed nearby human occupation. The campus Nature Trail follows the edge of the wood along the eastern side and ends near the visitors' car park.

Alexander Wheaten

References
1. Hill Rev. D. I. (1969) *The Ancient Hospitals and Almshouses of Canterbury.* Canterbury Archaeological Society. P 7.
2. Ibid.

19. The Radfall

The Radfall is a band of woodland which runs between two wood banks north-east from Tyler Hill near Honey Wood and along the eastern side of Thornden Wood. It is the remains of an ancient trackway. The name is derived from the term 'rod fall' used by woodreeves in the Blean two hundred years ago to describe 'one rod of underwood marked out when any new hedge is made. The wood standing thereon is taken to (the woodreeve's) use under the name of 'rodfall'.[1] The Radfall passes between Honey Wood and Great Hall Wood near Tyler Hill, then through Timber Wood until it forms the boundary between Thornden Wood and West Blean Wood. It is over 2 km long and varies in width around 20m. Medieval banks are prominent and ditches, which form the boundaries on both sides, are still apparent.

The Radfall lies on London Clay with some gravel cover on which grow oak standards, coppice chestnut and birch with some Hazel towards the north.

The origin of The Radfall may be as a droveway and in medieval times had become the road from Canterbury to Herne, but this became overgrown. When a great deal of underwood was to be found there, the woodreeves of the adjoining woods, Thornden and West Blean, began to treat it as their perquisite, as if it was a 'rodfall'. However this practice ceased when both woods came to be managed by Messrs. Cluttons on behalf of the Ecclesiastical Commissioners in the 19th century.

Ancient woodland indicators are rare within The Radfall. Although woodland hawthorn and wild service were noted in an earlier survey the wood is not particularly interesting botanically.

Good oak standards are present and the tree canopy provides 40 – 80 % cover. Some standard oaks have been cut in recent years and a large proportion of the area has been coppiced within the last 10-15 years. Where chestnut is dense there is little ground cover, but bramble, bracken, honeysuckle and moss are present where the ground is more open. A few ant nests can be seen.

Although The Radfall is some distance from any main road several paths and rights of way give access including a major track from Tyler Hill to West Blean Wood. It should not be confused with the two Radfall Roads mentioned elsewhere.

William Holmes and Gerry Flack

References
1 Lambeth, T S 6 Statement of Customs , 7 September 1805
2 Lambeth, T S 5 Survey of the Archbishop's woods in Kent (1759).Blean Rep. 1992, 199

20. East Blean Wood

East Blean Wood, now 277 acres, is so called because it is next to West Blean Wood, both being at the eastern end of the Blean. It is a plateau wood with shallow valleys.

History and Archaeology

East and West Blean Woods represent the section of Blean granted to St. Augustine's Abbey before the Norman Conquest. Henry VIII bestowed them on Archbishop Cranmer in part-exchange for eight great parks of the Archbishopric which he coveted. They remained in the endowment of the Archbishops for over 300 years until they were transferred to the Ecclesiastical Commissioners.[1]

The archaeology shows that this is not the whole story. The wood is divided by a woodbank into a north-western (smaller) and south-eastern part. The greater part of this bank is on the south of its ditch and thus belongs to the main wood; but after turning a corner the ditch changes sides and the bank becomes less massive. This indicates that at some time the wood was divided between St. Augustine's and a northern neighbour. The two owners made a bank to mark the boundary and shared the work in the same proportions as the areas of woodland that they owned (roughly two-thirds and one-third). The Abbey (like other ecclesiastical landowners) did the job well, and the neighbour rather perfunctorily. The Abbey woodbank marks the parish boundary between Chislet and Reculver. Archbishop Sheldon recorded the area of the wood as 160 acres in 1664, evidently representing the Abbey's ownership south-east of the internal bank.

This was not the only sub-division of the wood. At both ends the main woodbank abuts on massive banks representing ownerships carved out of the wood at some earlier date. Two banks were added to mark the later subdivision of the north-western ownership into three.

We cannot say whether any of the original external boundary of the wood survives. The 1801 Ordnance Survey shows a very complicated zigzag boundary, evidently resulting from successive subtractions and additions to the wood. Most of this was lost to further encroachments in the 19th century. The wood (like Thornden Wood) has a highway running through it, which is unusual; much more often such a road is really a lane between two woods, with a woodbank on each side.

This or some similar wood was presumably the source of the timber for Littlebourne Barn. The oaks in the barn are smaller than most of those in the wood now; it would not now be difficult to find bigger oaks for the great posts than were available in the 14th century. The present oaks in the wood are generally less crooked and sinuous than those used in the barn.

William Somner, the Archbishop's woodreeve, described the wood in 1611 as being divided into ten compartments, the underwood being of one to twelve years growth. About 20 tons of timber were felled in 1664 and 40 tons in 1707. In 1815 *'the coppiced wood [was] in great measure hornbeam'*, as it still is. Hasted in the 18th century found the Blean to be most mostly oak, so the hornbeam may have been planted.

Soils
This wood lies to the east, where London Clay peters out in favour of the older Thanet Sands. Soils appear to be a very acid, silty sand containing loess but little clay. The wood is wet with many springs.

Vegetation
This is an ancient, relatively natural, coppice-wood. There are about ten acres of modern forestry in the form of Scots pine plantations about 30 years old, still alive but neglected and reverting to hornbeam-ashwood.

The wood shows a sequence from chestnut and birch on the leached hilltops through hornbeam to hornbeam-ash on the lower, wetter slopes. There appears to be no beech. Oaks are mainly sessile, sometimes concentrated into particular areas, sometimes scattered among the underwood. There is a strong tendency, as in some south-east Essex woods, for pedunculate oak to occur on the wetter less acid soils. Oaks seem to be all timber trees (little or no oak underwood). As in other Blean woods oaks are prolific but do not flourish; they stop growing on reaching a small timber size and then go hollow. Hazel is widely scattered, holly mainly on banks.

As in other woods, features such as areas of dense oaks or of pure chestnut coppice often stop at rides, indicating effects of past management superimposed on the natural variation of vegetation. Chestnut is probably not an ancient feature; however some occurs as occasional stools scattered among other underwood, suggesting that it has spread by seed away from the original introduction.

Notable in the ground vegetation is the abundant heather, springing up from seed in recently coppiced areas. There are patches of several acres of periwinkle (*Vinca minor*), a clonal plant suspected of being introduced.

Hornbeam stool sizes about 8ft in diameter, as noted by the research group, indicate ancient woodland and be remarkable anywhere except in Blean Wood. There is much coppicing.

Being an ancient wood, ancient woodland indicators plants and trees are present. There are wild service trees and various plants including cow-wheat, attractive to the rare heath fritillary butterfly. The presence of heather suggests that the wood was not always dense woodland.

Present Status
Kent Wildlife Trust, manages the wood and have created a car park next to a road which crosses the wood from the east (near Hoath) to the road from Herne to Canterbury, which came into existence in the seventeenth century. In at least five places public footpaths emerge to the countryside around; the significance of so many footpaths is not entirely clear. The wood is part of the Blean Woods National Nature Reserve.

Alexander Wheaten and Oliver Rackham

Reference
1. Lambeth Palace MSS TC4, TS1, TS3 and TS7.

21. Great Hall Wood

Tyler Hill is a village two miles north-east of Canterbury. It boasts a memorial hall and an adjacent playing field which are on the east side of the Chestfield road. There is a car park here and an excellent map of the nearby woods. The prominent bank of

The Radfall marks the southern edge of the playing field and access to Great Hall Wood is gained by walking along this boundary of the field from the hall keeping this archaeological feature on the right hand side. The entry point to the wood is at the corner of the field. On the Tithe Map this wood appears as Paddock Wood.

The Radfall continues in a north-easterly direction and forms the northern boundary of Great Hall Wood. To the north lies Honey Wood. The footpath lies roughly parallel to the Radfall on its southern side. This track takes its course along a high plateau and Great Hall Wood lies on south facing slopes with the land dropping down to the valley of the Sarre Penn (or Fishbourne). The southern boundary of the wood is marked by a fine briar and oak hedge which has not been laid for many years. Agricultural land separates the edge of the wood from the stream and on the far bank lies Little Hall Wood. This sister wood lies on the shady north facing side of the valley and it has been planted predominantly with hornbeam. Judging by the long abandoned wire work lying in parts of the hedge, hops were once grown in the farmland of the valley bottom. Nearby is a converted oast and a line of willow pollards mark the bank of the stream. These support a good number of poles and one wonders whether they had originally been planted as a convenient supply of hop poles. To the east of Great Hall Wood lies the "remnant" of Paddock Wood. A well preserved bank separates these two woods and it stretches all the way from the high plateau to the cultivated land of the valley floor.

Great Hall Wood is a coppiced wood. Oak coppice and chestnut coppice predominate but beech coppice and a small amount of hazel coppice also occur. The standards are almost entirely of oak with only a handful of mature beech trees. Birch has gained a foothold in most places and sycamore is trying to establish itself alongside the tracks. Indeed, sycamore seedlings (and broom) feature wherever the wood opens to admit more light. The banks of the Radfall retain rainfall and the damp and shady conditions have proved ideal for self seeded hornbeam. Holly and butcher's broom also colonise the Radfall. The ancient drove road makes strange viewing here since for much of its length three banks may be distinguished. There are a number of depressions in the ground scattered throughout the wood with holly around the edges. Perhaps gravel was removed in times past.

After periods of continuous rain the pits regularly fill with water. The largest of these is as much as 25 yards across and up to 5 feet deep. It is situated in the west of the wood and an old extraction track appears to lead from it down to the once metalled road. Here in the western half of the wood the ground is almost completely covered in bracken. To the east bramble tends to take over. Wood sage and Great Woodrush, *Luzula pilosa* are common but in the wetter parts *Juncus effuses,* the Common or Corkscrew Rush is more prevalent.

Finally, it was a great relief not to be attacked by wood ants! In two days we did not expose the surface and the soil is very poor. Elsewhere there are yellow archangel, ragged robin, bugle and ferns. For the most part, however, the ground flora of the wood is rather restricted, with much woodsage, woodrush, several species of sedge, wood spurge, bramble, bracken and ivy. The common spotted orchid grows along some rides and in clearings. It is increasing quite remarkably on the RSPB reserve now that the grass is cut and raked off after the flowers have seeded, simulating hay meadow conditions. Lousewort, too, is steadily increasing on the reserve, where it used to be extremely scarce.

At the western end of Radfall Road there is lesser periwinkle, with blue flowers among narrow evergreen leaves. Foxgloves spring up in open sunny places, particularly where there has been some disturbance of the ground. Other summer flowers include St. John's wort (mainly *Hypericum pulchrum*) and golden rod. Attractive to late summer butterflies and insects, the mauve pincushion flowers of devil's bit scabious persist into late autumn.

The wood has no natural ponds of any size and a pond was dug on the line of the Fishbourne stream in 1985, its edges soon colonised by a wide variety of plants. Kingfisher, moorhen and mallard were quick to find the new habitat, and in summer at dusk bats swoop low over the water in search of insects.

Large nests of the wood ant (*Formica rufa*) are found in well-drained places throughout the wood, usually built over the stump of a tree. Across some rides with short grass, narrow tracks can be discerned, regular crossing places where the grass has been killed by the formic acid which the ants secrete.

22. Herne Park Elmwood

This grove lies on the end of the Blean along the road from Greenhill to Calcott. This is a wide road, perhaps formerly a tongue of common , which forms a Holloway where it climbs the hill. The woodland forms the roadside verges on both sides.

The trees are mainly East Anglian Elm, *Ulmus minor* with some oak, ash, hawthorn and maple. The elms probably form one clonal patch, suckering under the road. They are well grown, about 30 foot high and (in 2002) almost free of Dutch Elm Disease. Ivy is abundant . Ground vegetation consists of bramble and alexanders - *symrnium olusatrum*.

This is unlikely to be ancient woodland, but it is of interest as an outlier type of woodland common in East Anglia and the East Midlands. Along with the ravine in Ellenden Wood it gives an indication of what woodland might have been like had any survived on the more fertile soils below the Blean.

Oliver Rackham

THE FRENCH CONNECTION

Chapter IX

It was suggested that a comparison of the Blean woods with a wood on the other side of the English Channel would be of interest. The Forêt de Guînes was explored in May 2001.

La Forêt de Guînes - A Comparison

The Forêt de Guînes lies approximately 11 km due south of Calais. Although separated from its neighbour by the Channel, the Forêt de Guînes is, with the exception of King's Wood near Challock, the largest area of continuous woodland near the Blean.

The Forêt de Guînes is at the heart of Les Trois Pays country, a district taking its name from the towns of Liques, Guînes and Hardinghen. Once owned by the Crown, the forest was surrendered by Charles VII in 1435 to Philippe the Good, Duke of Bourgogne, who was allied to the English. It was retaken at the end of the Hundred Years' War and returned to the Crown in 1504 on the death of Antoine de Bourgogne. The forest *'came into public ownership'* (*domanialisée* - the correct title is Forêt Domaniale de Guînes) after the revolution of 1789. Currently the administration is effected by the Office National des Forêts, 24 Rue Henri Loyen, 59004 Lille. Long ago the Forêt de Guînes may have been one of the *Bois de L'Abbaye*. If so it is possible that historical records of the wood might exist in the archive material of the ancient abbey of Liques.

Geology

To the north of the Forêt de Guînes lies the Marais (marsh) de Guînes. To the east is the town of Ardres. An ancient brick making industry was based close to the twin lakes nearby and it is entirely possible that it was dependent on fuel from the Forêt de Guînes. *'The field of the cloth of gold'* (Camp du Drap d'Or) is situated off the road between Guînes and Ardres. Here Francois 1st of France and Henry VIII of England famously jousted in June 1520. A ring of woods occupies the land to the south. One of these is the Forêt Domaniale de Tournehem. This was a strategic site during WW2; the V1 launching ramp is still visible at the edge of the wood near Journy. Munition dumps were hidden in these woods and thus they became a target for allied bombing. The vast marble quarries of Marquise dominate the landscape to the west. This is a fact of considerable geological importance for predictably the Forêt de Guines lies on chalk. Many large holes are located in the west of the forest and without doubt some of these are bomb craters. However, others represent sites where chalk has been extracted for the manufacture of lime.

Wood Use

The oak is the tree that is most prominent in the Blean. The underlying chalk may help to explain why beech occupies a similar position here. Many of these are magnificent specimens. A 6 foot diameter at the base is not uncommon and the height may exceed 100 feet. Epicormic growth is not a serious problem; maybe only one in a hundred is affected in this way. These timber beeches are felled at an age of around 120 years and they are exported to Belgium, Germany and Spain largely for furniture making. These trees are the major revenue earners. Smaller quantities of wood are used for fencing etc. but the bulk of the residue is sold for firewood. Every village has its own *boulangerie*, and ovens hereabout (both commercial and domestic) are wood-burning. Good fuel and kindling is essential for ovens to heat at all quickly and faggots of beech and hazel twigs are made by local unemployed folk. These they are allowed to sell to supplement their benefit.

Skips full of logs may be seen on the major rides. Woods of all sorts are to be found here but ash, beech and hornbeam logs were observed in the greatest numbers, the latter being especially prized. In this part of France there is a current debate concerning the respective merits of wood and bottled gas as fuels. Fortunately the wood lobby is both vocal and vigorous! Charcoal is not produced commercially at the Forêt de Guînes but there is a *charbonnier*, one of a family of artisans who practise traditional crafts, at Saint Joseph Village in the Marais de Guînes.

The Forêt de Guînes is a true forest. Here pheasant, rabbit, hare, wild pig and roe deer are all hunted. The last named are very important in local culture. Indeed the head of the *chevreuil* adorns the 30 centime stamp, the denomination required for a post card to the UK. The foresters and farmers have learnt to live with this animal. New plantations are protected by incorporating sycamore around the perimeter. The roe deer find the tender sycamore leaves much to their taste and hopefully do not seek a more varied diet. We saw no deer in the forest although we could smell them on the high ground in the west near the boundary with the privately owned Bois du Mont. Apparently at this time of year (May) the deer prefer to eat the cereals in the surrounding agricultural plain! When there is a consensus that the damage has reached unacceptable proportions, they are then culled. Their meat is thus a genuine *'fruit of the forest*'! Overall the *'deer problem'* is less intense here than it is in Kent. Unlike our fallow deer, the roe deer do not *'binge'* in May; the demands of their breeding cycle cause the fallow deer to choose the shoots providing most energy, typically those of coppice stools.

Boundaries

Ditches and woodbanks are found here but they are altogether fewer in number and of lesser size than those with which we are familiar in the Blean. Here the banks simply mark property boundaries; they do not form an integral part of woodland management and they do not appear to have done so in times past. Marker trees may be found but the pollarding has been strictly limited. One reasonably old beech pollard (*têtard*) was noted together with the remains of a beech/hawthorn hedge. For management purposes the wood is subdivided into 80 *parcelles* with corridors separating them. These *parcelles* are approximately 500 metres long and 250 metres wide. These units are quite distinct from *'our'* cants. Whereas a cant represents an area for a woodman to cut, a *parcelle* is a piece of woodland of particular character. For instance, in the north and wetter part of the wood *parcelle* 24 had hornbeam coppice, oak standards and a carpet of periwinkle; quite typical of the Blean! The adjacent *parcelle* 25 had a plantation of pine with a ground cover of moss and shield fern. Many pine shoots had been nibbled off and had dropped to the floor. This damage may have been caused by **red** squirrels for these animals maintain a presence here in the absence of the grey squirrel. *Parcelles* form an overall mosaic so that there are no great swathes of trees of similar type. The result is a forest rich in wild life (we were fortunate to see a stoat) and vibrant with bird song.

The forest is best approached either from Bouquehalt in the south-east or from Guînes in the north. There are car parking facilities at both points of entry and a tarmac road through the wood links them together. This road is closed to public vehicles but the forest is nevertheless very visitor friendly. Routes for those on horseback and bicycle are clearly marked and one is free to wander on foot. There are numerous picnic sites, well serviced with litter bins. The head forester, Monsieur Michel Verier, lives at the Maison Forestière de Campagne near the northern entrance. He manages the forest with the help of two assistants; major work is done by contractors. The forest was depleted of mature trees in World War One and had not fully recovered by the time the Germans vastly over exploited its remaining resources in World War Two. M. Verier considers his most important role as establishing a balance or equilibrium in the type and age of the various trees. He also does a lot of educational work with parties from schools and colleges. The TGV line skirts and cuts through the north-eastern flank of the forest on its way from the Channel Tunnel to Lille. The railway here is approximately 160 feet above sea level. The land slowly rises to a high point of some 500 feet in the south west, from which point it descends rapidly to Fiennes. M. Verier is responsible for all this afforested land apart from the highest strip in the south west, the Bois du Mont.

Trees

Near the Maison Forestière de Campagne stands Colonne Blanchard. This monument celebrates the crossing of the channel on 25th May 1785 by Jean Pierre Blanchard (a Frenchman) and John Jefferies (an Englishman). The two aeronauts took off in their balloon from Dover and landed at this spot in the Forêt de Guînes. As you climb the steps up to the column, the character of the wood is at once apparent for mighty beeches and mature hornbeams are all around. Unlike the Blean, it is quite normal for hornbeam to grow to maturity. It is also coppiced along with hazel; there is also some ash coppice. (Any oak coppice appears to be almost 'accidental') However, the overall impression one gets is not that of coppiced woodland. The soil drains well here and oak standards only come into their own on the wetter ground. Some *parcelles* have a mix of hornbeam and ash, an uncommon sight in Kent. (Spuckles Wood near Stalisfield Green is one rare example and some hornbeam-ashwood occurs in East Blean.) In other *parcelles* replanting has taken place with alternate rows of beech and ash. Birch may be found anywhere but it is by no means as invasive as it is in the Blean. Poplar, cherry, field maple, elder and dogwood are all present. Willow is found in the wetter areas but there are only a handful of alders. Conditions are unsuitable for chestnut; the complete absence of this tree makes a striking contrast with Kentish woodlands. Here there has never been a significant demand for chestnut poles, and if grown for its fruit the tree is better managed in different circumstances. A maiden tree will normally only produce a good crop of nuts after it has reached an age of 30/40 years; consequently fruit trees are usually planted where rapid growth may reasonably be expected. An interesting comparison could be made with hazel which is coppiced extensively in the Blean. However, hazel *'orchards'* are located more specifically on the south facing greensands of Kent.

Hybrids

As outlined earlier, sycamore is introduced around new plantations for their better protection; it occurs naturally on the steep slopes of the high ground. Blackthorn and hawthorn both feature. Common hawthorn is readily identified but the presence of the woodland species is a moot point. Classification of some hawthorns proved very difficult; perhaps we are dealing with hybrids here? The fact that only some were flowering did not help. We came across only three holly saplings struggling to establish themselves and yew is nowhere to be found. It is interesting to note that these two species are increasing in the Blean. M. Verier was horrified at the very thought of yew; he considered that it would be too toxic for deer and horses. In reality deer will happily browse on the foliage of the yew for their digestive system copes with the poison up to a point. However, research by Richard Williamson, the first warden of the Great Yew Forest of Kingley Vale near Chichester, has shown that *'bingeing'* on yew (especially in winter time) is often fatal. The berries also constitute a hazard.

The head forester dismissed the possibility of our finding *Tilia cordata*, so there is no obvious evidence of a lime/hornbeam succession in prehistory. The coniferisation of woodland was as fashionable in France as in Britain after the WW2 years. The Forêt de Guînes was depleted in 1945 and re-stocking with rapidly growing conifers made good practical sense too, for in this way a recovery might be effected more quickly. Corsican pine, Douglas fir, spruce and larch are all found here - the spruce especially is used for making paper pulp. Many places in this part of the world adopt the name *Quatre Vents*, a custom easily understood. The surrounding countryside is very flat and there is nothing to stop the wind! Somewhere in the landscape you will detect either a modern windmill or the remains of an old one. There was a great storm here in 1990 and much fallen timber was an inevitable consequence. This has all been meticulously tidied up and the wood sold.

Ground Flora

The ground flora is extremely attractive and varied. Lady orchids and twayblades are plentiful; there are only a few early purple orchids. Solomon's seal may be found anywhere except in deep shade; bluebells appear singly rather than in clumps. Perhaps the presence of wild pig explains their relative scarcity. Sanicle is extremely common; Burnet saxifrage, ground elder and cow parsley were other members of the umbellifer family we were able to identify. Of the labiates, there was a profusion of bugle, yellow archangel and ground ivy but wood sage was conspicuous by its absence. The chalky conditions here do not suit this plant.

Goosegrass and sweet woodruff were representatives of the bedstraws which could be definitely confirmed. The banks and ditches are full of comfrey; *Myosotis sylvatica* is rather more elusive. Cowslip, primrose and creeping Jenny all find a home here as do Lady's mantle, wild strawberry, tormentil and silverweed. Of the figworts, eyebright and a variety of speedwells were noted but there appeared to be little evidence of cow-wheat or foxglove. Of the Ranunculaceae, buttercups and lesser celandine were in flower; the odd flower of a wood anemone could still be seen. Solomon's seal and bluebell are Liliaceae already listed; others include Herb Paris and wood garlic - the latter only frequenting the damp parts of the forest. Butcher's-broom was not apparent. Heather is another common plant of the Blean which seems scarcely to feature here, but the two areas of woodland share red campion, violets, broom, wild rose, honeysuckle, bramble, lords and ladies, hairy wood-rush, ivy, willow herb, wood sorrel, wood spurge, dandelion, daisy, nettle, bracken and a number of *Cirsium* thistles. Other plants recorded included buckthorn, caraway, burdock, Herb Robert, greater plantain, bush vetch, enchanter's nightshade, winter cress and a variety of docks. With the exception of hairy wood-rush, we were unable to label the other rushes, sedges and grasses. It is important to note that these observations were made in mid-May, 2001.

The abiding memory of the Forêt de Guînes is that of the splendid beech trees. Natural regeneration takes place here for beech seedlings are everywhere. This makes an interesting contrast with the Blean where it seems that oak saplings only establish themselves in open areas. The Forêt de Guînes has many merits!

Fig. 9. 1 - French Translations

beech	hêtre	**alder**	aune	**hawthorn**	aubepine
oak	chêne	**hazel**	noisetier	**larch**	mélèze
ash	frêne	**willow**	saule	**holly**	houx
hornbeam	charme	**birch**	bouleau		

THE BATTLE OF BOSSENDEN WOOD

Chapter X

The Effect on the Nation

The small village of Dunkirk on Watling Street a few miles to the west of Canterbury is situated within the Blean. In order to understand the events which occurred around that village in May 1838, it is important to consider the place and time. Dunkirk had neither parish nor school. Much of the immediate countryside was heavily wooded, the farms in the neighbourhood being some distance away from the village..

By the 1830's changes were afoot in long established country practices. Threshing machines had been recently introduced; there was much agrarian distress and discontent. Farm labourers and woodmen had never been well paid; now they were losing their jobs as mechanisation was established. The Church of England exacted heavy tithes, the Archbishop opposed any reform and the big landowners imposed high rents. Only freemen could vote and rural workers were thus disenfranchised. Injustice was apparent for all to see. The stage was set for the entry of John Tom, alias Sir William Courtenay.

John Tom was born in St. Columb, Cornwall, ten miles west of Bodmin the son of Charity and William Tom. His parents ran a flourishing local inn and sent John to a good school at Penryn but he was transferred to another private school at Launceston run on fanatical religious principles by a certain Reverend Cope of non-conformist tradition.

At the age of eighteen John began work in Truro as clerk with a firm of wine merchants. His employers were well pleased with his efforts; so much so that he took over the business when the partners retired in 1827. He made a good marriage to Catherine Fulpitt, the daughter of a successful businessman and her dowry helped to build up the company. The Toms' future appeared bright until John joined the Society of Spencean Philanthropists named after Thomas Spence (1750-1814). He had preached that land should effectively be nationalised under a system whereby local people would form corporations in which the land was to be vested in perpetuity. The corporation would supervise the division of land in such a way that a man would farm a plot of land for a period of time before exchanging it for another. Moreover Spence advocated universal suffrage! By the standards of the eighteenth century these were seditious views and for the last years of his life Spence spent long periods in prison.

By the turn of the 19th century the government of the day was worried. They began constantly seeking out the *'enemy within'* who might undermine the ongoing war effort against Napoleon. The final defeat of Napoleon at Waterloo in 1815 made no difference; the wars had cost huge sums over a period of some 22 years and the national debt was vast. With the burden of high taxation and high food prices social and political unrest was the inevitable consequence

The security forces therefore recruited spies to infiltrate the Society of Spencean Philanthropists which had been formed after Thomas Spence's death in 1814. The spies incited the Spenceans to acts of violence and then informed the police. The use of these *'agent provocateurs'* secured the execution, transportation or imprisonment of a number of Spenceans. All of this greatly upset Tom and led to him joining the society.

At about the same time things began to go wrong for the Tom family. John's mother was admitted to a lunatic asylum in Bodmin where later she died. Then on June 17th 1828 a fire destroyed his business premises. These events preyed upon his mind and he began to act strangely, showing all the signs of his mother's insanity. However his condition improved towards the end of 1831 and in May 1832, apparently much restored, he sailed with a cargo of malt for Liverpool. Once the sale was completed however Tom disappeared.

In September of the same year John Tom burst upon the Canterbury scene calling himself Count Rothschild, also Sir William Courtenay, Knight of Malta. He took up residence at the Rose Inn, courted publicity, dressed extravagantly, persuaded people to part with their money on account of his charm and good looks, lived on promises and credit. He made out that he was charitably disposed to the poor and needy.

Until the 1820's large landowners were predominant in Parliament. However, the country's manufacturing base had been steadily expanding and increasingly industrialists now demanded a voice in Parliament. The Reform Act of 1832 gave this but in no way threatened landed interests. The new House of Commons still reflected property ownership, be it land or business. A general election with the new electoral arrangements was called for December 1832 but as the 1832 Reform Act had been passed by the Whigs, the Tories knew they would have little chance of winning. So the Canterbury Tories decided to damage their opponents rather than try to win the seat by asking Sir William Courtenay, as he was now known, to stand as an independent.

In 1832 secret voting was not yet known and hustings the order of the day. As a consequence the mob was an important factor in any election, the very people over whom Courtenay wielded influence. The Tories correctly calculated that Courtenay's candidature would bring nothing but trouble to the Whigs. Sir William's initial address contained these words:

> *'...the time is now arrived when the true feelings of English blood must proclaim... whether Englishmen will be free or... in bondage. Shew forth, Men of Kent, by your votes, that you will elect those only that will boldly and determinedly pledge themselves to annihilate for ever, the tithes, taxation...etc'.*

The wiser voters of Canterbury could assess this piece of rhetoric for what it was worth, but it can only be imagined how it was received by the multitude. Even *The Times* took an interest and Sir William got completely carried away by his new found fame. He addressed his supporters from the balcony of the Rose Inn and showered coins on the adulating masses.

However on December 12th, election day, Courtenay polled less than 20% of the vote. Undeterred he decided to contest the East Kent division. Polling took place on December 20th and 21st with the result declared by the High Sheriff on Barham Down on Christmas Eve. Of approximately ten thousand votes, Sir William secured just three! The electorate had correctly perceived him to be a self-important opportunist.

Sir William responded to these disasters by publishing a broadsheet much in the Spencean tradition entitled *The Lion*. This was a title he had also bestowed upon himself *'Lion of Canterbury'*. In it he advocated that the working classes could never have too good wages for *'they are the consumers to raise the taxes and circulate their money'*. He condemned the government's policy of flogging as punishment in the army as an *'infamous and degrading system'*. He opposed the Irish Coercion Bill suggesting that we 'should do unto all men as they should do unto us'. Unfortunately these admirable sentiments were buried in a lot of verbose nonsense. *The Lion* read like the ramblings of a mind that had lost touch with reality.

But he didn't stop there! On February 17th, 1833 H.M. Revenue Cutter *Lively* was watching a Faversham fishing-smack, Admiral Hood, off the Goodwin Sands which it suspected was smuggling. Realising the game was up, the crew off-loaded their cargo of spirits into the water. On seeing the tubs bobbing in the water, Lieutenant Shambler of the *Lively* gave chase. The Admiral Hood was intercepted and the tubs recovered. Charges were preferred against the crew of the fishing-smack and their trial began at Rochester Court on March 1st.

Sir William took it into his head to defend these men and thus reinstate himself with the men of East Kent. However, the evidence was incontrovertible so, in order to construct a defence, he claimed to have been returning from France the very same day. He had seen the tubs floating with the tide from the west so they could not possibly have come from the *Admiral Hood*. Further antics included challenging Shambler to a duel. The net result was that the Faversham men were convicted of smuggling and Courtenay was charged with perjury.

Courtenay's case came before the Kent Assizes at Maidstone in July 1833. Throughout his behaviour was bizarre and offensive, treating all with contempt. A guilty verdict was the inevitable outcome. Courtenay was sentenced to three months in Maidstone Gaol to be followed by transportation for seven years.

By now Courtenay's notoriety was such that the trial was reported in the national press. As a result a possible link was made between John Tom and Sir William Courtenay. Catherine Tom travelled from Cornwall to Kent and, by an accurate description of her husband's distinctive features, convinced the governor of Maidstone Gaol that his prisoner was John Tom.

When eventually the governor allowed man and wife to

meet Courtenay continued to play the part and rejected Catherine. However, Catherine was made of stern stuff and informed the prison doctor of her husband's medical condition and the family's history of insanity. Eventually the Home Secretary agreed that Courtenay should be transferred to the lunatic asylum at Barming, a short distance from Maidstone. Despite being dismissed by her husband, Mrs. Tom campaigned vigorously for his release fearing a long confinement would only exacerbate his mental condition.

Courtenay might have been mentally ill but by good conduct and relative rationality was able to convince the authorities that he was neither a threat to himself nor to his fellows. Whilst he could be pardoned for his crime, since he had previously been of unsound mind, he still had to be delivered to someone who could act as an effective guardian. Knowing that he would be unable to manipulate Catherine, Courtenay consented to be handed over to the care of Mr. Francis of Fairbrook, a simple but vain man, who had acted as a character referee in his trial. In November, 1837 he was allowed to live at Francis' home, Fairbrook, in Boughton-under-Blean.

Political developments
During Courtenay's confinement important political developments had taken place including the reform of the Poor Law. Until then, labourers whose wages were below the poverty line received a kind of supplementary benefit calculated according to the number of children to be fed and the price of bread. Thus employers were under no obligation to pay a living wage, honest ratepayers resented paying the wage-bill of unscrupulous employers and poor relief undermined the morale and self respect of the workers. The system was divisive and thoroughly resented.

Under the new law those fit and able now had to enter a workhouse if they wanted assistance. In May 1835 at Hernhill just a mile or so from Boughton, a gang of men had protested against this and similar demonstrations had occurred across other parts of Kent. Some were violent and those rioters caught were given exemplary sentences. Rural workers and their families faced a bleak prospect. Without doubt the Poor Law needed reform but it could be argued that the remedy was worse than the disease.

Courtenay realised this was a cause to espouse in rural Kent. He could fire up these passive labourers and lead them to the promised land. He began fraternizing with the workers, spoiling their children and flattering their wives.

Courtenay's host was disturbed by this course of events for he employed some of these men on his farm. If they conversed freely with his guest they might get ideas above their station. He and Courtnay began to quarrel and during one spat Courtenay displayed a pair of pistols. This brought matters to a head and Francis ordered him out of his house. Courtenay was happy to go. He was now much in favour with the nearby household at Bossenden Farm, Dunkirk and removed himself there. He had done well out of his relationship with Francis making the journey to his new host's home on the back of a '*borrowed*' horse! It was to serve him well in the coming days.

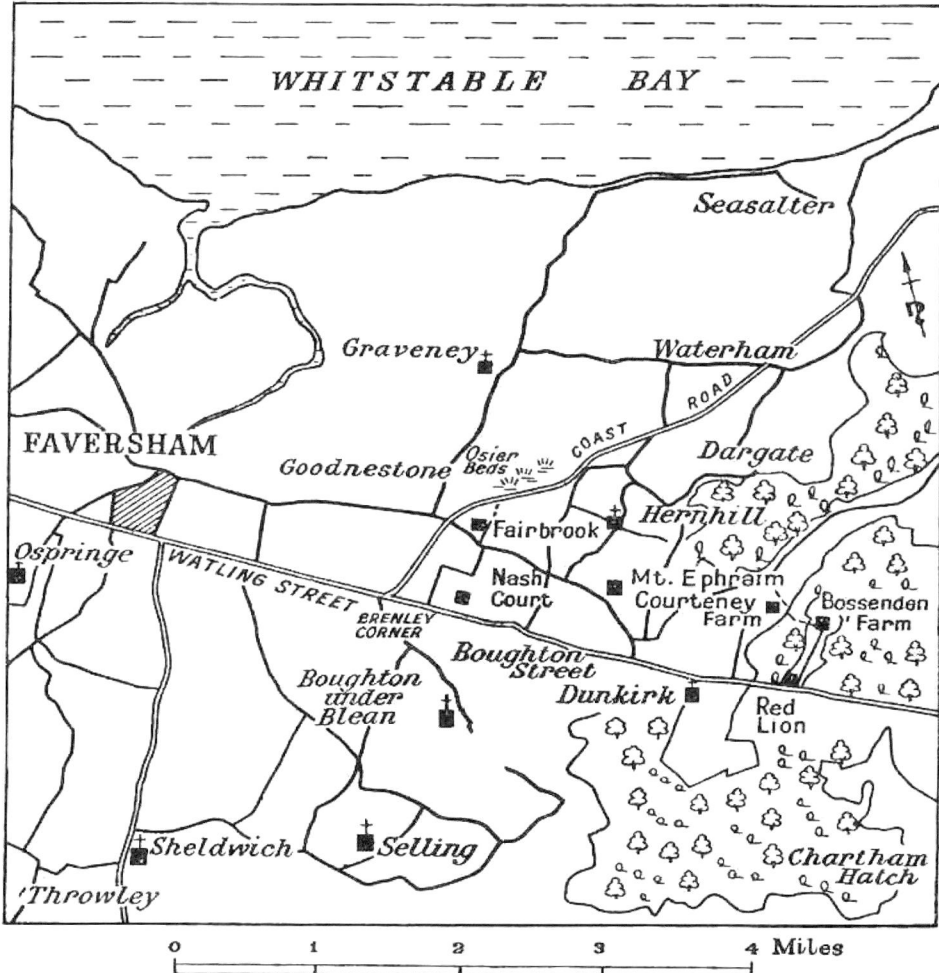

Fig. 10.1: The village of Dunkirk and Bossendon Wood

Courtenay was welcomed by the Culvers of Bossenden especially by the ladies of the household. He was also made welcome in the cottage of William Wills, a smallholder living with his family near Fairbrook. Wills had a sister, Mrs. Hadlow, who lived near Hernhill. Both became his fanatical followers.

Up to this point Courtenay had commiserated with the uneducated folk of the area about low wages, unemployment and the evil of the Poor Law. Now he promised that if they trusted him and followed him when called, they could take the land from the lords and divide it amongst themselves so that each man had the means to support his family. He claimed to be the reincarnation of Jesus Christ; this was the second coming.

The Ville of Dunkirk had no church and no school. The nearest clergyman the Reverend Handley of Hernhill was more interested in delivering admonitions from the pulpit rather than involving himself in genuine pastoral work. The local folk were desperate and gullible. Sir William was a powerful preacher and had enough knowledge of biblical texts to be able to twist them to his advantage. His apocalyptic vision terrified his simple converts and the climax of an evening sermon would often involve the discharge of both his pistols into the night sky.

Sir William now decided to try to expand his support base and on May 29th set off at the head of his followers through north-east Kent in search of new recruits. Riding 'his' horse at the head of the procession and with a banner depicting a lion he quoted from the Book of Revelation: *'...behold a white horse; and he that sat on him had a bow; and a crown was given unto him; and he went forth conquering, and to conquer'*. Sir William's horse was white!

Sir William did not conquer however. When the recruiting party returned tired and dispirited to Bossenden Farm, they had attracted only a few new converts to the cause. His impassioned rhetoric had been in vain.

Meanwhile members of the local gentry had alerted the Justice of the Peace, a certain Dr. Poore, to the martial nature of Sir William's troop of men who had been marching around the countryside. Dr. Poore was concerned to learn that the superintendent at Barming Asylum, believed that Sir William was still mentally unstable at the time of his release. Other information came to light, no less alarming. Mr. Curling, a farmer of Hernhill, informed Dr. Poore that Courtenay had seduced four labourers from his employment to go on his march. Dr. Poore made out a warrant for the arrest of Sir William.

The execution of this duty was entrusted to John Mears, the constable at Boughton-under-Blean. To be on the safe side Mears took along not only his assistant but also his brother Nicholas, in case there should be trouble. The three men set off for Bossenden Farm in the early hours of Thursday May 31st.

Back at the farmhouse, Sir William realised that his campaign was falling apart. Desertions from his band, which had never been more than forty strong had begun to take place. Desperate measures would be needed to hold them together. When one of his followers noticed the approach of the three men and recognised the constable Courtenay had to make a quick decision. He shot Nicholas Mears then thrust his sword several times into his body. John Mears and his assistant ran for their lives.

By murdering Nicholas Mears, Courtenay had bonded his men together by terror. He exhorted them wildly, saying that no weapon could harm them for he, Courtenay, was divine and had come to lead them to salvation. Realising that news of the murder would quickly reach the authorities and that he must embolden his men for the final showdown he ordered his men to head off for Fairbrook, recruiting or coercing any they met on the way.

Meanwhile the two constables had reached Mr. Curling's farm where they passed on the terrible news. Curling's son set off to find Dr. Poore for authorization to call out troops from Canterbury and the two constables continued to Faversham where they sought out Mr. Knatchbull, a local magistrate. Knatchbull knew all about Courtenay as his father had been one of the victorious candidates in the East Kent election of December 1832. Not only did he issue a warrant for the arrest of Courtenay but he decided to deal with the matter himself. He assembled a posse of seven constables together with a similar number of other men on horseback and rode hard to Boughton. Here he made a rendezvous with Dr. Poore who informed him that Courtenay's band was nearby at Fairbrook and that soldiers were on their way.

Dead or Alive
Ignoring Dr. Poore's call for caution, Knatchbull determined

to confront Courtenay direct without waiting for the soldiers. However, it soon became apparent that whilst Knatchbull's men would have been taking an outrageous risk had they taken a frontal attack there was absolutely no need for them to do so. Courtenay gave a blast on his bugle, a signal for his men to return to Bossenden Wood and fight on familiar territory. Knatchbull sent a few men to keep the retreating band under observation; and continued to the Red Lion in Dunkirk. Here he met Dr. Poore who by now had been joined by one hundred soldiers under Major Armstrong. Dr. Poore read the Riot Act to the crowd outside the inn and the military, having learnt Courtenay's location in Bossenden Wood set off to capture him dead or alive.

Major Armstrong himself led a party into the wood through Old Barn Lane whilst his second in command, Captain Reid's detachment was ordered to enter the wood to the east through Bossenden Farm. Things went disastrously wrong and Lieutenant Bennett of Reid's party was shot as he advanced to arrest Courtenay. After killing Bennett, Sir William collapsed under a hail of bullets. Catt, a man enrolled as a special constable, succumbed to *'friendly'* fire.

Though Sir William's men, armed only with staves, fought with fanatical courage the odds were hopeless and in no time eight of his party were dead and seven injured, one so seriously, he died the same day. The rest were taken prisoner.

The fall-out from these events was considerable. *The Times* reported the battle and the public developed a macabre interest in the affair. A week later the bodies of the men who had fallen in Bossenden Wood were interred in the churchyard at Hernhill. A correspondent of *The Times* wrote this of the funeral:

> *'Never was I more pained than I was by the spectacle of universal sorrow, amounting almost to despair, which it was my misfortune to behold... Would that those who in high places are intrusted with the administration of justice had been present to witness it, and to calculate the effect which the loss of life already experienced, and the remorse felt by those deluded men and their wives and families is now producing in this part of the country'.*

By the standards of the day justice did prove lenient for the

The Battle of Bossendon Wood

hapless prisoners. In all eighteen were charged with the murder of either Nicholas Mears or Lieutenant Bennett and all found guilty. Normally this would have resulted in sentence of death but the judge, Lord Denman realising these uneducated men had fallen under the spell of the charismatic Courtenay sentenced the three most heavily implicated to be transported, the others to short prison terms.

The Battle of Bossenden Wood was debated in Parliament. There was much soul searching. How could such events have come to pass in the environs of Canterbury, the long established centre of Christian pilgrimage? How could people be duped by a madman such as Courtenay?

The answer was believed to lie in education and in June 1839 the Whig government decided to increase education spending by 50%. The Archbishop of Canterbury opposed the proposal in the House of Lords but the bill was passed before the end of the year. The attitude of the senior clergy of the established church met with widespread condemnation. However, some Anglican consciences were stirred by the criticism and a fund set up enabling a church and school to be built at Dunkirk.

The use of soldiers to maintain public order had led to the massacres of Peterloo in 1819 and of Bossenden Wood in 1838. As a result a bill was introduced in 1839 to enable Justices of the Peace to establish regular police forces.

So the Battle of Bossenden Wood had a profound effect upon the life of the nation. Society at large began seriously to debate issues of education, social justice and policing. Most importantly there was a feeling that those simple men, who had been so misled by Courtenay, had been badly let down. John Tom or Sir William Courtenay had damaged many people, but his life and death set in motion changes that were for the good prompting a public determination to address many of society's ills.

Sources:
1. *Battle in Bossenden Wood - The strange story of Sir William Courtenay'* by P.G.Rogers; Oxford University Press, 1961
2. *The New Encyclopaedia Britannica*, 1990
3. Various web-sites
4. HMSO - Ordnance Survey Map
5. Dawes family, Mount Ephraim, Hernhill - Map of Bossenden Wood

A Sustainable Future

Chapter XI

Time present and past
And time future contained in time past
      T.S. Eliot - 'Burnt Norton'

As with time so it is with woods. More than any other ecosystem what we see in the woods today is related to decisions taken by people many years ago. What our children will see in the future will depend upon decisions taken today or in the past. In this essay I consider some of the factors which will influence the Blean in the future.

Today the Blean Woods are renowned by conservationists for their size, their plant communities, their scarce invertebrates, and their birds. The Blean Woods National Nature Reserve at 495 hectares is the largest area of broad leaf woodland in conservation management in south-east England. Church Wood, Ellenden and East Blean Woods are now proposed as Special Areas of Conservation under the European Habitats Directive as outstanding examples of the nationally scarce Stellario-Carpinetum community of oak hornbeam woodland. The Blean is one of only two main strongholds for the heath fritillary butterfly in England.

To the commercial forester the Blean Woods currently provide little opportunity for economic return. Conifer plantations provide a limited financial return but current forestry policy does not permit further planting of conifers on ancient woodland sites. The management of broad-leaves is dependent on subsidy.[1]

To the historian and archaeologist the Blean is an increasingly valued resource with a well documented history which can be related to the present woods. To the wider population of Canterbury and East Kent the Blean remains largely unknown compared to other countryside sites in East Kent. Car parks at Clowes Wood and Blean Woods attract less than 100,000 visitors a year. A survey of visitors to the Canterbury countryside in 2000 showed a low level of awareness of local woodlands.[2]

The future of any wood will depend on the interaction of

biological, economic and cultural forces. All of these are changing rapidly at the start of the new millennium.

In the immediate future prospects for the Blean look good. The designation of substantial areas under European and UK wildlife legislation, together with a presumption against the loss of woodland means that there is unlikely to be major loss of woodland to development or agriculture, or conversion of broadleaf to conifer. Currently more than 1,100 hectares in the UK are designated as Sites of Special Scientific Interest under the Wildlife and Countryside Act, and a further 900 hectares are designated as Sites of Nature Conservation Interest.

However such protection is not absolute. The late 1990's have seen the loss of Brickhouse Wood, a Site of Nature Conservation Interest, to a landfill site. It is possible that there could be further loss of woodland to transport links, or a new reservoir if proposals for a reservoir at Broad Oak are resurrected. At the same time in a large area of wood it is difficult to regulate small-scale damaging activities. There are frequent attempts to clear parcels of wood for residential or commercial use. In 2000 half a hectare of scarce wet woodland in Denstead Wood was damaged by the dumping of hardcore. Alone such attempts may be insignificant, but cumulatively they can have a significant impact.

The England Forestry Strategy (Forestry Commission 1999) represents a radical shift in government forest policy with an emphasis on the non-timber benefits of woodland, notably amenity, biodiversity and recreation, and support for new woodland planting. To what extent these aspirations will lead to changes in the Blean is unclear, but there is potentially support to build on the Blean's unique advantage, its size, and extend and link existing woodlands to create an even larger woodland.

The character of any woodland reflects, in part, the aspiration of its owners. In the last fifty years there has been a significant change in the ownership of woodland. The Ecclesiastical Estates of Canterbury have sold most of their holdings and now the main owners are conservation organisations, the state and bank pension funds. This has led to a new phenomenon: the management of woodland primarily for conservation, the consequences of which are only beginning to be seen. The first attempts have focused on the continuation or re-establishment of components of the historic landscape. There has been successful conversion of conifer plantation back to broadleaf woodland in Blean Woods and East Blean National Nature Reserves; heathland has been recreated on Blean Woods National Nature Reserve and there is continued support for coppicing although it is no longer economically viable.

More recently consideration is being given to a less interventionist woodland management where large areas of woodland are left unmanaged (Peterken 1996) and to integrating nature reserves into the wider countryside so that they are not isolated islands. The Blean lends itself to such approaches because of its large size. The new management plan for Blean Woods National Nature Reserve (English Nature et. al., 2001) has as objective *'To manage 75% of the existing high forest as non-intervention woodland.'* The Kent Wildlife Trust has agreed in principle to develop this approach in the woods to the South of the A2 highway where it is seeking to acquire significant areas of woodland. Such areas of woodland are likely to be very different to the woods we know today.

Climate change is likely to have a significant impact on the ecology of the Blean. A recent review suggests that increases in temperature between 0.5 and 2°C are likely to change the boundaries of many tree species in the United Kingdom leading to shift in areas of forest development and a change in composition of current woods. (Hassell et. al. 2000). Bird watchers are looking forward to the arrival of species from Europe such as Black Woodpecker and Honey Buzzard and it is likely that there will be similar changes in the invertebrate fauna.

The Blean is unusual amongst large blocks of woodland in that it has no significant populations of deer or other large herbivores. However this distinction may not last long with the continued growth of deer populations in southern England and increasing feral populations of wild boar. Both deer and boar may be a significant component of the Blean ecosystems in the future. The presence of these herbivores will have a significant impact on management decisions about woodland management. Will it be the favoured management if there is a large population of deer?

The future of the woodlands is dependent also on both macro and micro-economic influences. If woodland management continues to fail to provide a competitive economic return the survival of woodland will depend on society having sufficient wealth to support the more intangible benefits such as recreation, carbon storage and biodiversity. Continuing economic growth and expansion of housing in the south-east is not necessarily a threat to the woods of the Blean. For example there is potential to achieve new woodlands through the planning process. If timber production became economically viable again then there might be pressure to promote profitable species or management practices.

The future of the woods will ultimately depend on their wider cultural value. There is wide support for wildlife and biodiversity in principle, but this is not necessarily reflected in understanding or concern about local woods. (L. G. Bride pers. comm.).

In conclusion, the future of the woods is safe in the foreseeable future although economic and biological factors may mean that the woods are very different in the future.

Brian Watmough

Bibliography

1. English Nature, RSPB and Woodland Trust. (2001) Blean Woods National Nature Reserve: *A Joint Management Plan 2001-2006*.
2. Forestry Commission (1999) England Forestry Strategy: *A New Focus for England's Woodlands*. HMSO.
3. Hassell, J.E., Briggs, B, & Hepburn, I R.(2000), *Climate Change and UK Nature Conservation: A review of the Impact of Climate Change on UK Species and Habitat Conservation Policy*. ADAS.
4. Kent County Council (2000) *Survey of Rural Tourism in East Kent: A study for Kent County Council*.
5. Middleton, P. in prep. *Commercial Forestry in the Blean*. In: Buckley G P & Watmough, B R (eds.) *The Ecology and History of the Blean*.
6. Peterken, G.F. (1996) *Natural Woodland, Ecology and Conservation in Northern Temperate Regions*. Cambridge.
7. T.S. Elliot (1935) *Burnt Norton, The Four Quartets*. Faber & Faber.

Brian Watmough is Countryside Officer at Canterbury City Council. The views expressed here are his own.

Glossary

(Words not defined in the text) Taken from The Blean 1st Edition.

Ages. Names applied to periods in the development of human skills and culture in England.

STONE AGE - earlier than 2,000 years BC (Before Christ) or 4,000 BP (Before Present). The Stone Age is divided into three stages: Palaeolithic (ancient + stone) for earlier than 10,000 BC; Mesolithic (middle) from 10,000 to 4,500 BC; Neolithic (new) from 4,500 to 2,000 BC.

BRONZE AGE – 2,400 to 750 BC

IRON AGE – 750 BC to AD 40 AD (Anno Domini = Year of Our Lord).

After those 'prehistoric' ages the names adopted include Roman Britain from AD 40 toAD 410, The Dark Ages from AD 410 to 700, Anglo-Saxon England from 410 to 1066, The Middle Ages (or Medieval) from 1066 to 1536 and, thereafter, Post-Medieval.

BAST - Fibre from a tree's inner bark, especially of lime. Anciently used for cordage.

BATT - The trunk of a felled timber tree. More commonly butt. Before felling = bole.

BIODIVERSITY - Biological diversity is the variety of life on Earth. The term refers to all species of plants and animals, their genetic variation and the complex ecosystems of which they are part.

BRICKEARTH - Infrequently found land areas of surface deposit offering high fertility for agriculture. Thought to have been created by wind-blown dust (loess) where it resettled to enough depth upon a bed of, for example, London Clay.

BRYOPHYTE(S) - Plant(s) of the botanical division Bryophyta; including mosses and liverworts.

CANT - A compartment of coppice as a working section. The cant area may be marked for each crop of poles, by cutting a boundary line (a 'wash'), or by durable markers; usually pollards or stubs. These living markers are sometimes found combined with woodbanks.

CARBON STORAGE - Trees employ carbon in their growth. Absorbing it during their lifetime, they release it slowly after death and decay

COPPICE - The underwood of broadleaved tree species harvested every few years by cutting to near-ground level and then allowed to grow shoots again from the stool (stump).
    Woodland managed for producing such underwood.
    To cut underwood.

DEERPARK
    An enclosed pasture of many acres to foster and control deer; traditionally fallow deer in England.

DEN - A wild animal's lair.
    Saxon place-name suffix frequently found in parts of south-east England.
    It denoted a seasonal feeding ground for swine, especially of acorns and beechmast

DENDROCHRONOLOGY - A system of dating using the characteristic patterns of annual growth rings of trees to assign dates to timber.

DOLLY - A woodsman's name for a short, forked stick used to strip thorns from bramble stems.

DOMESDAY BOOK - "A record of the lands of England made in 1086 by order of William 1." (OED) Note: primarily a record of land tenure, not a topographical record.

DROVEWAY - A recognised route for moving farm animals. Transhumance.

ECOSYSTEM - A biological community of interacting organisms and their physical environment.

ENCLOSURE ACTS
The term refers usually to the many private Acts of Parliament passed in Georgian times (especially George III 1760-1820). This enclosure of open fields and commons towards more efficient agriculture was relatively little seen in Kent because of its existing farm ownership structure.

EPIPHYTE - A plant growing on another plant but not a parasite; e.g. moss on a tree.

EPOCH - See table of epochs in text. ' –cene', e.g. Eocene, is from Greek kainos = new.

FAGGOT (OF WOOD)
Faggot-making, a great, ubiquitous industry for firing materials. The demand dwindled with the introduction of fossil fuels.

(ROYAL) FOREST
An extensive land area suitable for hunting. Owned by the monarch and subject to special Laws of the Royal Forests. Foris = outside, or beyond, the common law. Created by Norman and early Plantagenet kings. No royal forests in Kent. (Compare Sussex = 7)

GRUB - 'grubbing- out' is to destroy and remove tree roots.

HECTARE (HA) - Quick conversion: 1 hectare = 2.5 acres (2.471), 1 acre = 0.4 ha (0.40), 1 square mile = 2.59 sq. km = 259 ha = 640 acres

HIGH FOREST - The term distinguishes tall, relatively massed, trees from coppice or scattered parkland or hedgerow trees. Traditionally managed for sawn timber products. Note: Where coppice has overgrown to reach a height impractical for slender pole products, it may be said to have 'turned into high forest'; thus foretelling a changed woodland habitat but probably not a valuable timber potential.

LAYERS (WOODLAND) - Tree layer, or canopy. Upper branches and twigs.

SHRUB LAYER - Shrubs, saplings, lower branches of mature trees.

FIELD LAYER - Wild flowers, ferns, saprophytes.

GROUND LAYER - Mosses, fungi. loam A fertile soil of clay and sand containing decayed vegetable matter. (OED)

LONDON CLAY - A geological formation resulting from seawater deposits of more than five million years ago (Tertiary deposits). Landscape features are plateaux and low hills. The chief soil-base of the Blean, stretching from near Boughton-le-Street on the A2 to Herne on the A291. A bluish clay, weathering brown.

MESOLITHIC / NEOLITHIC / PALAEOLITHIC - See Ages

PANNAGE - Woodland food for farmed swine. Acorns, beechmast, roots, etc. In Domesday Book the woodlands of Kent (and some other counties) were measured by their capacity to feed swine.

POLLARD - 'A tree which is cut at 8-12ft above ground and allowed to grow again to produce successive crops of wood.' (Rackham 1990)

RAPTOR - Any bird of prey, e.g. an owl, falcon, etc. (OED)

SAVANNA(H) - A grassy plain in tropical or sub-tropical regions with few or no trees. (OED)

SCRUB - a) vegetation consisting mainly of brushwood or stunted forest growth;
       b) an area of land covered with this. (OED)

STADDELL / STANDLING - Two of many vernacular terms used in coppice management for stems allowed to grow on to timber dimensions. Others include storers, tillers and waivers. Most such terms are obsolescent if not obsolete.

STOOL - A cut stump of a broadleaf tree species intended to grow new shoots as a crop.

STELL - An enclosure formed by pollarding at about chest-height and then layering the resulting branches to form a low hedge.

STUB - A tree pollarded at chest-height (or lower than normal pollards) at a position where a distinctive marker is needed, perhaps in conjunction with a boundary bank.

VASCULAR (PLANT) -Vessels in plants for conveying sap, etc.
WEALD / WEALDEN - The once heavily wooded region including parts of Kent, Sussex, Surrey and a corner of Hampshire. The name has been employed for geological description and vernacular architecture. (From Old English = wald, wold)

© **Geoffrey Roberts 2004**